ECLIPSE

Books by Mary Summer Rain

Nonfiction

Spirit Song
Phoenix Rising
Dreamwalker
Phantoms Afoot
Earthway
Daybreak
Soul Sounds
Whispered Wisdom
Ancient Echoes
Bittersweet
Mary Summer Rain on Dreams
The Visitation
Millennium Memories
Fireside
Eclipse

Fiction

The Seventh Mesa

Children's

Mountains, Meadows and Moonbeams
Star Babies

Books on Tape

Spirit Song
Phoenix Rising
Dreamwalker
Phantoms Afoot
The Visitation

ECLIPSE

Mary Summer Rain

HAMPTON ROADS
PUBLISHING COMPANY, INC.

For information write:

Hampton Roads Publishing Company, Inc.
134 Burgess Lane
Charlottesville, VA 22902

Or call: (804) 296-2772
FAX: (804) 296-5096

e-mail: hrpc@hrpub.com
Internet: http://www.hrpub.com

If you are unable to order this book from your local
bookseller, you may order directly from the publisher.
Quantity discounts for organizations are available.

Call 1-800-766-8009, toll-free.

Library of Congress Catalog Card Number: 98-73922

ISBN 1-57174-121-6

10 9 8 7 6 5 4 3 2

Printed on acid-free recycled paper in Canada

For Rose Marsac

You've never been forgotten

Foreword

The moon, known by ancient civilizations as the Great Mother who ruled the waxing and waning tides of life and knowledge, has been the traditional multicultural symbol of fertility, representing both the physical and the intellectual since the dawn of spiritual ideology. Goddess of attained Wisdom, of new and renewed life. Rebirth. Intellectual illumination. Revelations and insights.

In light of this beautiful, long-held philosophy, it would follow that the full moon signifies an enlightened mind, brightly illumined with knowledge and comprehension, while the new moon represents the shadowed darkness of confusion and ignorance.

But what of the transitional stage of the moon in eclipse, where knowledge is temporarily hidden from perceptual view? Shadowed and obscured. Not quite within obtainable grasp. Symbolizing the intermittent spells of forgetfulness or the clouding of the answers to life's seeming mysteries.

Throughout life a compelling inquisitiveness of mind sparks an eternal quest for knowledge. As children, curiosity is continually enlivened by wonderment; as adults, that wonderment shifts to the desire for a deeper understanding that, hopefully, leads to attained Wisdom.

As we strive to accomplish this goal, we research, study, and then spend a great deal of time contemplating that which we've intellectually absorbed. Oftentimes, our endeavors reveal multiple conclusions engendered by the multifaceted and intertwining aspects of reality. Thus, do we realize that relativity frequently plays a vital role when deriving an ultimate solution or answer to any philosophical inquiry. Yet, there are times when, even after extensive contemplation has been applied, answers and resolutions remain shrouded in mist, and clarity becomes a nebulous specter we cannot seem to grasp. The moon's eclipse, therefore, represents that which Consciousness inherently knows—The Knowing—but the limited human memory has forgotten—a state of selective amnesia that can, once again, be illuminated by the igniting spark of a singular key word, phrase, or expressed thought that reawakens our sleeping ancient memory.

This book, hopefully, will be the spark that awakens that ancient memory within and chases away the darkness that shadows the brilliant knowledge of the spirit's intellect.

ECLIPSE

SPIRITUAL PHILOSOPHY

Is there such a place as hell?

The ideology of a place of physical torture for a nonphysical soul is ludicrous. If ever there were a legendary land right out of mythology, the place called hell would be the prime candidate. Ever since the Stone Age, primitive cultures endeavored to imagine an afterlife suitable for the reward of good and the punishment of bad earthly behavior. Heaven, of course, was usually depicted as a land of light, which some cultures called the Eternal Summerland. Sun, stars, and the airy clouds *above* was clearly a practical place to locate this wonderful destination for good people. And hell was associated with the heavy darkness *below,* where bodies were buried.

Not all cultures or spiritual philosophies recognize the theory of hell. Buddha taught the beauty of reincarnation, which precluded the idea of hell. The Hindu's Krishna taught that hell is lived on earth for those who succumbed to lust, anger, or greed.

Those cultures believing in a hell all borrowed their related concepts from each other. The Greeks borrowed from the Babylonians, who adapted theories from other cultures of their time. The underworld of the Egyptians, as detailed in the *Egyptian Book of the Dead,* is an elaborately conceptualized myth, combining the ideas of judgment, heaven, hell,

11

and purgatory. The early Romans placed hell as a location beneath Italy and, as in the Egyptian belief, the Roman hell was composed of caves, rivers, gates, and judgment. The Shinto religion of Japan believes in a region beneath the ground called the "place of darkness," where all aspects of misery and misfortune dwelt. The idea of a place such as hell is a sadistic theory originating within patriarchal religious belief systems in the Middle East, for the purpose of keeping women morally obedient to dogmatic laws and culturally submissive to the male-dominated society—in conjunction with controlling all the faithful adherents.

Over time, this practice, as observed by other religious groups, was seen as a viable and effective method of controlling the behavior of their followers. After making modifications to the concept by way of extending its reach to all believers within a specific religion, the idea of hell was quickly assimilated as a major tenet of their own dogmatic formulation. Other religious sects soon followed suit until the idea of a place called hell became a universal belief. Christianity, being the newcomer religion on the historical block, borrowed from the preceding cultures and, as time passed, had to make official revisions to its original dogma by adding the concepts of purgatory and limbo. Limbo was a tenet of Catholicism that designated an afterlife place of eternity for all unbaptized babies and, supposedly, is no longer touted by Catholic theologians. Curious, yes?

As decades of belief slipped into centuries and on through ensuing millennia, the concept of hell has been exacerbated by such imaginative writers as Dante Alighieri in his famous *Inferno* and John Milton, with his *Paradise Lost*. And we'd be remiss to omit mentioning the terrible visual depictions that strike horror within our sensibilities through the complex painted artistry of Bruegel's and Bosch's famous renderings of death and hell. Thus have we ended up with a wide variety of depictions of all manner of human suffering when, in reality, no such event occurs.

The spirit of this theory is one of *internal* pain and suffering. Hell, that is, its true concept, is meant to symbolize the *pain of rejecting God*. It is the *dark void* within our being that evidences itself when we choose to distance ourselves from the Divine and voluntarily absent ourselves from God's light, love, and compassion. A place within the etheric realm such as hell is completely nonexistent. No one dies and goes directly to hell, because there is no such place.

When an individual intentionally and, in full Consciousness, rejects God, that one's spirit, upon physical death of the body, rests within what can be called a place of comfort and compassion whereby the spirit is engulfed in divine love. Remember, it is only the *physical* reasoning mind of the human person's current incarnation that made the choice to reject God; it was not the person's *spirit,* which knew full well of God's existence.

Taking this further, how would it be logistically possible to physically torture something that is not physical—doesn't have a body to punish? Our spirit forms are immaterial and luminous. We have lived for centuries with this wild, threatening concept of a terrible and terrifying place as a possible destiny if we don't live a good life. As young children, hell and all its cruel demons and devils have been used as scare tactics to keep us in line (and give us nightmares). Each generation continues to perpetrate the myth without giving it serious contemplation by way of reason and logic. Like a fairy tale, it is told and retold without question and, before long, becomes an accepted tenet of one's belief system.

A more accurate ideology regarding hell would be something like the following statement: *When we turn away from the Divine, we experience emotional loneliness and mental anguish.* This then would be the true torment in our lives. This then is our *living* state rather than a reality that is designated as a possible destination upon physical death.

It is interesting to me, having been brought up in a Catholic school where the nuns taught the fire-and-brimstone concept of hell, that today, the Church's stance on this has dramatically changed to one of caution to not take the biblical images of hell as *literal* interpretations, but rather now points out that they *symbolically* represent a state of voluntary spiritual isolation.

Was Mother Teresa an angel?

What? This question gave revealing insight hidden behind the inquiry and causes me some concern as to how this correspondent views the general character of his fellow human beings. I wonder why it would appear to be beyond reason to attribute Mother Teresa's humanitarian and selfless qualities to being above and beyond human potential? Are we being swept away by the weekly angelic fantasies portrayed on serialized television programming? Or have we become so cynical as to find it impossible for one (or more) of our sisters or brothers to devote self completely to others through the quality of genuine empathy and selfless acts of goodness? Has perception of humankind become that bleak? Sunk so low?

The shadowy ideology behind this question clearly infers that we are believed to be a race of people incapable of compassionate behavioral responses, that we are too consumed by ego to set self aside in deference to the welfare of others, that we are an apathetic lot devoid of the basic emotional responses of common decency. It infers that such selfless devotion to another could never come from a human being, but only from a high spiritual being, only an angelic one. A question such as this reveals a hidden perspective that is usually voluntarily concealed or is buried deep within the questioner's own subconscious.

Mother Teresa was a beautiful example of true human potential. She was born in Skopje, Yugoslavia (in what is now Macedonia), on August 26, 1910, and named Agnes Gonxha Bojaxhiu. She was not an angel or an angelic being, but rather a human being who exhibited the angelic qualities that are inherent in all of us. Love, Unconditional Goodness, and selflessness are priceless jewels we are all blessed with possessing. They are part of the treasure of natural riches we all have. Whether we choose to share or hoard those riches is up to each of us. It's a personal, conscious choice, our behavior. A personal choice.

New Age books are suddenly leaving me unfulfilled. Why?

Perhaps you've reached that saturation point that comes to all avid readers who center on a singular subject matter. It happens, you know, especially after one has gained a considerable level of knowledge and personal attainment. After this occurs, there is a sharper and more discriminating discernment applied to the content and quality of the text. Soon after perusing three-quarters of a book or even before you've completed reading a couple of chapters, you find it more and more difficult to push onward. You're bored. The book is too obviously predictable or elementary; it's shallow and your intuitive insight kicks in to ignite that spark of Knowing that informs you that the material is not quite credible or that it is redundant.

For example, I'm in the habit of keeping several books going at one time. One or two are for study and research and one will be purely for leisure reading, usually a novel or biography. For years the novels I chose were medical mysteries. It began with Robin Cook; as time went on, more and more authors began making a name for themselves in the genre. However, the more I read these, the quicker I was able to predict who the villain was and what the outcome was going to be. How many mysteries can be written about Ebola or genetic engineering without it becoming so redundant that you begin to pass them over while browsing the New Releases shelf in the bookstore? You've suddenly realized that you've got germ and gene burnout. You're tired of repetitive storylines. It's time to move on, expand your horizons.

So you see, this matter of reading material leaving you cold isn't confined to the New Age genre; it's more a matter of personal development combined with literary repetition regarding a specific subject matter. If you're interested in the so-called New Age subject, I suggest you broaden this scope of interest into the naturally related nonfiction areas of physics and philosophy. These fields will greatly expand your knowledge base and deepen your understanding of "natural reality." This can be compared to looking at a children's picture book illustrating Roman or Greek mythology characters, then reading more in-depth text on these gods and goddesses and, finally, delving into Roman and Greek history, including their historical philosophers, to gain a full-bodied understanding of the civilizations from which these basic myths were generated.

Expansion. Knowledge expansion, like an ever-widening pond ripple, keeps subject matter from becoming stale and stagnant. There's no reason to have an interest in a subject unless you're prepared to stretch and pull it through its related issues. Keep researching, studying, contemplating. If the literary offerings have become stale, reach out and let your feet do the walking to a different, related section in the bookstore, where your mind will thrill with the potential of knowledge expansion and the sudden and delightful appearance of new wonders to contemplate.

Celtic lore is full of fairies. Do they exist? If so, do they have souls?

Celtic lore is indeed rich in fairy legend, yet you've singled out one species of these so-called "little people." We also hear colorful tales told of gnomes, elves, leprechauns, devas, sylphs, undines, pixies, green men, sídhes, banshees, and sprites—these not only originating from the Emerald Isle, but also from many other lands.

Many ancient myths, legends, and fairy tales can be directly traced back to a specific incident that generated the developed theory, specifically, an incident such as the unexpected sighting of an unusual and rare phenomenon. A couple of examples of this would be through my own woodswalking experiences, when I quite unexpectedly found myself three feet from a forest observer. The tiny woman made no move, yet her almond-shaped ebony eyes held mine locked on hers. Skin light brown in color and glossy black, her straight hair flowed to her knees. The slim feminine form was unadorned. I looked away, then back again to find her gone. Other incidents include darting points of sparkling lights dancing about me when out in the woods at night, spirit wolves that sit beside the trail and take note of my passing, owls that are not owls, and whisperings among the pines. There's more, but these examples are enough to get my point across.

To claim I definitively saw a fairy would be presumptuous. I did see a very small person, perhaps a being like those the Celts call "little people." All I know is that I saw what I saw and, for me personally, that validates the existence of these types of people. And it would be impossible to make such powerful eye contact with such an individual without perceiving her soul.

Whether we don't particularly believe in the existence of these little folk, yet immensely enjoy the many and varied tales written and told about them, or whether we do emphatically believe in their existence or even such a speculative possibility, we win either way, don't we? They certainly give us hours and hours of interesting probabilities to ponder over.

Why is suffering the only way to spiritual perfection?

Wait a minute. Perfection? There is no physical, behavioral, or spiritual perfection here on earth. No one is perfect. No one exhibits perfect behavior or attains perfect spirituality. Aren't those attributes of the Divine Being? Doesn't the state of perfection belong to the Trinity alone to claim as a divine and absolute trait? I've just posed two questions that weren't meant as questions, but rather were a subtle mechanism prompting one to an introspection that leads to an affirmative conclusion.

Earthly perfection is a contradiction in terms. So let's delete the word "perfection" and replace it with "attainment" or maybe "maturity." Spiritual maturity. Now, back to the question, which correctly asks: why is suffering the only way to spiritual maturity? It isn't. It isn't the only way. At least not of itself, it isn't. It only appears that way because different degrees of suffering go hand in hand with the attainment of other spiritual attributes gained while making one's journey through life. Many of these attainments are powerful, yet subtle. However, in gaining these, one most remembers the suffering involved in their development. Long suffering is the *by-product* of attainment, not the *impetus* for it.

Spiritual maturity develops after one has conquered behavioral immaturity, after one has gained the eight aspects of the powers of Wisdom, which were explained in *Fireside*. For example, one of these powers of Wisdom is Silence and, mastering this power can be a long and arduous journey, which one could interpret as suffering, while gaining the self-control necessary for success. This singular power of Wisdom involves the ability to instinctively hold one's tongue, control reflexive verbal responses, and temper the urge to give unsolicited advice. Gaining the power of Silence carries deeper ramifications, which are oftentimes at odds with one's personality because Silence entails no verbal move to control, manipulate, or lead others in any way. No boasting or having the desire to exhibit one-upmanship. No prideful comments (or thoughts), no criticism, no more rude or hurtful utterances, no repeating of hearsay.

So then, the long journey toward spiritual maturity can indeed cause one suffering while she or he diligently works on the control of unspiritual behavior; however, this does not mean that the "suffering" alone is what makes one spiritual.

What is prayer?

True prayer is probably not what you think it is. When we hear the word "prayer," we usually conjure up an image of someone kneeling with bowed head and palms together. This is not a correct image, at least it isn't the singular image to associate with prayer. Likewise, when we think of prayer we think of pleading requests made of the Divine. A request connotes "asking" for something. Why is this? Why are we always *asking* of God? This means that people are, more often than not, asking God for something rather than *giving* something of self *to* the Divine. This "giving" should be forms of thankfulness, gratefulness for what we already have: health, basic needs met, a loved one, companionship, natural talents, inherent insight, an ability to produce income whereby we maintain a state of being reasonably self-sufficient and independent, etc. These are real blessings we should be thanking the Almighty for. To pray for "things" is absolutely ludicrous and exhibits a detrimental attitude of self-absorption. It indicates "want" rather than "gratefulness." Praying for wealth, status, material possessions, or to win a competitive sports contest screams of the egotistical "I" of self. Do you really believe the Divine responds to ego-generated requests? Now you might be led to think something like this: "Well then, I'll pray for the health or wealth of another!" Or, "I'll pray that my friend wins the award, or my son wins his football game!" Nope. Transferring the self-centered focus doesn't fool the deities one bit. No matter how you look at it, it's still the ego of someone who you're attempting to stroke and gratify.

Issues such as health are a blessing. If one wishes to pray for such a gift for self or others, rather the prayer be a true prayer than an "asking" event. Phrase prayers to represent an understanding of destiny rather than your own will.

Now, back to that mental image that most often presents itself when we think of prayer or hear the word. Remember that visual? The one with someone kneeling in supplication with head bowed and hands together. Why is this singular image conjured up all the time? Instead, why is it that other impressions aren't presented before the mind's eye? Impressive visuals of someone hard at work—putting forth their best effort? Or a presentation that depicts someone helping another? What about when you avoid spreading gossip? That's a form of prayer because it is seen as an active spiritual deed in the eyes of the Divine. Spiritual *acts* are a beautiful form of prayer. They are a form of prayer because they are interactive deeds of spiritual goodness that are highly pleasing to the Supreme Beings. Giving comfort is prayer. Being an unconditional friend is prayer. Volunteer work is prayer. Giving possessions away without a single grudging thought is prayer. Sharing your time, being someone's sounding board, appreciating a beautiful day, compassion, averting a confrontation, and having genuine Acceptance are all superlative examples of precious prayers that are gifts to the Trinity.

Prayer is not confined to a kneeling position nor any attitude of supplication. Prayer is not confined nor intensified by being within a place of worship. Votive candles, statuary, and incense do not enhance the depth nor the intensity of a prayer. Prayer is honoring the deities through pleasing acts of unconditional and instinctual goodness. Prayer is a way of life. Prayer is *living* goodness. In this manner are we fulfilling our spiritual potential on a daily basis. In this manner are we the magnificent *living lights* the Divine Source envisioned us to be.

How can a completed spirit who has returned to accomplish a specific spiritual mission end up deviating from it?

Will. By way of the will. Through choice.

Now let me explain further why this is so and how it can happen. While existing on the spiritual plane the spirit operates with full capacity of Knowing and purpose. It is brimming with anticipation to succeed in a specific earthly (or other physical planetary) mission. This spirit is strongly focused and centered on accomplishing the goal it was entrusted to attain and finalize. The spirit is biting at the bit to be about its way; after choosing its birth mother, who meets the best opportunistic conditions for this mission's beginning, the spirit enters into the physical.

BAM! Heavy body. Heavy atmosphere. Labored breathing to intake air. New sensations of pain and pleasure for this new spirit casing.

As this body grows and becomes an individual, its mechanized mind is inundated with matters of the physical. Philosophical, social, religious, ethical, moral, ideological, sexual, and identity concepts bombard the mind, all needing sorting out and prioritizing. This can sometimes be a difficult process for a completed spirit to accomplish. It is no longer solely the pure spirit it once was. Now it has a body whose mind is affected by electrical impulses and chemicals. The draw to physical pleasures is great. The draw to focus on the ego of self can be compelling. The focus on the identity of self can be overwhelming because of the very nature of the physical. The ego can become an obsession. Physical pleasures, such as drugs, alcohol, sexual experimentation, narcissism, and others often mix with a growing attitude of personal superiority whereby the individual now uses his spiritual mission as a manipulative tool to demand reverence, obedience, and submissive responses. In other words, the mission goes to his head and control of others becomes the paramount goal in life. Oftentimes, when this goal isn't going according to plan or begins falling apart after being successful for a number of years, the individual finds self unable to manage the situation and often resorts to more severe measures to get the control back. These measures frequently slip into violent behavior, complex fabrications, and intense psychological dramatization with those around him in order to gain sympathy and attention. Attention for self becomes the greater goal and any means are utilized to obtain it. But the individual can sense when those around him are tiring of the sympathy giving, the ongoing attempts to soothe and help; when apathy begins to show on the faces of those he associates with, an alienation of friends begins to occur. He ends up pushing everyone back instead of gathering them to him. He throws it all away with no place to go. He has hardened himself to his loved ones and chased them all away with manipulative maneuvers and violence. He has turned his friends away who have finally concluded that all the comfort and conversational hours of help have only served to feed the situation and give it stronger, more destructive energy. He finds himself despising the mission, becoming jealous of it getting more attention than he is and turns his renewed efforts to undermining it in any way possible. He blames the mission for the deplorable situation he finds himself in. He blames all those connected with said mission and, therefore, in his unstable mental state, believes that these connected individuals must also hate him too for the way he's acted. Hate and blame are now his to cast about.

With the mission losing priority, the physical takes its place. Love. Seeking physical pleasure. Controlling others through the facade of love and its dramatic overemotional displays all take priority now. Yet it's too late. He has abandoned that which others once admired him for (the spiritual mission they recognized he was here for). Now others are still willing to give him a chance, but when his manipulation begins to be obvious, they are too intuitive and independent to allow this in their lives. Again the individual is shot down, rejected. This type of individual cannot stand rejection. It strikes a devastating, fatal blow to the ego, which the individual will not let go of. And after experiencing a consecutive series of them while still trying to gain attention through the use of false love, after proposing marriage to woman after woman and being turned down, what's left for this person?

A completed spirit is merely another human being while in the physical—a human being with a powerful spiritual

task to accomplish as his/her quest in life. Yet that human being is no pure spirit walking the planet. That human being is
subject to the pull of physical temptations just as every other
human being is. That human being's mind is affected by
drugs, alcohol, chemical imbalances, electrical impulses, and
the attraction of sexual experimentation just as easily as others are. This is just one example of the many influences that
can deter and interfere with a completed spirit's mission.
The possible individual paths are as numerous and as diverse
as the entities walking them. What makes the difference is
free will, a focused mind, determination to carry the mission
to its conclusion, resisting the physical attractions, and, most
importantly, an intense recognition of *spirit* as sole identity
rather than a "self."

This generally held concept of completed spirits who are
here on the planet being so high and mighty that they are as
little gods and goddesses with no temptations or human
frailties has got to go. Let me share something with you regarding this issue. While making his life journey, Jesus often
confided in Mary Magdalene. One of his concerns was his
identity, which he himself occasionally questioned. He had
doubts about whether or not he was accomplishing what his
mission was designed to do. He was subjected to gossip because he associated with those society perceived as being
"less favorable individuals" and because he felt no compunction to avoid them. This was because he saw everyone as
beautiful spirits and loved them all equally. He danced, celebrated festivities with gusto, drank, and enjoyed participating in games that were sometimes those of chance. He was a
human among humans, experiencing life as it presented itself, all the while taking every opportunity to spread his
truths and way of the Word. His mission was not for those of
high status alone, but for every sheep found roaming upon
the land. Yet . . . self-doubts crept in. Doubts regarding who
he really was, doubts about his effectiveness, doubts of suc-
ceeding. What made Jesus succeed was his determination,

mission focus, balance of identity, and will. Jesus, like the completed spirits here to accomplish a spiritual task, has been completely misunderstood. The *real* Jesus is unknown and has yet to be revealed.

If the Divine is all forgiving, why do we have to work karma out?

Karma isn't for the Divine; it's for us, the individual spirit. Karma, the process, has nothing to do with God's forgiveness. It has to do with presenting a purified presence before God when we're ready to return to the Divine Essence. Would you give a present to your father and have him open it up to see a tattered and soiled shirt? The same principal applies to the purpose of karma. Presentation.

Of course the Divine is all forgiving, yet that attribute has absolutely nothing to do with the reason for karma. No matter how purified you manage to get your spirit through the times of extended incarnations, upon completion and the presentation of self to God, the Divine Mind will certainly *know* all you've done and experienced. All the dirty deeds will be clear to God, so there is already forgiveness there. See? It's a fact that God is pure and so, that which returns to the Divine Spirit, must also be as pure as possible.

I've perceived varied misconceptions regarding karma that are causing people extreme anxiety and confusion. The most psychologically damaging of these is the "reason for misfortune" or "having a physical affliction," which I will address through another question posed in this book.

Karma is not the catchall answer to everything bad that happens in one's life. It's become an easy out. A scapegoat on which to place blame, instead of understanding or facing personal responsibility. It's convenient to shift blame to another individual or some popular spiritual concept to cover the actions of self without having to bear the heavy burden of accountability. I find it interesting when I hear someone claim that karma is the cause of misfortune, yet anything wonderful happening in this person's life is due to nothing but *their* cleverness. Huh? Go figure. That isn't even rational. More than anything, that shows ego, and ego has got to go long before one is in the properly prepared condition to be presented before the Divine.

This reader's question sounded as though God would not forgive our transgressions unless we went back and fixed every one of them. Not so. The Divine Minds forgive unconditionally.

Are there spiritual aspects associated with being a victim of sexual abuse and, if so, what does this do to one's spirit?

This inquiry came from someone who was abused as a child and wonders about spiritual ramifications.

Such events do not negatively impact the spirit essence. The essence of one's spirit remains whole, yet absorbs every life experience of each incarnation as a separate facet of the spirit's totality. Cell memory, if you will, exists. This is how the spirit's experiential "carry-over" traits evidence through unique skills and child prodigies. Indiscriminate cell memories of the spirit can frequently transfer through to a future life incarnation. This, though, doesn't directly affect the spirit essence itself.

Let me try to make this clearer. Imagine your spirit as being likened to a mainframe computer database. Every thought and action of each life is entered and stored. They become cell memories of the spirit. Each lifetime forms a new facet of the main crystal that is your spirit (computer) holding the experiential input.

Now, as one journeys through life, that former input from any previous lifetime can be adeptly accessed by Consciousness or it can naturally be present as a sort of spiritual cell memory if it was an especially strong event or personal trait. The experience of sexual abuse becomes part of your current-life experience and is entered into the computer as being such. That's where it remains as part of your overall physical experiences for that specific lifetime. In future incarnations, that event may be a strong cellular spirit memory and, in some manner, be allowed to affect the current life through a variety of reactive ways, such as shunning the opposite sex, an aversion to sex, being an advocate for the prevention of sexual abuse, choosing celibacy, working with victims of abuse, etc. This is a direct cause-and-effect (action/reaction) example of spirit cell memory and the mechanizations of same.

The questioner was fearful of negative effects left upon the spirit due to current-life sexual abuse. This should not be a worry or concern. The spirit takes in all experiential events as neutral input without judgment; what turns it positive or negative is how each cell memory is *psychologically* processed in the future incarnations. It can be a forged tool that serves as an impetus to exhibit positive or negative behavior associated with the issue. It can generate an attitude of advocacy or aversion. Psychologically, it can exhibit itself as a help or hindrance. However, it's very important to realize that this evidences *only* within the psychological functioning (behavioral traits) of a future incarnation and *not* within the *composite* spirit essence itself, which remains strong with the knowledge that all experiential events are merely absorbed as fragmentary components of its totality.

Now, at this point, a deeper thinker would come up with a question that naturally comes on the heels of where my response has taken it, so let's take care of it next.

If the spirit essence absorbs all life experiences as neutral input, how is negative behavior recognized and categorized as being necessary to earmark for karmic correction?

The neutrality aspect references the effects upon the spirit itself, which is nil. However, this does not mean that positive and negative deeds and thoughts are not *recognized* as such.

These, in and of themselves, are earmarked by their very nature, automatically; elsewise, how could a spirit end up tending toward an overall healthy (good) or ill (dangerously negative) soul composite that evidences or bleeds through into future incarnations? We know that this occurs because, through this concept, we are witnesses to the manifested goodness of a Mother Teresa or the expressed vileness of an Adolph Hitler. In this manner do individuals outwardly reveal that inner state of their spiritual beingness.

Each spirit possesses an inherent Knowing of one's personal spirit condition. In addition to this Knowing, each spirit, while occupying a physical form housing a mechanized brain, understands correct behavior and spiritual rightness. This then leaves one's behavioral actions and responses contingent upon the free will, the conscious and voluntary choices made in life.

Is a spirit held karmically responsible for negative deeds performed while in a body having mental dysfunctions?

If the thought process of the mechanized brain is hampered through chemical imbalance, a malfunction of the electrical impulses, or other types of physiological abnormalities resulting in mental impairment, the spirit does not recognize these deeds as negative ones. It's almost as though the deeds never happened at all.

When an Alzheimer's parent becomes combative and strikes out at his/her adult child, is that parent responsible for that behavioral action? Of course not. When that same parent makes things up, such as lies about the adult child or shouts out cruel and hurtful comments, is that verbal negativity something the spirit needs to answer for? No. Likewise, mental aberrations resulting in psychotic and schizophrenic behavior will not carry karmic responsibility.

It's important to understand that to incur negative karmic debt, one has to have performed the offending negative thought or deed (or act of omission) during a state of full Consciousness and awareness of such deed through the free will choice of a *stable physical mind*. Granted, it's human nature to want someone to pay, and pay dearly, for the heinous deeds we see done to others on a daily basis; yet if the perpetrator is not of sound mind and did not perform such act with full, stable mental capacity, how can personal responsibility or accountability be deemed an inevitability or held to unconditionally? Just as the social justice system takes this into account by incarcerating an unstable perpetrator in a mental health institution instead of finding them accountable and sending them to prison for life, so too does the soul recognize these same types of acts as being categorized as such.

Because of the atrocities that resulted from the mind of Hitler, many of us would like to believe a sane individual could not have conceived such misery, much less convince others to carry out his philosophy; however, Hitler knew exactly what he was doing and that's what makes it so frightening and makes every other soul shudder at the thought.

Please tell us the true story of the life of Jesus. Overall, history has given us a mere sketch of the real individual.

I certainly agree with your idea of history being a mere sketch of the man. There was so much more depth, complexity, and scope to his personality. The everyday activities that made up the greater part of his life *in between* the overemphasized events that were reiterated in the gospels are hidden from view. Why is this, I wonder? His deeds and words (few of them) are recorded, but why not his very *thoughts*? Why don't the gospels reveal his personality? His doubts, pleasures, loves, and inner concerns?

What we have in the Bible is a designer savior. Designed by the poor memories of those who were with him. Designed by a desire to be recognized as one who spent time with him and, supposedly, knew him on a personal basis. Designed by those wishing to present the image and persona of a miracle-producing god, one who was their close friend. Ergo . . . ego wrote the biblical gospels.

But wait! *Fresh* gospels have been discovered! Fresh historical air now comes escaping out from the pottery found in Nag Hammadi by a modern-day Bedouin. Scroll after valuable scroll saw the first light of day after two thousand years of waiting for their glorious daybreak. Scroll after scroll and codex after codex, written by those who wished to *retain* truths that they saw being altered in the name of some new religious philosophy that would one day be called Christianity, sent shock waves that rumbled and tumbled through the fields of theology, antiquity studies, and archeological research. What was severely suppressed two thousand years ago and tagged as being heretical (as opposed to the new, designer gospels) by the founding men of budding Christianity, suddenly reappears as though reborn or resurrected.

Combining the Nag Hammadi cache with that of the find unearthed in Qumran, we become enlightened to an individual called The Righteous One. We also learn the truth of the Feminine Principle, the Divine Mother, Sophia (embodiment of Wisdom) who was the Creatrix, and the Goddess who birthed the lesser-revered individuals such as Melchizedek is revealed. Through these ancient, preserved truths, we learn of the true divinity of God's divine relatedness of the Trinity, which includes the feminine aspect of the Shekinah, . . . which Christianity, through its patriarchal bent, dubbed the Holy Ghost . . . then changed it to Holy Spirit. The Shekinah was eventually downgraded by the patriarchal, ancient-time cabalists, by demeaning the original matriarchal, feminine concept to one that connoted a term solely associated with "God's spirit evidenced in the world." But I'm digressing.

The questioner's concern was of the historical individual called Jesus. The unearthed truths infer that The Righteous One could be none other than Jesus. BUT, that would mean that Jesus *survived the crucifixion!* It would mean that he walked the earth and continued teaching for over *twenty years* after his alleged sacrifice! Is that the truth that the infant Christianity tried to suppress and therefore tagged as being a heretical belief, because the foundation of their religion was based on the sole premise of Jesus dying for your sins? What would undermine their foundation of faith more than anything would be to discover that he did not die at Golgotha. Are those who Christians call heretics the real truth bearers? Oh, so many wonderful puzzles to unravel! Well, they're not really puzzles anymore, are they? The truth of all these matters seems to be coming to light, one way or another.

When people die from natural causes, their spirit is released from their body in a gentle manner, but when they die in a forceful manner such as an accident or murder, the spirit is forced out roughly from the body causing it to become vengeful or confused, whereby it may linger for months or years. Why?

The singular key word within this question is "may." This concept is classed under "usual" circumstances; however, it is not a carved-in-stone rule.

Violent deaths, those that are sudden and unexpected, are not deaths that are prepared for. Because of this aspect, the spirit is literally forced out of the body, which naturally *can* cause considerable confusion, feelings of unjustness, or even some thoughts of retribution. Those anticipating a near-future death get their affairs in order and are prepared. Those leaving suddenly most often have left much undone. Unfinished business, whether it be a need to see justice carried out, affairs put in order, or other situations, is usually the cause for a spirit to linger around the physical for a time.

Yet those who die after having been in anticipation of the event still may linger for a time, too. Perhaps there are difficulties in regard to carrying out the last wishes of a will and the deceased is intent on ensuring his/her desires are adhered to. Perhaps some business that should have been taken care of had been overlooked. Perhaps there are final good-byes to express or the spirit wishes to give comfort for a time to the bereaved. The reasons vary greatly.

Death from murder can often involve a lingering spirit. A suicide most often does not because the individual's focused mind-set was to escape, get out of here, off the planet to a far, far better place. Accidents can go either way. Death resulting from a prolonged illness usually entails a speedy journey into the spectacular beauty of the Beyond. It's what the ill individual was waiting and waiting for, anticipating, wanting to experience. The death of an infant or young child also prompts a quick return to the Hereafter because strong emotional ties have not had the time to develop the intensity of strength powerful enough to compel a lingering event.

It is more the rule, more the actuality, for a spirit to speed into the Beyond than to linger. This is why it's so vitally important to understand the truth of this concept. I see so many people claiming to "feel" some deceased individual's spirit around them when, in fact, it's nowhere about in the physical. The so-called psychic advisers need to grasp a deeper understanding regarding this because, seriously, most often, the spirit of a friend or loved one cannot be contacted. Why? Because it's gone onto greener valleys and is involved with its spiritual work of advancing into a more purified state. Don't forget, once on the other side, bettering and upgrading the state of the spirit becomes a single-minded focus and one is rarely available for "call-backs" or parlor conversations.

This issue, remember, is addressing the *general* populace of humanity, not specific spiritual entities whose mission is to assist the physical and can be contacted through communications. The distinction is important.

Please dispel the belief that to accept Jesus Christ into your heart absolutely absolves all sin and saves your soul. I'm so tired of hearing this.

An individual of intelligence doesn't buy this. In the first place, it's not logical. This statement says that "no matter what crimes you perpetrate, you're completely forgiven as long as you hold Jesus Christ in your heart." *Belief* in Jesus is far different than *living* as though he were *dwelling* in one's heart. The fact of the matter is that if one lived life while constantly and forever truly believing Jesus lived within the heart, that individual would not have a single bad or unkind thought, much less perpetrate an unspiritual deed. See? It doesn't wash. It's a contradiction to begin with. In addition, forgiveness comes from the Divine and is automatic. It's a given because of the Divine Being's magnanimous attributes. It has nothing to do with Jesus at all. Humanity must keep its concepts straight. Jesus, while walking the earth, forgave sins *in God's name.* Jesus did not allege to forgive sins in the name of Jesus. He was messenger, a server for One greater. So let's get on the right track with this. Forgiveness is a given, with or without Jesus, or Buddha, or Allah in your heart. There are absolutely no conditions placed on whether or not God forgives people's transgressions. It is done *unconditionally!* Please, let's get with the program here.

Does the whole spirit reincarnate each time or does a portion remain behind in the spirit world until all karmic debts are met?

The *totality* of the spirit incarnates each time. Each incarnation forms a brand new facet of the whole living crystal of the total spirit. Through Consciousness, every incarnation has access to every formerly formed crystal facet of itself. In this manner do we oftentimes experience those specialized traits and memories that are unique to a particular facet, such as unexplained skills, knowledge, cultural or ethnic attractions, and recalled memories. These are the "carry-over" experiential traits of former incarnations that formed within that specific facet of the spirit's total living crystal. Each incarnation forms another facet and adds its own unique characteristics of the experience. One facet may be imprinted with an Irish ethnicity and an analytical proficiency. Another facet of one's total spirit crystal may identify with a life lived within an ancient monastery and contain a fascination with old texts or theological mysteries. The individual who formed this facet may have been a mystic. In this manner we are all things, a composite of every life lived and every event formerly experienced. A current child prodigy who becomes the much-touted media marvel, such as an accomplished pianist, has retained the skill that was developed to proficiency in a former life and has been permanently imprinted on that specific crystal facet. The skill "carried over" into the current life experience.

Our facets do not break off into pieces at any time. They are not left scattered about in different dimensions. We are not fragments of our self. We are whole.

Evidence of this wonderful wholeness comes to the fore when retrogression occurs. This can be instigated naturally through instances of memory bleed-through, deep meditation, or hypnotic therapy guidance. As a personal example, the last complete facet formed within my own spirit crystal was that of an individual indigenous to North America, an American Indian. Now, during the formation of this *current* incarnation facet, memories from that formerly formed facet have carried over strongly. Coming to realize that an American Indian ethnicity was a strong aspect of my *total* self, I couldn't ignore certain inherent traits and inner promptings that drew me to that culture, traits that comprised my totality. Memories compelled me to recapture certain of those remembered aspects and consciously integrate them into my current experience. By doing this, I gained a beautiful sense of completeness. Now that this has been accomplished, I understand that I am a *composite* of every ethnic culture I ever experienced and the "who" of me is not defined solely by any singular faceted culture or ethnicity, talent, or physical characteristic. One facet of the spectacular spirit crystal represents a single *fragment* of the "who" of you. One unique experience does not make a total individual or spirit. One unique experience *adds* color and dimension to create the ongoing formation of one's composite spirit essence.

By using the analogy of a "crystal," I believe it's a more accurate visual than that of "computer." Some spiritual philosophical concepts are better clarified by going with the computer symbolism, others by using the crystal. Both are effective representations that serve to unscramble the often confusing concepts.

Now . . . I'm not sure I should expand on this questioner's inquiry, but being naturally prone to carrying ideas to the hilt, I suppose I should take this concept one step beyond the generally recognized theory.

The questioner asked whether or not we leave a portion of our spirit behind when incarnating. The definitive response was a resounding No. However, let me take the basic concept and digress, or rather I should say, let me defer, to *other* spiritual beings who have this ability and frequently activate it.

There are "angels" and there are "angelic spiritual beings of light." It is extremely rare for a real angel to occupy a human form. They could, but it is not normally within their realm of operation to do so. However, as I stated, there are angelic beings who do frequently take on human form. These beings can also occupy *several* human forms *simultaneously* without diminishing their effectiveness in any way. This event is precipitated by the gravity of a mission and deemed the best manner to achieve optimum success. An example of this concept manifesting was when an angelic being occupied the human form of Mary Magdalene and Thomas at the same time.

Mary Magdalene was never the wanton harlot Scripture alleges her to have been. She was confidante, consort, and first disciple to Jesus. She was despised by the apostles, especially Peter, for being a mere woman and appearing to be Jesus' favorite among them. She was highly intelligent, wealthy in her own right, exhibited a unique understanding of Jesus' concepts, and led a large group of women disciples after establishing a women's spiritual center. Later in life her mission was to be a helpful companion to Jesus' mother.

Thomas has also been misrepresented in scripture. Thomas was never a doubter, but rather displayed the same analytical mind Magdalene had. When among the group of apostles or with Jesus out in a public crowd, he would intentionally generate questions for the prime purpose of compelling the others gathered there to think deeper. The other apostles resented his fine mind and, because of this resentment, depicted him as simply a doubter who had to have everything proved to him. Thomas was a devoted and favored member of Jesus retinue. Later in life, Thomas remained in close contact with Mary Magdalene and frequently visited Jesus' mother to give assistance however he could.

Revealing this information was my choice to do. I've done so because the reality of this questioner's initial concept is *only an option of choice for angelic beings.* People need to understand this distinction.

Each time I introduce a new or rare spiritual concept, I open up a probability for the human mind to latch onto such theory and claim it as their identity or experience. Yet this penchant will not deter me from attempting to present the truths as I've come to know them to be. What people *do* with information is their choice and responsibility, not mine. My responsibility is to clarify the spiritual philosophical concepts as best I can and do this without reserve or fear of any type of reprisal, though they be many.

Did fire-breathing dragons once exist as described in the Bible?

The paleontologists would have a field day with this one. What of the lumbering Tyrannosaurus rex? The Stegosaurus stenops? Brontosaur and Triceratops?

Evidence of these prehistoric creatures abounds in today's world of discovery, so how can we say that, in ancient times, evidence wasn't also found? Bones. Imprints of footfalls in stone. An individual chancing upon these prehistoric samples two thousand years ago would most likely have scratched his/her head and then come up with the fun idea of spinning wildly imaginative tales, don't you think? To go as far as claiming these creatures lived in biblical times is too great a stretch. Says more than a little about the biblical stories, doesn't it? How is it that current society categorizes prehistoric creature interaction with humans to Greek, Roman, or Celtic *mythology* or *legend* and, on the same hand, continues to declare these same types of creatures as being *real* when recounted in the Bible? What's going on here? Which is it, mythology or truth? Now I've asked the same question the inquirer did. Clearly my question was not a question, though.

How do we protect ourselves from psychic mind control, from elementals, black magic, jealousy, and hatred?

The answer is contained in the question. Control of others is born through the victim's permission of it and is sustained through submission. Control, psychic or psychological, cannot survive in a state of resistance or neutrality. It manifests by way of someone *permitting* it to invade his/her life and becomes a powerful growing force of manipulation when it is submitted to. Control exists only when it is *allowed* to.

Frequently this permission is not recognized for what it is. Fear gives permission to control. Insecurity gives permission.

Lack of personal responsibility gives permission. Paranoia and indecision open the door for control to walk in. Asking advice indiscriminately gives others control. Not realizing your own personal power shifts that power to others, who will then use it through your own control mechanisms.

Black magic is fear-based. Mind control, psychic or psychological, is not control and cannot gain a foothold if one doesn't allow one's mind to be manipulated or brainwashed. The key to preventing this from happening is *knowing* one's mind, knowing what one believes. Jealousy? Hatred? Why should these negative attitudes even affect you? Acceptance, remember? Having neutral Acceptance of the attitudes of others is one of Wisdom's beautiful and incredibly strong powers. Why should one feel controlled just because another individual hates them or is jealous? We must not invite these same negatives to affect us by allowing their damaging qualities to enter our sphere of beingness. A healthy mind recognizes negativity when exhibited in others and does not internalize it. Wisdom is the name of the personal power that protects one by repelling negativity through recognition, acceptance, and understanding that it belongs to the mind of someone else. Internalizing the negativity of another opens self to same. It gives permission to enter without resistance. It *invites* control with welcoming, open arms and, before you can finish saying Rumpelstiltskin . . . you're snagged, caught fast in the web of negativity.

Is it dangerous to invoke spirits or do ceremonial magic?

Whether it's dangerous or not, why on earth would one wish to do so? For entertainment? Certainly not as a serious endeavor. Invoke which spirits? The spirit of whom? Whose spirit is more powerful than the Divine's or the angelic beings'? To invoke any lesser spirits makes no sense at all. If one must call upon those of power, do so. If it's so vital that you seek the ones with the greatest power, then call upon those who possess it and have the wherewithal to use it. Seek assistance from the *highest* source. Calling upon lesser spirits will only bring grief.

Ceremonial magic. Games. Ego. False sense of power.

How does one tell the difference between a dream and an out-of-body experience?

As real as some dreams can appear, they will contain some type of inconsistency or illogical aspect: running in slow motion, seeing a lamp in the refrigerator, perceptual distortions such as exaggerated facial features, overall scenic presentations that either display a macro or micro view, etc. All these features indicate a dreamscape event.

An out-of-body event signifies a spirit journey and seeing life through the projected perception of the spirit's inherent awareness of the current Consciousness. This means that one sees world reality as it is presented in the framework of the third dimension (unless one is traveling into other realities by way of Quantum Meditation). Out-of-body perception takes in what is real, current, what is happening *today*. Visuals will not show a lamp in the refrigerator. They will not distort the characteristics of people's faces nor present a macro or micro view of a scene. Out-of-body viewing sees the same things you see with your physical eyes. The difference between what the spirit eyes see and what the physical eyes see is that the spirit will see whatever it intends to see at whatever chosen location the mind wishes to travel to in order to see it. And that's the Tao of out-of-body experiences.

Is maturity fostered by daily decisions to follow the Ten Commandments?

There are different types of maturity and, since you didn't specify which one you were referring to, I have to think you were implying spiritual maturity.

Making daily decisions to follow the Ten Commandments can certainly lead to spiritual maturity; however, the key word here is "decisions." Spiritual maturity comes from living the Ten Commandments naturally, without applying conscious decision-making choices.

The act of *consciously* choosing to make behavioral responses in accord with the Ten Commandments is, in essence, a method of self-training toward the goal of the maturity you seek to gain. In this manner is the decision-making process one of great value. To have to *think* before one makes a move, in order to determine spiritual value assessments, is a sign that one is intent on walking on the path of The Way and is expending every effort to adhere to that determined life of goodness.

The personal effort expended during this process affords great rewards in the form of gaining increasing measures of personal power through sudden insights, which spear as a ray of light from the embodiment of wisdom. While on this conscious, decision-making path, one is oftentimes surprised by the increasing frequency of unexpected epiphanies that enter the mind as explosions of clear understanding. Expending the effort to live life according to the Ten Commandments brings multiple side benefits. Attaining the spiritual maturity comes when the walk upon this path becomes effortless and thought applied to making spiritual behavioral choices becomes an unnecessary step to actions.

Is entering an altered state of consciousness to reach one's spiritual potential (abilities) dangerous?

This question sounded reasonable until the inquirer added the word enclosed in parentheses. The individual is equating "spiritual potential" to "abilities." Abilities? These are not the goal of reaching spiritual potential. The *living* of *Unconditional Goodness* is the goal. The attainment of *Wisdom* is the goal. Abilities? Nada. What is it with this incredible fascination with abilities? Is it a power thing whereby people are misunderstanding what true power is? Is it ego? Is it the egotistical, self-inflating capability to be able to claim psychic talents? What? I don't compute this attitude that mixes up spiritual priorities in respect to the qualities that equate to higher spiritual attainment.

Listen. An individual who can easily perform remote viewing, travel out of body, use telepathic skills at will, give evidence of psychokinesis, and utilize psychometry can also be the most spiritually bankrupt individual walking this planet. *Psychic abilities do not define a spiritually aware or highly developed spiritual state of being.* Please, this is so important to truly understand. Psychic abilities are *of the mind.* Most psychic skills only show that someone is a mentalist. They do not, in any way, prove spiritual development. Mental. Spiritual. The two are not interchangeable synonyms for each other. Their conceptualities are not related.

Sadly, I've noticed a general inclination for the populace to elevate an individual who possesses mental abilities to the status of spiritual guru. This is only because people don't understand the difference between Spirituality and mentalism. This, therefore, is how ingenious mentalists stroke their huge egos through attracting the misguided seekers who perceive the individual as a great, accomplished spiritual leader. The seekers, then, shower said imposter with reverence, commitment, loyalty, and end up gifting him with ever-increasing power. Eventually the mentalist/guru becomes a master manipulator. And a brand-spanking-new cult is birthed. So please, stop the tendency to equate mental contortionists with spiritually developed individuals.

Oh, now I suppose someone will say, "Well, doesn't the term 'psyche' refer to the spirit?" And I would agree with that. Where the problem arises is how society has misplaced the psyche word into the real category of mentalism. Right from the outset, concepts were mixed. A psychologist would have a completely different definition and set of conceptual theories regarding the "psyche" word. As a general rule, let's begin to untangle this mess by training ourselves to use the word "mental" when referring to mental abilities and use the word "spiritual" when referencing aspects related to the spirit.

Now, before I forget, let me return to the original question. Let's reword it for the purpose of maintaining its proper context. "Is entering an altered state of consciousness to reach one's spiritual potential dangerous?" Personally, I see this question as being bass-backwards because usually the *attainment* of one's spiritual potential *precedes* the experience of slipping into altered states at will. Well, at least that's the way it's supposed to happen, theoretically, anyway. However, there are more exceptions to the rule than there are rules to count. I'm big on living a life of Unconditional Goodness as one's singular goal, which, if successful, quite naturally carries gradually increasing measures of wonderful side effects, such as a new gentleness to one's character. Acceptance of others' behavior becomes a more natural response; meditation becomes easier to do, as are serenity, ease of slipping into altered states, increased moments of inspired wisdom, and deeper insights. These accompany the ideal of living by way of Unconditional Goodness. So to ask about going into altered states first is very much like thinking the horse needs to be behind the cart for the cart to move up the road. "Is it dangerous to force altered states?" Not as a rule, it isn't. Not if you're spiritually strong and spiritually minded. But why is doing that so important? What does it prove? Where does it get you if you're not already *there* spiritually? The way I see it, if you want to reach your spiritual potential then . . . be spiritual. You accomplish this by living a life of Unconditional Goodness. What on earth is more important than that?

I don't believe in a place called hell, so where in the hell did No-Eyes have you journey to then?

I explained this in *Daybreak,* but perhaps you missed it or I need to word it another way. Sure, you're right about there being no such place as hell, except in legendary tales.

Remember when there was an experience recounted in my books when I felt I was walking through some type of vileness while going up to her cabin? Do you recall how terrified I was? The event I experienced was a minimal exposure to humanity's negativity, its greed, jealousy, hatred, vengefulness, cruelty, and violence. The place I went to (which I called Hades) was along the same vein, yet brimming with the maximum level of those same negativities. For some reason, my spiritual mentor felt I needed to experience how heinous people's basest behavior, attitudes, and thoughts were if they could be *sensually* experienced. The descriptive characteristics of the senses I detailed were as though reality were presenting a face, a smell, a sound to hatred, greed, cruelty, etc. The stenches, the grotesquely distorted features and postures, and the soul-shuddering sounds of these negatives were horrendous. The event can be compared to how Scrooge's partner, Marley, appeared in spirit with massive "chains" wrapped about him. The chains represented the "weighted" spiritual effects that his greed and the dark deeds of his life forged on the spiritual dimension. So, too, was my journey a presentation "representing" the unseen vileness people's behavior really causes. Another example can be compared to the hidden mirror of Dorian Gray. The man remained young and handsome, while all his evil deeds were manifested upon the image of his hidden and shrouded portrait, where his true self was hideously depicted.

Imagine, if you will, being able to see what envy's face looked like and hear its true voice. Imagine hatred putting out a specific odor for all to smell. The true spiritual effects of human vileness is what my journey was all about. It taught me a great deal. Its experience was invaluable. Being surrounded by the sensual aspects emitted by such base emotions brought home the hideousness of such behavior. Hell. It was exactly like being surrounded by hellish beings. If there were such a place as hell, it would be right here where all the tormented and vile humans hide their gruesome selves behind a smiling mask and cover their true stench with cologne.

Are the revelations of all the bad happenings at the end of time in the Bible true?

Yes, they're *symbolically* true. This subject matter was covered in *The Visitation*. The catch is this: what constitutes the so-called End Time? Everyone seems to be shuddering in their boots, preoccupied with this End Time thing. By looking symbolically at Revelation, we see that the major portion of the story has already manifested over time. Many of the concepts refer to internal, personal events occurring in one's own life which bring about inner turmoil that eventually leads one to a state of spiritual transformation. Revelation was a dream, don't forget. And dreams are mostly symbolism. This fact has been ignored and, because of this monumental oversight, it's caused unnecessary anxiety, fear, and apathy.

If someone has died and their spirit has gone on to do other work, how can people on earth still contact that spirit? How can a reincarnated spirit be contacted?

What? Why in heaven's name would anyone want to contact a singular facet of someone's spirit crystal? That's like going up to the grocer and saying: "I knew you in your last lifetime when you were a financial analyst and I desperately have to talk to you about that portfolio you advised me about. Let's do lunch!" Though you may have the right guy, that guy most likely has no idea of what you're talking about. He is someone altogether different now. He has a new ethnicity, a new name, maybe a different gender, too. Former relationships are severed, new ones have been forged. New philosophies or spiritual beliefs may be in evidence. Only memories of the now are retained.

Instances have occurred where two or more people have reconnected after having shared former life experiences together. I would never say never to that. Yet these instances were usually managed through mutual recognition and strong memories of each other. There has been proof of several spirits reincarnating time after time together and, while in the physical, made recognition of each other. Note: these, though are not twin souls. But to try to contact and reconnect with great-grandpa who has died and reincarnated again as Prince Tumbutu in Africa is . . . not wise. Not a good move. Definitely not a good move.

What are dark forces?

When you hear that phrase I hope Satan doesn't come to mind. Probably does, huh? Well, I suppose that's a natural response; however, it would be wrong. Oh, I'm not saying that an evil entity is not a dark force; I'm saying that evil entities are only the tip of the icy berg.

Maybe the real dark forces are so well disguised that people tend to not recognize them. These forces are experts at concealing themselves, masking their darkness with false light, and smelling flower fresh. They wear illusionary masks and walk among you, work beside you, and reverently sit in the pews on Sunday morn. Is the answer getting warmer yet? They preach, sell you fast-food, pick up your garbage, and manage your money. The banker, the clerk, the preacher, your lover, all have the ability to carry dark forces in the form of negative attitudes, thoughts, emotions, and deeds.

The dark forces are the greed, hatred, jealousy, prejudice, racism, sexism, and egotistical negatives I wrote about in previous responses to related questions. Dark forces are powerful forces manifesting evil evidence in the world. Why is it that we don't recognize unspiritual attitudes as being a powerful force of darkness in our lives? It's so clear, so obvious . . . so real.

If I stood beside a racist and cryptically whispered in his ear: "Watch out! There's a dark force here!" he'd snap his head around looking for some type of evil-looking character lurking in a shadowed corner. He'd never in his wildest dreams imagine that I was referring to himself, because people don't normally think of negative attitudes as being dark, dangerous, and a damaging force harmful to the world. Same would happen if I whispered the identical words of warning to an egotistical preacher or a chauvinistic man, or a self-centered woman. Every one of them would look elsewhere, everywhere but within. These negative attitudes of humanity represent the greater portion of evil (dark forces) loosed upon our society, yet other representations are here, too.

There are spirits who have given no care to their spirit's condition, no concern for nor effort applied to correct past negative behavior (karmic correction). As time passes, these types of spirits become imbalanced by way of the negative far outweighing the positive. Nor does this matter to them. Eventually negative behavior becomes a way of life to them. It has become a habitual behavioral pattern, a comfortable pattern. They eventually come into the world with no care to do good or be good. Ego has been allowed to overtake self. If something doesn't directly serve self, then it's not worth the effort to expend time on nor give attention to. If someone is in their way, the dark individual takes removal measures. If there's something they want, they take it whatever way they can. Respect for life's sacredness is a foreign concept. The manipulation of others and the control of all situations are paramount. These are just a few examples of how a dark force living among you will behave. Yet not all these shadowy spirits incarnate. In this case, they do their dirty work through attempting to negatively influence and manipulate humanity by way of instilling damaging thoughts, desires, and spiritual concepts which conflict with The Way. Doubt is a favorite tool of theirs. Skepticism and suspicion are usually their second choice for weapons of destruction. Watch for these insidious signs in your life. Watch for the cleverly hidden dark forces that daily brush your shoulder as they pass or pause in your shadow. Learn to recognize their faces. Pick up on the underlying stench beneath the cologne. Attune your ears to the grating voice behind the honey-coated tongue.

Is it possible to exist in two realities at once?

Sure, but I want to clarify the fact that this is manifested through the spirit's Consciousness and not the *embodiment* of the spirit. We are not talking about simultaneous incarnations here. We aren't referring to a splitting or fragmenting of one's spirit. What we are talking about is being able to broadcast one's Consciousness to cover a multiplicity of dimensional locales. This can be accomplished and it is done.

For the sake of keeping within the bounds of this question's specifics, my response focuses on the example of Quantum Meditation, which facilitates mobility of one's Consciousness through multidimensional realms of reality and vibrational frequencies. While the meditator's body remains in the third dimension (one reality) Consciousness can expand out to a different dimensional locale (second reality). By doing this, the meditator is actually in two places at the same time. The physical body is here, while the Consciousness is elsewhere, each dimension being equally real. By the way, we also see this happening during a comatose state.

If the questioner is intending to mean a *physical* existence in two different *realities,* then that's entirely different. That would interpret as having a dual physical body. No, that doesn't happen. Please don't confuse this with the spiritual body that Consciousness can manifest to use while making journeys by way of Quantum Meditation. That's a far stretch from talking about two "physical" bodies.

As already explained in a previous response, only angelic beings can manifest experiential incarnations within multiple bodies simultaneously. This capability also encompasses the utilization of varying dimensional realities.

So, how did I just answer this question? The spirits of humans cannot *physically* exist in two *realities* at once. Humans can park the physical body in the third dimension and have the conscious travel to other realities. All other types of simultaneous, multiple-reality experiences can only be manifested by angelic beings. Hope that helped to summarize my answer.

I've been a Catholic all my life, yet find the Church's attitude toward appointing women as priests (or pope?) antiquated and sexist. Though I try to ignore it, I'm really irritated by this. Any calming words?

I don't know if my words will be calming or more infuriating; I suppose that's going to be left up to you. Let's face it, the Church is a staunchly patriarchal institution. There's no getting around, over, or behind it. However, we can peek *beneath* it and sneak a look into its highly guarded, secret past. Shhh, walk softly with me now as we descend down into the depths of the basilica's dark catacombs, where no member of the general faithful is allowed to tread. We're going to see what's been long buried.

Oh my, look what we've found. A pile of old, brittle texts. We'll carefully take one codex from the stack and have a peek. . . .

Our little adventure was well worth it, for the following is a portion of the history we uncovered.

Centuries before the emergence of Christianity, belief in the Mother Goddess was the prime spiritual concept of nearly every world culture. She was represented by different names according to the various cultures. In Canaan she was known as Asherah; in the land of Sumer she was called Inanna; in Greece she was worshipped as Demeter; in Cyprus, Aphrodite. In many ancient belief systems she was known to be a virgin birthing a savior who sacrificed himself to save others and had subsequently resurrected. She birthed a messiah. Over and over again the scenario was retold throughout history.

Up to the second century C.E., the bustling city of Alexandria was the gathering place for freethinkers. Intellectual spiritual thought (Gnosticism) and the openness to innumerable alternative ideological concepts were welcomed without reserve or judgment. Among these widely held concepts was the belief that the Holy Spirit was feminine. Other mores of the time included the attitude that women were equally as intelligent as men and had equal legal rights. There were as many women scholars and spiritual leaders as there were men, however, it was the women matriarchs who were perceived as being personally responsible for the maintenance of the integrity of spiritual concepts, which, consequently, remained pure from generation to generation.

Belief in the Divine Mother was found to be alive and thriving in almost every culture. The ancient cabalists believed that the Shekinah was God's former spouse and that all wisdom originated from her magnificence. And, in some of the oldest Talmudic texts, it was said that angels were *created from her splendor.* Furthermore, long before the time of Moses, multicultural beliefs throughout the civilized world held that the *Divine Mother gave* each culture tablets on which were recorded the Rules of Right Living.

By the middle of the second century, the sex of the Goddess was altered to that of a male when men changed her into a god and Alexandria experienced a massive spiritual upheaval through the growing strength of a newborn religion called Christianity. The newfound Christian church, specifically the leaders forming Catholic dogma, had no tolerance for any spiritual beliefs that ran counter to their newly devised tenets. The Church leaders' righteous arrogance declared all religious concepts that were outside its realm to be punishable acts of heresy. The Church's foundational precept was built on the birth, teachings, suffering, death, and resurrection of the Son of God . . . a man; therefore the formerly held beliefs in the Divine Mother Goddess as Creatrix (and more) were declared anathema and deemed a conceptual priority to eradicate forever.

So then, the intellectual freedom and spiritual diversity that Alexandria had thoroughly enjoyed for centuries was now suppressed and those individuals who had been recording the ancient beliefs on scrolls were forced to sequester them away to preserve their integrity. These scrolls and codices also included detailed historical events of Jesus' life. Many of these last were secretly hidden away because they were too revealing and explicit for the Church's taste when it began the process of choosing "official" gospels to sanction. Some of these hidden caches were found in pottery within caves around Qumran and Nag Hammadi in December of 1945. What's interesting to note, particularly relevant for the woman who asked me this question in her letter, is that, historically, the long-held and solidly based matriarchal societies and Divine Mother beliefs were smothered and relegated to myth and legend *after* the dawn of patriarchal Christianity.

Let's see, what other secret did we unearth in the catacombs? Oh yes . . . *Pope Joan!* We discovered that there indeed *was* a woman pope. Her name was Johanna, but she altered it to her brother's name of John when she was forced to take on a male identity in order for her high intelligence to be recognized in the ninth century. She was elected pope in the ninth century and remained so for two years, until her true identity (gender) was discovered after she had the misfortune of having a miscarriage in the middle of a papal procession. Some historical records refer to her papacy, but her name was officially deleted from the papal succession list in the seventeenth century. Joan (Pope John) reigned after Pope Leo IV and before Pope Benedict III. To hide her reign, the dates for Leo's reign was extended two years and forever stayed on the books that way. However, in 1276, Pope John

XX altered his title to John XXI in recognition of Joan's legal and rightful reign. Today, if you happen to peruse the *Catholic Encyclopedia,* you'll not see Pope John (Joan) listed within the chronology of historical popes. Nope. What you will find is Pope Joan listed as an entry word. Beneath her name you'll read that she is a myth, a legend, which *somehow* got started back in the ninth century. Funny thing, though, while down in those catacombs we came across an unusual chair with a hole in the seat. It looked like an ornately carved, adult potty-training chair. This, we find, is called the *sella stercoraria* and was used for nearly six hundred years during medieval papal consecration ceremonies for the purpose of a "chair exam" and was instigated *after* Joan's reign. Its purpose? It's rumored to have been devised to ensure that the new papal nominee was indeed a man after being checked out by an appointed examiner. Today papal representatives will not deny the existence of this chair and that it was used during "papal consecration ceremonies," however, there's a big "but" here. They also claim it was solely used because of its impressive carvings. There is no entry word in the *Catholic Encyclopedia* for *sella stercoraria.* Another curious bit of related history comes to mind here. Beginning with Benedict's reign, papal processions altered the standard route. Forever after Joan's reign, the ceremonial processions *detoured* around the street where Joan miscarried.

So. We managed to uncover some good stuff. I hope the questioner hasn't become more infuriated. For further reading on Pope Joan, I suggest a wonderful historical novel written on her life, *Pope Joan* by Donna Woolfolk Cross, published by Ballantine, ISBN: 0-345-41626-0. For a peek at some of the gospels that the so-called heretics stashed away, check out *The Gnostic Gospels* by Elaine H. Pagels and published by Vintage, ISBN: 0-679-72453-2; also try *The Nag Hammadi Library* edited by James M. Robinson, published by HarperCollins, ISBN: 0-06-066935-7.

If I believe in God, does that make me a Christian? Since I know God can't be proven, does that make me an agnostic? Or, since I even mention that God can't be proven, does that make me an atheist?

Good grief! It sounds as though you don't know what you are. That's okay, neither do I. At least I thought I once knew before I did quite a lot of spiritual evolving and have come to realize that, if beliefs must have a name, I'm a Gnostic.

Let's get your first issue out of the way. Believing in God does not make you a Christian. The deity word you chose was "God," not "Jesus." That makes a difference. Believing in God could mean a multitude of divine entities such as Allah, Buddha, Great Spirit, Jehovah, Divine Mother, Mohammed, Yahweh, Jesus, or Kali, or Parvati, or whoever. Belief in only one of these, Jesus, supposedly makes one a Christian. But Christianity has put additional conditions on its requirements, such as also demanding the belief that Jesus died for your sins to save humankind. What if someone believed in Jesus and knew he did not die on that cross? Does that make a heretical Christian? Or does that negate the right to call oneself a Christian at all? It's all very messy if you ask me, and you have.

So, first we establish that believing in God does not make one a Christian. Next, are you an agnostic if you believe that God can't be proven? No. We see *possible* and *probable* evidence in our world for the existence of God, but we cannot seem to make it conclusive enough for all to agree on. Realizing this fact is simply admitting to *reality* and doesn't necessarily have anything to do with Spirituality or placing one into a terminology cubbyhole. This same rationale applies to your concern over possibly being labeled an atheist if you mention that God can't be proven, especially since you already stated that you *do* believe in God.

Thus far we've clarified that believing in "God" does not make you a Christian. That realizing God can't be proven does not make you an agnostic. That mentioning the fact that

God can't be proven does not make you an atheist. Okay, I've given my response to all your questions. I have one of my own to pose. Why are people so obsessed with labels?

I used to call myself a Catholic. Then, after untold, unexplainable spiritual experiences, and after doing years and years of extensive research and listening to my intuitive senses, I came to realize that Catholicism was a far too patriarchal, ritualistic, contradictory, and materialistic religion for me. It was stuffy and unyielding. It wasn't near to being the universally inclusive and tolerant belief I'd come to know by way of the Within. At an early age I was repulsed by the Church's claim that it was the "one and only way to salvation and all others be damned." That bold arrogance sickened me as I saw so many good people in the world who weren't Catholic. It did not wash. Eventually I came to know that the threats of damnation for not doing this or not doing that were groundless and I pointed my feet in another direction. So then I thought I was a *nondenominational* Christian." This term seemed to fit for a while until my worldview and experiences with the so-called Christian sects repelled me. The backbiting between them, the scrabbling over whose minuscule tenet differentiation was more right than the others', the fanaticism, chauvinism, prejudice, and the intolerance of other beliefs revolted me so completely that I didn't want to be associated in any way with the term . . . Christian.

So now what was I? I was a plain "nondenominational." Terms kept falling away. I realized that in no way was I physically, mentally, emotionally, or soulfully connected to any kind of man-made "religion." I'd come to realize that I was a "spiritual" person. I embraced Spirituality and rejected religion. Now that "religion" was out the door, there was no need for a term to describe what I thought I was. *"Nondenominational"* went into File 13 and I was left with . . . well, for a while I had no word for what I was. Then a phase of intense research ensued. I read and read and read some more. Huge insights came as exploding epiphanies. Flashes of knowledge, ancient memories, words, phrases came to me as a great Knowing. And there was no religious sect within which to confine them. There was no religion to box them in, no preacher who said the right words, no guru, or conceptual theology existed which embraced what I'd come to comprehend and *know*. The spiritual philosophy that came as an eventual inherent Knowing was bigger than them all. It was big. It was *really* BIG! It was of the Universal Consciousness of the Divine Source. A Universal Spirituality, or that which had no threats, no confinements, no chauvinism or racism. It had no ego, no arrogance, or materialism. It had no judgment, no damnation. It . . . just . . . *was*.

So here I sit typing this response into a computer for you. In concluding these comments, I ask myself, "So, what am I?" And the answer comes quickly, without giving thought, "I'm me." If someone is nosey enough to ask what my religion is, I say, "Divine Spirituality." Then watch as they either quickly change the subject or walk away scratching their heads.

We will never be a unified family of humanity if we don't toss out the obsession with terms and labels that only serve to separate and compartmentalize us from each other. Get rid of the cubbyholes that only serve to keep us isolated from one another and continually hold us at odds over petty trivialities. Let's get rid of the terms, labels, and names. In other words, toss the intolerance out the door with the name-calling. Who cares what you spiritually believe, as long as you're a good person? The Divine Aspects of the Trinity do not relate to the inconsequential terminology humans have devised to define their religious beliefs. The Divine Aspects only care about whether or not one is a good person. Why should we fragment the Trinity's generous criteria into minuscule compartments that we *think* are necessary to create?

Is it possible to reincarnate several times with the same name? Example: Karen?

Sure it is. This happens all the time. You see, when we're still in spirit and in the process of analyzing which earthly mother is in the best position to present us with the optimum criteria we need to begin our new journey, we look for meeting the needs of geographical location, ethnicity, spiritual beliefs, to name a few. A name is not part of these criteria. A name has no bearing whatsoever. So then, it's possible to even sequentially choose a mother for many consecutive incarnations who will name you Karen. You can end up being many Karens, or Joes, or Carmelitas. This happens more than you'd probably imagine.

I heard that the Lord's Prayer is entwined with the chakras. True?

No. This prayer was put together by using various sentences and phrases that were allegedly spoken by Jesus throughout his lifetime. It was pieced together from fragments. One particular sentence always bothered me. "Forgive us our trespasses *as we forgive those who trespass against us.*" As "we" forgive? This is asking *God* to forgive as *we* do. Huh? God is asked to follow *our* behavior? Isn't that more than a little backwards? God forgives unconditionally. Do we?

No, the Lord's Prayer is not entwined with the chakras. We hear a lot as we make our journey through life. I can't agree more with that. We do hear a lot.

I have a hard time accepting reincarnation because I was abused as a child and can't believe that that was my karmic destiny.

Well now, wait a minute, please. Your conception of reincarnation is a bit skewed. First of all, you're clearly under the impression that *everything* that occurs in your life is karmic and that's just not so. I myself experienced some psychological abuse in my youth regarding my gender, yet I never once believed that it was karmic, because it wasn't.

In life we have multitudes of experiential events happening on a minute-to-minute rate of occurrence. *Every* little mishap, devastating event, blessing, or joyful situation is not karmic. Life happens—the good and the bad, the joyful and the sorrowful. That's the reality of life. I have two personal sayings: "The definition of life is—shit happens" and "The definition of life is—magic happens." Know what? Both are true. Just because you happen to be in a convenience store when it's robbed doesn't necessarily mean that the situation was karmically induced. Just because you won the lottery doesn't mean the happy event was karmically induced or that it was destiny. See?

Life is watching bad things happen to good people and good things happen to bad people. Rhyme or reason are haphazard. Trying to go figure can spin one in dizzying circles. The spinning finally stops when Acceptance comes into one's heart. So in the end, it's important to fully understand a concept or ideology before rejecting (or accepting) it out of hand.

When we die and pass through the Light, can we come back to visit our living loved ones whenever we want?

Not specifically whenever we want, but whenever it is deemed necessary to assist someone. Don't forget, the time spent on the other side is usually short—very short. Spirits are eager to continue working on the purification process. This means incarnating again, which brings a new set of loved ones into play.

Is Jesus living on this planet now?

No. Isn't it interesting that, when one thinks of the Second Coming or the physical manifestation of a divine being on earth, everyone automatically assumes it's Jesus? And what if the reality of this Second Coming didn't involve any type of deity "descending" to earth but rather is meant to mean *our individual spirituality ascending to the level that equates to The Way?*

I read somewhere that there's a God above God. What's up with that?

What's up with that is a multitude of different versions of deity hierarchy. There are ancient writings that detail a Creatrix who is positioned separately from *the* God you usually think of. In addition to this Creatrix are lesser gods, some male and some female, who emanated from the Divine Mother. It's quite an interesting story.

Do we have to be baptized in order to go to heaven?

The purpose of baptism is to absolve original sin. I have a big, big problem with that. Firstly, what is original sin? The only reason we're here trying desperately to purify ourselves is because we're already working our way back to God. God forgives unconditionally, ergo, why do we think some ceremony will *bring* God's forgiveness to us?

Secondly, who has authority equal to God's to do this forgiveness? Some ordained preacher? Who ordained the preacher? Another human? The Catholic nuns taught the children that *only* those baptized as Catholics were absolved of all their sins and would see salvation. When I was in high school, a boy in my class was newly baptized and do you know what the nun said about him? "Class, we have an angel sitting in the room." She led us to believe that just because this terror of a boy was newly baptized, his soul was without any sign of sin—pure as the driven snow. Oh, phooey! He was no different from the rest of us. He was like an overweight, overaged Dennis the Menace sitting there trying to look like he had some golden halo hovering above his head.

Thirdly, just the fact that we're here on this earth proves the fact that we do not have to be baptized to have this original sin absolved. Why? Well, get a clue . . . how many *times* does *one soul* have to go through this absolution? How many incarnations have to be subjected to the same ceremony over and over again???

God forgives unconditionally. Now I know I keep repeating this, but I feel I have to. It's too important to forget. God *already* forgave us our transgressions. We don't need some religious sect to claim that only they can manage this for us. That's religious control and manipulation. That's the use of false power through using the threat of damnation. That's power by instilling fear tactics.

Is Wicca a form of Satanism?

Wicca, in its true, ancient form, was a spiritual philosophy that honored the Mother Goddess who was perceived as the Earth Mother symbolizing fertility (soil), birth, and loving-nurturing. Does that sound anything at all like Satanism? Please, I surely do not want to come across as though I'm being sarcastic in any way, but a little in-depth research into the historical background of subjects like Wicca can go a long way. As with every theological belief, spin-offs occur. Some lose sight of the originating concept and take it upon themselves to add or delete aspects to alter the pure form. The ancient theme of Wicca was to respect nature and celebrate its many faces, including the planting time and harvesting season. Festivities were held so that the farmers could feel like they were active participants in Mother Nature's process of being fertile and fruitful. The phases of the moon were recognized as affecting planting and harvesting times. Annual feast days to make these seasonal transitions were celebrated with gatherings where dancing, sharing, and general merriment took place. Wicca was a joyful appreciation of Mother Earth and all the bounties she provided. In its pure form, the ancient form, Wicca was a women's way. It was a way to give respect and reverence to the Mother Earth Goddess . . . the Creatrix of life.

Does it take a special gift to be a Light Warrior for the Creator?

I need you to convey to me exactly how you're defining a "light warrior," because your question leads me to the conclusion that your definition is different than mine. "Light warriors" are the same as those who have been referred to as "living lights." Both of these terms refer to anyone who lives a life of Unconditional Goodness and has chosen to walk the path of The Way. These individuals have taken Acceptance into their hearts and they are without the negative attitudes of racism, sexism, materialism, etc. The only power on earth they recognize is that of spiritual wisdom and the only higher power they bow to is that of the Divine Source. These individuals live quiet lives while actively working to uplift the level of spirituality whenever the opportunity presents itself. Giveaways are a way of life for them. These giveaways include possessions, a helping hand, comfort, being a sounding board, etc. "Light warriors," or "living lights," don't recognize an ego of self but solely that of the Divine Aspects of the Trinity. In this manner do they live life attending to the Divine Way instead of their own.

So then, if these qualities are the "special gifts" you're wondering about, then it should be exciting for you to learn that you can be a "light warrior," too.

Is the notion of the "evil eye" in any way associated with the Egyptian's Eye of Horus (Uchat or Ujat)?

No, no. The evil eye is believed to be an intense stare backed by powerful mental energy filled with dark intent. In other words, hatred. It's supposed to incur some type of death curse.

The Uchat (Eye of Horus) is just the opposite. The representational design was painted on the sides of sarcophaguses and also placed within the wrappings of mummies as a form of *protection*. Before the symbol was finally assigned to Horus, it was first associated with the Goddess of Wisdom and Truth, *Maat* (Mayet). Her great wisdom was equated with Maat's "all-seeing" eye through the power of her pure integrity and unparalleled intellect. Her "Eye" was always painted on both sides of ship's prows.

Were the druids an evil group?

No. I've noticed that there are some negative misconceptions about this spiritual group, but it's undeserved.

Someone gave me a cassette tape supposedly channeled by Melchizedek. Should I be listening to tapes like these?

This question, like the ones people ask me regarding certain book titles, is one I can only respond to by giving an indefinitive, neutral reply.

Listen, this is important: Don't ever let anyone tell you what you should or shouldn't read or listen to. This is giving away your power to choose for self what you believe. I always tell people to be avid readers, to expand their knowledge base as wide as they can take it. The more well-read one is, the more certain aspects of your chosen subject matter will cross-reference with another's. Eventually certain concepts will stand out and you will begin to become more intuitive while reading. Your discernment will become honed to a razor-sharp edge, giving you the ability to quickly determine the viability of material rather than plodding through it with indecision. Don't ever let anyone tell you what you can and can't read. No book is blacklisted. No subject matter forbidden. No censorship to gaining a broader scope to one's knowledge. It is *your* responsibility to *yourself* to make *your* own decisions.

Historically, there have been many people with the name of Melchizedek. There appears to be a current trend for individuals to take on new names—the biblical ones are most popular, followed by those nature-related names that were adopted by the flower-child generation of the sixties. Presently there are several individuals calling themselves Melchizedek, all claiming the identity of the same biblical character. This Melchizedek, according to some Christian Gnostics, was considered a lesser god (below those of the Trinity)—a savior who was perceived as being higher in divinity than Jesus. He is alleged to have been born of the Goddess Sophia and believed, by some patriarchal adherents, to be the awaited-for entity of the Second Coming. Personally, well . . . like I said, it's all up to you to decide.

What is a Christian? I mean, what defines this religious designation?

Bottom-line designation is the basic belief that *Jesus Christ was the Son of God and that he died for our sins.* Different Christian sects will make additions to this basic tenet, such as a mandatory belief that you have to take Jesus into your heart to attain salvation, necessary baptism for salvation, etc. Some sects claim Jesus Christ as being Lord God, that Jesus is the one to return for the Second Coming, and that all prayers will be answered if asked in his name. These are the elemental dogmatic beliefs of Christianity.

Someone told me that you claimed to be Jesus. I find that hard to believe.

Smart lady. I find that hard to believe, too. The rumors about me are outrageous and wildly outlandish to the point of being just plain stupid. It's a fact that well-known people are easy prey for the public and, with that in mind, the public has a virtual field day. I've also heard that some people think

I've claimed to be some goddess. Total idiocy. Not a shred of truth or rationale to that stuff.

I'm confused about the validity of astrology. At times it seems to make scientific sense; at other times it has the feel of being heretical. Comments?

Heretical to what? We are born of matter. Matter is influenced by other matter. Doesn't the waxing and waning of the moon affect the tides and all fluids, including those of the body? Since the moon is a celestial body, why wouldn't it be probable for the magnetic properties of other celestial bodies to also affect our physical and emotional selves? Astrological aspects can influence us in both subtle and dramatic ways. Our *belief* in these influences does not make them real; they're inherently real *despite* whether or not the little human minds give them credence.

Who really wrote the gospels of the Bible?

Thomas the apostle wrote some notes. The mother of Jesus kept a diary. Mary Magdalene recorded an extremely personal and revealing history of her time with Jesus and his mother. *Unnamed* individuals wrote of Jesus' life and teachings *two centuries* after his death and *borrowed* a few of the apostles' names as authorship. These last writings actually made it into the official version of the Bible as gospels. Well, after all, Magdalene's records weren't known about because they'd been partially burned in an accidental fire, and the diary of Jesus' mother is still concealed until the right time manifests for its revelation. It's just as well because those leading the patriarchal new religion of Christianity would've never taken a woman's word as official gospel anyway.

The oldest gospel fragment is a papyrus fragment found in Egypt. It was a portion of a 130-page Greek codex of John's, believed to have been written around 125 A.D.—years *after* his death.

The "official" gospels were written in uncials (capital letters) with no punctuation, spacing between words, divisions, or headings of any kind. No signatures were in evidence, so early Church leaders assigned names borrowed from those of Jesus' inner circle of disciples. What's interesting is the numerous amount of inconsistencies these gospels reveal when comparing them to each other. For example: In Matthew, Jesus was circumcised at eight days and the ceremony at temple was on the fortieth day. In Luke, Jesus and his parents are fleeing to Egypt during this same time period. Another example: Matthew has Judas dying from suicide, a hanging. Yet in Acts, Judas dies from an accident, a fall. Other questionable recordings involve geographical errors that represent not only inconsistency, but impossibility.

Religious scholars have reached a general conclusion: The canonical gospels were taken from a source popularly known as "Q" or the *Gospel of Q* (Quelle is German for "source."). This lost work was believed to have been written in Aramaic, Jesus' tongue. Who really wrote the gospels of the Bible? Theologians agree that they don't know; neither do I. What we do know is who *didn't* write them from their graves.

Does exorcism really work?

Historically, Catholic "experts" performed this rite as a routine ceremony. In modern-day society, it is a rarity because the Church has moved out of medieval thought and into reality, where 99.9 percent of reported cases are now referred to psychiatric professionals for evaluation and subsequent treatment.

Exorcism by humans does not work. Dark entities are neither affected nor controlled by religious people. Religious accouterments such as holy water, the crucifix, Bible, or alleged sacred words of power hold no manipulative sway over a dark entity. Though recorded success of exorcism is in evidence, it was only because the entity tired of the game and didn't want to play anymore, not because of any priest's or minister's feeble power.

Yes, Jesus was said to have driven out seven devils from Mary Magdalene. This story is a tale spun of ignorance, for Magdalene was not possessed. What was assumed as possession in this ancient-time incident was nothing more than a physiological affliction she evidenced—a tremor of the right hand (which Jesus healed). On the other hand, Jesus did drive out dark entities from others. And why not? He was someone the entities *did* fear and could be easily controlled by.

What makes special objects holy, blessed, or sacred? I'm specifically inquiring about devotional objects "blessed" by priests or other religious figures.

Belief, nothing more than *words* claiming that it is so. Humans have no power to bless, only the deities of the Trinity do. Know that all life is sacred, for it has come from the Divine Beingness. It is the height of spiritual arrogance to think a holy card, rosary, prayer book, or other religious item holds more spiritual influence or power if it was supposedly blessed by a human ordained in a man-made religion than one of these same items bought off a store shelf.

Blessings are gifts that come in many forms. Good wishes are a form of blessing given to another. A beautiful day or a safe journey can be counted as a blessing. But for a blessing to represent a special sacredness or power, it has to come from the Divine Source.

Is there such a thing as mortal sin?

No. It's no because the Divine is all-forgiving and a serious offense against The Way committed during one incarnation cannot condemn the entire multifaceted crystal of one's composite spirit. To condemn a spirit for a grievous infraction committed during one lifetime would be as irrational as believing your entire body is going to be terminally affected by a stubbed toe.

Each incarnated experience presents new opportunities and results in different behavior than the preceding one and, ideally, each subsequent life experience is a little more spiritually aligned than the one preceding it. Transgressions occur. People falter. Mistakes are made. However, these do not condemn us because, when all is said and done, people are the *sum total* of *all* experienced lifetimes . . . not just one.

What is "The Knowing" you keep referring to?

The Knowing is the inherent, intuitive knowledge of "What Is" (gnosis). The Gnostic ideology of personal, insightful knowledge and inspirational epiphanies became a target of spiritual contempt with the dawn of the Christian era, when the Church deemed it necessary to form a concrete dogma for the faithful to be confined within. The Church decided what people should believe—all else was declared heresy and became the cause for severe punishment, imprisonment, and execution. Yet, The Knowing couldn't be smothered or killed. It lived within the spirit, where it remained in celebrated hiding until societal rationale again gained firmer ground, permitting tolerance for a wider range of philosophical ideologies.

The Knowing is gnosis. Gnosis means an "inherent or intuitive knowledge of spiritual matters." It is sometimes associated with the terms "mysteries" or "esoteric," but only because ignorance perceives *spiritual intuitiveness* or *spirit memory*, or *spirit intelligence* from an uninformed, antiquated, or religiously prejudiced standpoint. The Knowing becomes more evident and pronounced in those individuals who have not taken their religious upbringing as being the sole way to God or salvation. The Knowing is given fertile soil in which to blossom when the individual expands her/his knowledge base through an active, lifelong thirst for knowledge. Serious contemplation deepens The Knowing. The attainment of Acceptance and Wisdom expands it out into the universe, where the Divine Universal Minds await the touch of our extended quest for truth.

Do you think Mother Teresa should be canonized as a saint?

No, because it's a designation that's too specific to one religious sect. As far as I know, the Catholic Church is the only religion involved in deciding who's a saint and who isn't. The strict criteria used to make this decision are confining and include proof that verifies that the nominee manifested at least one documented miracle that was accomplished through prayer. In addition, some individuals whom the Church beatified before canonizing were later demoted from the sainthood designation. This says to me, why doesn't a saint remain a saint?

Most historical personalities who were later canonized as being an "official saint" were individuals who, today, in this modern society of Religious Right fanatics, would've had aspersions cast and accusing fingers pointed at them because of their "New Age-like" behavior. Most "saints" were mystics who exhibited some type of spiritually eccentric behavior such as communing with the Goddess-essence found in nature, having visions, participating in communications with angelic beings, initiating new or foreign spiritual concepts, involuntarily manifesting the physiology of the stigmata (bleeding from the hands or feet as Jesus did from his crucifixion nails), slipping into states of altered consciousness, etc. As backward as it seems (and is), today the Christian Right would denounce this spiritual individual as being an agent of the devil. Today we are witnessing a return to the ignorant, accusatory, spiritual attitudes of medieval times.

No, I don't think Mother Teresa's life and behavior should be picked apart, analyzed, and judged. I don't believe anyone or any singular religious sect can claim the right to so judge the life of another. We can all be saints by way of behaving in a spiritual manner. It doesn't take the proof of having performed a bona fide, witnessed "miracle through prayer" to live a saintly life in the eyes of the Divine. Anyway, who are humans to think they have the spiritual superiority to determine this designation for others? What's more important here? What's our spiritual goal . . . being "light" in the eyes of the Divine or in human eyes? Societal recognition is peanuts contrasted to being given the nod by God.

The Religious Right organizations are becoming dangerous extremists. In a Colorado for Family Values newsletter, they justified their plan to make discrimination against gays and lesbians a legal activity by claiming that it was "a struggle over the very survival of our culture's Judeo-Christian" foundation. We're going backward. When is the prejudice going to end?

For the record, this letter was from a married woman with two children who has become tired of seeing prejudice everywhere she looked.

Clearly, as I stated in my former response, society's level of tolerance is diminishing. Finger pointing makes people's egos puffed up with self-righteousness. Wisdom remains an elusive power for these accusing ones. Acceptance remains a rejected gift of grace. While attempting to "save" society, they are destroying it. The days of the Inquisition are returning with the same preponderance of ignorance.

This woman's letter exploded a spiritual outrage within me. It appalled me. It churned my insides and made my spirit sick. Why? Not just because of the prejudice, but because these sanctimonious people were actually attempting to make discrimination *legal!* And they call themselves Christian? Do they not know that the term itself is supposed to mean "following the way of Christ?" Do they even *know* Christ's ways? No, they know not the true Christ. In their boasting way of reciting biblical passages by rote, they indeed do know the Jesus of the *Bible* . . . they know not the *true* Jesus of reality, though. They know the glamorized and sanitized version of Jesus. They haven't seen the ancient gospel writings that included character and behavioral recordings of Jesus-the-*man* that were left out of the making of the official canonical gospels. *Jesus . . . loved . . . everyone!* Jesus never differentiated from nor gave preference to any distinguishable differences in those he met. Listen, do you realize how many beautiful statements he made during his life? Don't you realize how many wonderful concepts he attempted to instill on an hourly basis? The Bible is nothing but a reiteration of the same sayings and events over and over, but what about all the thousands of sayings and events that happened *between* those recorded ones? What about what he whispered to the pauper or what he laughed at with the prostitute? Or what about the merry, impromptu jig he stopped to do with the gay sheepskin trader? Jesus *despised* prejudice. He despised it with a passion. One evening, while having a heart-to-heart talk with Magdalene, he confided to her that "discrimination is like a plague that infects everyone it touches." He likened it to drinking from a poisoned well. And now, "Christians" are calling for that same despicable attitude to be legal. This is evidence of behavior *contrary* to Jesus' teachings. It's deliberately poisoning our spiritual waters. And any perspective or action that runs counter to the attitude of Jesus must be that of the devil's. Isn't that what these Christians claim? Isn't this theory the foundation of their self-righteousness? So what's the true reality of what we're seeing happening here? Moves to counter Christ's teachings and personally held attitudes. Ergo . . . Christians doing Satan's work through perpetrating intolerance, condemnation, and persecution. That's the bottom line here. That's what it shakes down to. The pitiful aspect of this whole issue is that these self-righteous people are not only hurting others, they're also twisting a blade deep into the very heart of the Divine . . . all the while, doing it in Jesus' name. How sacrilegious can you get?

What is the true nature of Jesus dying for our sins? He lived to teach us, so how could his dying serve a purpose for us?

Why would Jesus have to die for our sins if God already forgave us those sins? Makes no sense. We do not have to seek God's forgiveness because that's naturally already there. Forgiveness.

How does reincarnation work when there are twins who know each others thoughts and are so much alike?

Being an intuitively linked twin (or other unrelated person) doesn't affect the individual you are. You are still a facet of your own total, composite spirit. This composite spirit is a separate entity unto itself. The twin is a different, separate entity unto itself. The mind link that twins often exhibit is of the physical . . . the mind. It's mental. It is not bound to the spirits of each. The twins may look identical, act the same, be dressed alike, and manifest identical thoughts and Knowings, yet their life paths are totally different. Their karmic records are different. Every baby born represents an individual, composite spirit. The key word to remember with this concept is "individual." The conceptual rumor of the reality of twin souls or soul twins is just that, a rumor. It's a misnomer generated from a desire to explain why some individuals seem to be so much alike or are so close to one another. One of the explanations for this phenomenon is nothing more than an intuitive recognition of someone we spent a past life with. It's possible to identify several people in your life who possess this commonality with you, but it doesn't mean that you were physical twins or have a twin soul (which doesn't exist anyway).

Physical twins are individual people. Physical twins house individual spirits. Each spirit has separate pasts, different paths to walk, and uniquely different karmic aspects.

Now, this question automatically led me to an associated one, which someone is sure to come up with while reading this response. Let's get into it next.

Do Siamese twins have one or two souls?

If the physiology of these twins manifests two individual heads, then there are two souls. Likewise, if the heads are joined and can be successfully separated, then two souls are in evidence. The *mind* is the key. Generally, two minds mean two souls. If there is one head and multiple appendages, then that is not evidence of true Siamese twins; it's a physiological abnormality of a single individual with one mind and one spirit.

How does reincarnation verify with adoption?

I'm not sure you meant to say "verify." Perhaps using the word "associate" would better fit the conceptual idea of your question. You see, adoption is a circumstance of life and doesn't, in itself, have any related way of concretely proving out (or disproving) the basic theory of reincarnation. What the inquirer wonders is how the life circumstance of adoption affects the adoptee's spirit's original choice of a birth mother who was seen to best present that spirit with certain criteria required for the current life experience.

Many times the probability of the chosen mother's offspring being adopted is *foreseen* while the spirit is still in the process of looking over its physical life choices. In this case, the spirit is choosing the birth mother *because* the adoptive mother (or parent) is known. This means that the *secondary* (adoptive) parent was the one who the spirit based its projected criteria on. So then, the adoptive parent was, in essence, the *intended* chosen parent. In the event that an adoption was not foreseen by the spirit before entry into the physical, then this event becomes a facet of destiny that most often *improves* and *upgrades* the quality of one's basic criteria that was predetermined by the spirit before birth. So whether the adoption was foreseen by the spirit or not, the situation most often represents a better set of circumstances associated with the spirit's original plan.

Does accumulating indulgences really lessen one's time spent in purgatory?

Since I'm not sure how many Christian sects believe in the concept of purgatory, I think this question is extremely Catholic. I think I need to first explain purgatory for the benefit of the general readership.

Purgatory is believed by Catholics to be an initial destination to which the spirit first goes after physical death. Purgatory is the destination for those spirits who aren't pure enough to enter heaven, yet aren't bad enough to be condemned to hell. In purgatory, one exists in a quasi-hell situation, where suffering and torment "purges" the soul of all wrongdoing residuals for the purpose of attaining a state of purification before being able to enter into heaven. Okay, that covers the place.

Now we need to define what these so-called "indulgences" are. The Church decided that certain sins carried with them certain degrees of seriousness. An extremely grievous sin was called a "mortal" sin. A lesser degree of sin was called a "venial" sin. Correspondingly, a mortal sin took a great deal of time being neutralized in purgatory through greater torment and suffering, less time for the smaller, venial offenses. After time in the physical, a person's soul would accumulate a whole mess of sins to have to eradicate through years and years of suffering in purgatory before being purified, the Church came up with what it called "indulgences" to shorten a spirit's time spent in purgatory.

Indulgences are specific prayers and acts of good work that have been determined (measured) to provide certain weights of merit or redemptive qualities, and are given in consideration against sins committed. In other words, the recitation of certain prayers and the performance of certain deeds could lessen one's time in purgatory. When I was a child I had holy cards placed in my prayer book. These had beautifully inspiring pictures on one side and a long prayer on the back. At the bottom of the prayer was a note in parentheses that informed the faithful how many years you could save yourself from suffering in purgatory each time this prayer was said. (I used to say a lot of these prayers! No way was I going to have to suffer in purgatory any longer than I had to. I was putting prayers in the bank like crazy!)

However, through enlightenment we now realize that the recitation of certain prayers won't save us X amount of years in purgatory because *every* incarnated *life* is a journey into this symbolic purgatory. It's *here* where our spirits have planned to balance out and neutralize negative karma that we've previously incurred. It's *here* where we attempt to bring the state of our composite spirit into a more purified condition through good thoughts, works, and words. The here and now is our beautiful chance to make it all happen. It's a conscious choice of mind and will determine how our spirit's condition is kept and maintained. We can work on repairing and cleaning, or we can slack off with indifference to make it more impaired and dirty depending on our current, daily (hourly) behavior. Once again, purgatory is the here and now, not some imaginary, mythical destination for the spirit.

Responding to this question has brought home an interesting (and unsettling) fact about the concept of indulgences that I was taught as a child. These indulgences were really a method for the Church to foster self-centeredness, to gain control through instilling fear of punishment. In reality, these are prayers said to save *self*. How utterly selfish that is . . . how incredibly self-centered. I always thought we were supposed to say prayers for *others*.

Can priests forgive one's sins in the confessional?

I alluded to a facet of this "forgiveness" subject when I previously responded to a related question. The questioner's wording of the above inquiry specified the exact "where" this forgiveness was taking place. It added another dimension to the question. Let's get rid of this compounding aspect by clarifying that, theoretically, a priest can allegedly forgive sins (hear one's confession) anywhere. It doesn't have to be in a bona fide church confessional to be official or effective.

Okay, now to the main question here. Can a priest really *forgive* the sins of others? He can forgive all he wants, but the fact is, God *already* forgave us the moment after we committed the transgression. So . . . why the need for some human priest with false power that does nothing? These words may seem harsh to some; yet I don't see the need to mince words and serve them on a designer cracker, when these issues of spiritual reality are so important. Don't you think a penitent's remorseful attitude, by its very nature, means anything at all? Don't you think the words "I'm sorry, God," or "God, please forgive me" have any merit or spiritual effectiveness? Do people really believe that God does not or will not forgive them unless they confess to some human religious figure? What sort of mind-set is that? Our relationship to the Divine is a personal one. It's between you and God—no intermediaries required. No one (human or otherwise) is necessary to intercede for you. *You* commune with God. *You* pray and beg forgiveness. And . . . God responds.

An additional aspect to this confessional and priestly forgiveness concept is that, after the confession of the penitent has been heard, the priest will give a penance. This penance is in the form of saying a designated number of specified prayers chosen by the priest. The prayers and their numbers are supposedly meant to correspond to the seriousness of the confessed transgressions. So the penitent leaves the confessional, goes and sits in a church pew and says maybe ten Hail Marys and thirty Our Fathers as penance for his/her recently confessed sins. Then everything's supposed to be fine and dandy again. But where are the words of *God* that state the rules for such a form of penance? Who came up with this? Who decided that ten Hail Marys neutralized the sin of stealing a lipstick or that twenty Our Fathers was penance for being a Peeping Tom? Where is it written that Jesus devised this system?

It isn't. It was devised to increase men's power. It says, "Only by coming to *me* to confess your sins can you be forgiven and stay in the Church." It's control and manipulation. Only God has the power to forgive. Nobody forgives sin in God's name because sin is against God and its forgiveness is personal. Forgiveness is One-on-one. Also, how can prayer be equated to penance? Isn't the whole idea of penance related to being some form of punishment? How can prayer be punishment when it's a beautiful form of communion with the Divine?

Did Eve cause us all to be born with original sin?

Wait a minute. If we're both thinking of the same Creation myth, I seem to recall that it was the alleged nasty *serpent* that did the tempting here. It was the serpent that introduced and initiated the original concept of temptation. And what was he offering? And why was he offering it? The archangel Lucifer (he *was* an archangel) offered Eve the "fruit of knowledge" because he believed that God's children shouldn't be expected to make their way without having knowledge. He believed that true children of God should be able to make intelligent choices in their life and not be left in dark ignorance. Lucifer had pleaded with God to gift the children with knowledge but nothing was done about it, so the archangel intervened because he took pity upon the new human creations and took it upon himself to even up the children's chances for making more knowledgeable decisions.

Isn't it interesting that "knowledge" was that which was forbidden us. Isn't it interesting that God supposedly denied people knowledge and that the seeking and taking of knowledge was claimed to be the first sin of humankind . . . the Original Sin? What's even more interesting is that it was the *woman* of the human pair who was interested in gaining knowledge. And forever after, women have been blamed for it. The great temptress. Weak and evil. The cause of the Fall. How ignorant societal thought has remained.

The acceptance of knowledge is not the Original Sin. Neither Eve nor the serpent had anything to do with this thing called Original Sin. The initial falling away from God was when the created spirits wanted to experience the physical after observing the pleasures that animals enjoyed. When the spirits left the ethereal world behind in deference to their desire for physical pleasures, they allegedly committed the first sin by abandoning God's side for pleasurable, physical experiences on earth. That is what the Original Sin was. This is why we work our way back to God by "resisting" the earthly negatives and behaving in a more spiritually minded manner. *Living in the physical with a mind to the spiritual light* is how we evolve back into the Light. Eve was the first human woman. Eve was God's perfect creation. Eve recognized a need for knowledge and reached for it. That was not a sin . . . that was myth that slithered out of the human mind's search for a scapegoat to blame.

Do angels have souls?

Sure they do. All intelligent creations of the Creatrix who possess an awareness of the Trinity's Divine Essences have souls.

Are relics valid?

A relic is a relic is a relic. The dictionary explains that a relic is merely a remnant, a fragment. The definition can be expanded to include the inference of an object of great age, or that associated with a particular historical event such as a

World War I relic or one from the Crusades. These objects can also be further defined as being specific to a culture or religion. This questioner's intent was to inquire about religious relics and whether or not they're valid. Referring to my opening statement: a relic is a relic is a relic. All relics are valid objects in that they're a fragment of a whole or a fragment left over from an event or historical period. However, the questioner is wondering whether or not the belief that a religious fragment (bone sliver from a saint or piece of the cross) truly contains special powers of healing, protection, etc. The questioner is asking about the validity of this claim by religious sects. The answer is no. Yet claims to the contrary come from the incredible power of the mind (faith), that we see so much evidence of in the instance of so-called spontaneous healings during highly charged revival meetings. These are not true healings and represent religious hysterics that trick the mind for a short time into believing one has been chosen to be the blessed recipient of a miracle and has actually been healed. The intense desire to believe can temporarily override reason and logic.

This same principle applies to the alleged magic (powers) of religious relics and other objects of devotion. A rosary blessed by the pope has no more power or divine sanction associated with it than one bought right from a shop or street vendor. Water is not made "holy" just because a priest has blessed it. A bone fragment from a saint or an alleged splinter from the crucifixion cross will not endow special graces upon the owner. These and items like them are just relics of something that once was whole. Inert. Inert except for the molecules slowly moving around inside it to give it form.

This question relates to all objects that people conceptualize as being holy, blessed, or sacred. How is it that society has such a strong tendency to pick and choose that which it deems sacred. All of life is sacred. *All* that has been divinely created is sacred. Man-made objects are not. Man-made objects such as religious devotional items are not sacred in and of themselves, yet they are a "means" to prayer, which *is* sacred. We need to keep perspective on this issue.

I'm not a Catholic, but watching the TV news about Denver's archbishop being elevated to the level of cardinal made me question why his new red skullcap symbolized his being a new "prince" of the Church? If the next level up from cardinal is the pope, does this infer that the pontiff is "king" of the Church? Why such terms of royalty?

I have to admit that I have no idea why these terms are an integrated part of the sect. It does seem odd, especially when Jesus is referred to sometimes as *"Prince* of Peace" and *"King* of Heaven." I've never heard of a time when the pope was called a "king" at least not that I can remember. I, too, saw the same newscast and the identical irony crossed my mind. I hadn't known that a cardinal was called a prince of the Church. If they use the term "prince" as a hierarchy placement marker in the religious order, who then would be "king"? The utilization of a term of royalty disconcerted me and I immediately connected it to the Church's fascination with royal robes of gold and silver threads, its amassed treasure of jewel-encrusted objects, its phenomenal collection of artworks by the world's great masters, and the Italian marble halls.

And, I wonder, why are underlings expected to kiss the pope's ring? I could see wanting to kiss the feet of the Divine Being, whose essence manifests in the physical, but to do so for a *human* leader of a religious sect strikes me as being almost disrespectful and irreverent to God's face—an affront to God. This is merely my personal opinion, mind you, yet . . . kissing a ring? Prostration before a human? I haven't the answer for this questioner, only an opinion that is in agreement with him.

Do you happen to know the age of the oldest gospel discovered to date?

Generally scholars are of the opinion that the oldest gospel fragments date back to the second century, around 125 A.D., but there exists a small fragment of what is believed to have been written by Matthew, which is referred to the *"Magdalen fragment."* It is called this because it's held at the Magdalen College at Oxford. Some scholars believe this dates back to 70 A.D.; however, this date is vigorously disputed by many other highly regarded scholars. A problem with dating has recently arisen, though. Scientists have discovered a glitch with the radiocarbon-dating (C-14) process, which I will address in another question specific to the discovery.

What if God turns out to be a Goddess?

My first reaction to this question was to say, "So?" Then, after giving it additional thought, I smiled with the image of how that actual eventuality would literally knock the patriarchal pants off the religious leaders! Maybe that mental impression wasn't a very "spiritual" one, but hey, it'd still be funny. Anyway, humans are the ones who made God in their own image. Who says the real God/Goddess has gender? Seems to me the Divine Being would be hermaphroditic. If the Divine Essence is All, then the Divine Beings would possess female and male aspects. The Essence would be the Supreme Being . . . as in *really* "SUPREME" Being and be the God of All *and* the Creatrix *and* the Spirit Essence. This idea of God being a male or a female is silly. It's silly because the Divine Being . . . is . . . All! It is because of this fact that I use both the male and female terms for this Divine Essence interchangeably, depending on whether I'm speaking about the Father Aspect, the Mother Aspect, or the Spirit Aspect. I'm not being feministic . . . I'm being real. And, returning to the questioner's idea—if God did turn out to be a Goddess . . . what a kick!

I respect and accept the religious beliefs of others; however, I am not so tolerant of them when certain groups try to force their beliefs on me and try to come into my home to do it. Do you experience this too?

Sure I do. Who doesn't?

Usually, when strangers appear at my door, I keep my identity hidden. Most often, these strangers are asking directions and they go on their way without ever knowing who I am. However, when these religious folks appear, I very clearly introduce myself as Mary Summer Rain. In response to this they blush, smile, and quickly proceed to tell me to have a nice day. Next thing I know, they're getting back into their car and hightailing it out of my deep, dark woods. Sometimes the misconceptions about my work have their up side. But before I came upon the idea of identifying myself to cure the problem, I'd tried other options that failed. I'd even gone as far as buying a bright, red sign for my driveway gate that said: DO NOT ENTER—RESTRICTED AREA—HAZARDOUS MATERIALS STORED HERE. I was so excited when I found that sign in our local Ace hardware store (this being a mining area, you know), that I bought it with the full intention of firmly nailing it to my gate. Then reality set in when Sally asked me how I was going to handle all the calls from the sheriff's department, from curiosity seekers, and from raging environmentalists? Uh-ohh. Bad idea I had. So now the sign hangs in the basement to remind me that overkill is not the best solution for some problems.

Tolerance. Yes, I certainly will agree that there are times that strain religious tolerance to its limit, aren't there? There are times when we can barely contain the urge to get in another's face, or we feel like jumping up and down and pulling our hair out while screaming at the top of our lungs. Well, we'd at least succeed in making a colorful spectacle of ourselves and looking quite crazy if nothing else. Who knows, it might even work if they think you're really crazy. I've been known to pull a few antics in my time; keeps life spiced up. A little spontaneous hilarity goes a long way in relieving stress.

If you don't want to act crazy or hang a "hazardous materials" sign, try maintaining politeness while stating that you respect their religious beliefs but you have your own and you'd appreciate it if they extended the same courtesy to you. Or you might inform them that the biblical gospels were all "written" *after* the apostles died. Then again, it might not be a great idea to engage them in any type of conversation. You may have to resort to attaching a Health Department quarantine sign to your door and, if that doesn't work, you might try gifting them with some of your own spiritual material . . . like a Summer Rain book. It worked for me.

Are slivers of wood claiming to come from the true cross real?

No.

Loved your dream book, gave them as Christmas presents last year. Though it's one of the most comprehensive dream symbol books on the market, there are still a few words missing. Will you be adding to the book in the future?

Thanks for the compliment on the book. And there are a *lot* of words I left out. I got my first clue when, upon receiving my copies right off the press, Sally looked up the word "inner tube" and guess what? Uh-huh, it wasn't there. Ever since that day, I've been keeping a running list of words and their meanings. So far I'm up to approximately 1,600 new entry words. At some point in the future, when I think the list is complete enough, I plan to put out a revised, updated version of the book.

Why are the ancient spiritual belief systems now perceived as myths and legends?

In this questioner's letter, he referred to Egyptian gods and goddesses. He mentioned Celtic goddesses and other cultural feminine deities. This individual thought the old beliefs were beautiful ones and wondered how it came to be that the only divine female left in our society was the "Earth Mother" concept.

In a response to a previous question, I explained how the newborn religion of Christianity actively attempted to stamp out the old beliefs that centered on the Goddesses in deference to belief in a single, male deity and religious central character by the name of Jesus. A large part of this stamping out involved a complete and total reversal of feminine deity and Feminine Spirituality perception. Whereas before it was viewed as being a nurturing and creative concept, now it was painted as being "of the devil." Now celebrations of the turning seasons and harvest time were tantamount to "dancing with the devil." This is how the nature spirituality of Wicca became to be seen as a vile evilness to be weeded out, persecuted, and erased from society in order to cleanse itself of "Satan's destructive influence" upon souls (particularly female souls). As far back as the end of the first century, the infantile Christian founding fathers had zero tolerance for the old, long-held, and revered beliefs that centered on the Divine Mother. In an attempt to soothe the public's growing discontent with its compulsory New Order, the Church bent a bit by declaring itself the "Holy *Mother* Church" and elevating the role of Jesus' mother by calling her the "Blessed Mother" and "Holy Virgin." In this manner, the unwilling faithful were somewhat placated. Though Holy Mother Church thrived and blossomed, no woman could possibly be given any appointments within it because these were medieval times and, as every man knew, women just didn't have the intelligence to grasp spiritual concepts nor be able to understand enough to preach its tenets. Women were simple-minded and, once a month, "unclean" and not permitted within the church during these times. Centuries later, the Inquisition effectively handled the problem of the dwindling faithful who were beginning to return to their former matriarchal ways and embrace the comforting Mother Goddess by claiming all contrary beliefs to be an act of heresy against God and Holy Mother Church. In droves did the faithful return to the Church for fear of their lives, and so it has remained through time. Utilizing fear to control the faithful worked wonders. Fear of damnation and of losing one's very soul if one strayed away from the Church. Fear of not confessing one's sins, fear of being excommunicated from the "one and only, true" religion. Fear of condemning your baby to an eternity of never seeing the face of God if it isn't baptized in the Church. Fear made the Church grow and grow. And it became richer and richer. But as huge as it has become today, women remain confined to servile roles. This is not a personal, feminine attitude of sour grapes, it's just historical fact and the only way this question could be answered.

Today there is more freedom of intellectual thought. More and more faithful are taking a closer look at recorded history. The Divine Mother is gaining a firmer hold on the ground she once held. People are recognizing the signs of manipulation through the use of unfounded fear. They are waking up out of a deep sleep and opening their eyes to the Light. The Shekinah has returned. She's back!

My friend believes prophecy comes from the devil. Why?

I think you should ask your friend that question. You also mentioned that your friend was a Fundamentalist Christian. It's fact that this sect is overly fascinated with Satan and all aspects of him. They are awed by their perception of his power. They appear to spend more time claiming to fight off "Satanic attacks" than revering God and living a life of daily Unconditional Goodness. Their mind is bloated with thoughts of Satan and fear of him. Their societal perception is colored a deep, Satanic blood-red, where most of what they see is skewed toward a Satan-tinged color. If these individuals indisputably accept the biblical chapter of Revelation as being a prophetic dream of John's, then why on earth wouldn't they accept prophetic dreams visited upon modern-day people? The deities of the Trinity are as alive today as yesterday. Biblical times didn't possess a monopoly on angelic manifestations nor the possibility of people having spiritual intuitiveness, and the experience of visions. What I've personally found contradictory (and spiritually arrogant) is when these Fundamentalists have their in-home meetings and fall to the floor in ecstasy while listening to their group leader become "filled with the Lord" and speak God's words *through* them—in tongues! Well, hello . . . that's channeling! Yet when others outside their sect claim to do the same thing, it's immediately seen as the *devil* speaking, therefore you're doing Satan's work and they quickly stick out their arm and practice finger pointing. How is this so cut-and-dried, black-and-white distinction made? How is it derived? Is being a Fundamentalist the criteria used? Is being a Fundamentalist what makes the channeled words "sacred" while the channeled words given to others are evil? That mind-set sounds just like that of Holy Mother Church. We're right; you're wrong. We are of the Light, you are of the Dark. If you're not with us, you're against us. We are God's chosen, you are not. What crap. What arrogant, self-centered, spiritual crap that is. And I don't apologize for my choice of language, either. I'm not looking to win any Favorite Person of the Year award; I'm looking to talk straight and be real here. If some spiritual perception or concept is twisted, skewed, or stinky, I'm going to come right out and say it smells like a rose or it smells like shit. I'm not doing it to be funny. I'm doing it because it's *not* funny. It . . . is . . . not . . . funny the way people accuse others of being in league with the devil. It is not funny to harbor damaging and vindictive intolerance within your heart. It is not funny to hate others.

"Intuitive Spirituality" exists for everyone. It lives everywhere because it comes from the Universal Mind of the Divine Aspects. This intuitiveness is a *connection* to those Supreme Minds. It is not prejudice. It is blind to our differences of gender, race, our spiritual philosophy, our age, and ethnic genes. Intuitive Spirituality, which I've referred to as my own coined term of "The Knowing," is never selective. It exists as the air we breathe, the water we sustain ourselves with. It is Truth in pure form. It is without impurities of false thought. It is there. It is here. Without and Within. Nothing can affect it. It leaves its effect on everyone who comes in contact with it. Epiphanies. Epiphanies that come as heart-welling explosions of spiritual light and wisdom change one forever. You are never the same again. Don't you dare, don't you *dare* point your self-righteous finger at any of God's children and shout, "DEVIL!" Because when you do, you blaspheme against the Divine Mind of God.

Does my spirit guide communicate with my daughter's guide?

I can't conclusively say that it does, but I wouldn't know of any reason why it wouldn't, either.

Communication between entities on the Otherside realm is much like a highly sophisticated Internet system. All information is spontaneously available. Cross-referencing is continually in process. Interaction is a given. After all, the guides and angelic beings are hard at work for the purpose of uplifting the spiritual level of physical beings everywhere. Being involved in constant intercommunication with each other is a necessary function for manifesting this goal. It's like an Internet system without machines. Pure mind is a wonder to behold.

Does God sometimes intervene because of our prayers?

Let me put it this way: The Divine Minds *hear* all prayers. The Trinity's compassion is unbounded and has no limits.

This compassion makes a wave in the ethereal, which, in turn, activates angelic responses. What did I just say? *The Divine's compassion puts angelic beings into action.* Though the Divine doesn't *personally* answer through *action* to respond to prayers, the Divine's *reaction* of compassion *causes* the response. This response is carried out by the angelic beings. The bottom-line answer would be: yes, indirectly.

Are evil spirits causing the horrible crimes that are being increasingly committed now?

It would be so easy to shift the blame for these crimes onto some unseen force in the world, yet that isn't the case. The dark force that has grown into such a cannibalistic monster is none other than Ego with a capital E. This is a generation of the self. It's been manifesting and growing bigger, stronger, and uglier with each passing decade.

These crimes you're referring to are against life. They are against the sacredness of life itself. How has that been lost? It's been smothered by a growing sense of self-importance. The ego. The "I's" have it. The "I's" are in command. We hear a resounding chorus echoing across the land. "*I* want those shoes so *I* will kill you so *I* can *have* them." "*My* religion is right, yours is wrong, so *I* will point my finger at you and persecute you." "Only *my* race is the pure one, so *I* will annihilate yours." "*My* lifestyle is right, yours is wrong, so *I* will make discrimination against you legal." I. Me. Mine. My. EGO! Self-righteousness is egotistical arrogance twisted like putty and made into something that's supposed to resemble a pleasing gift to God. It's not! God sees it for the ugly thing it is. Intolerance is worked and reworked over and over in an attempt to call it something holy or biblically aligned—when it's not. God sees it for the shameful behavior it is. Ego is molded into a multitude of shapes that are supposed to resemble beautiful sweet-smelling attributes, but the Divine Minds are not fooled and are repelled by the stench beneath the cover-up. They are not fooled by the molded façades, the sweet perfumes, the false claims of "I *deserve.*" Humans are fooled. God . . . never. So let's not participate in any more elaborate cover-ups. Let's get rid of all the scapegoats grazing our browning pastures. When we're looking for causes, let's stop looking right and left. Let's begin by cleaning out our own barns first.

Is there such a thing as heresy?

Well, yes. Simply put, the word "heresy" merely means a concept contrary to an accepted one. Conceptually, "heresy" is a very harsh and unforgiving sort of term. It indicates an intolerance for variant thought. It forbids an opinion other than its own. It forbids it so vehemently that it extends itself to the "right of condemnation." We saw this at work during the Inquisition. We see it at work today with the Fundamentalists and Religious Right who actively accuse others of working for Satan, just because those others have a variant spiritual philosophy from theirs. Both conduct witch hunts based on ignorance coupled with the immaturity of spiritual arrogance.

Today, the concept of heresy, or of someone being labeled as a heretic, has no place in our world. By now we should have attained a higher level of evolution, intellectually and spiritually. It's bad enough that heresy existed in ancient times, but to carry it forward like it's been, is not something we should be proud of. We are all individuals. We have the right to learn and research whatever subject we wish. We have the right to form opinions, alter thought in deference to more precise ideologies, and be free to believe in whatever our contemplations have led us to. We have the constitutional rights that entitle us to freedom of speech and freedom of religion. We have the right to just . . . *be* . . . without judgment from others. We will not evolve further until this manifests.

I had occasion to be in someone's house who had gargoyles all over. I felt uncomfortable, as the demons were lurking everywhere. Was I just being silly?

My first reaction is to say, yes. However, I always tell people that their initial responses (feelings) about things are never "silly" until those responses have been examined and exposed as truly being such. When my children were young, I used to continually reinforce the idea that they shouldn't ever let embarrassment prevent them from asking questions, no matter how silly they sounded. If one never asks, one never satisfies a curiosity or increases their knowledge base.

First of all, gargoyles are not demons. They were never meant to portray a demon nor signify one. "Gargoyle" comes from the Latin word *gurgulio* (gullet), which refers to the act of "draining." The concept of gargoyles was originally conceived by Greek architects in order to resolve water run-off problems on roofs by creating marble lion heads on cornices. The water emptied out of the lions' mouths. Later, Gothic architects borrowed the clever idea and used these innovatively designed statues as drainspouts. A channel inside the gargoyle conducted the rainwater from the roof and propelled it away from the building walls by way of the spout in the creature's mouth. When these stone figures began to be used on churches and cathedrals throughout Europe, they were given a secondary purpose, that of warding off evil spirits. Gargoyles were perceived as a means of *protecting* a building from being infiltrated by dark forces. Today this last concept is the more popular perception of what gargoyles are.

I agree that these stone creatures can appear quite fearsome looking, but that visual presentation was the result of medieval thinking in that it was believed that only a "terribly fearsome" image could successfully repel evil spirits. However, some of them can be quite fanciful and amusing. I have an entire wall of bookshelves and, perched on one of the top corners, a large, stone gargoyle sits with its arms wrapped about its knees while looking down upon the living room. At Christmastime I give him a red Santa's cap to wear. This silent "observer" in my cabin has become an amusement for those who enter. He has never made anyone uncomfortable or skittish. In fact, I also have two gargoyle incense burners—one hangs on the wall and one sits on the woodstove. Another small, sitting gargoyle hangs one leg over the edge of a wall sconce as he watches us pass by him during the day. My cabin is full of all sorts of "little people" like miniature Yodas arranged with fairy figures as though they're sharing an afternoon conversation among Lilliputian crystal and amethyst standing stones; a mobile of twelve Yodas hangs over my desk (a handcrafted Christmas gift); fairy women with large stained-glass wings perch on the ledges of my office windows, the sunlight (and moonlight) turning the wings into gossamer points of light. There are little ceramic bunny families nestled beneath an entry table, a baby fawn peeks out from under an end table. And the bookshelves hold more than books; they contain East Indian totems joined by the multicultural religious figures of the virgin mother, Buddha, a brass statuette of Parvati (Hindu Daughter of Heaven Goddess), a colorful Egyptian Maat figurine, Selket standing with her golden arms outstretched. And atop the bookcases stands a large, hand-carved, wooden Norn (Scandinavian manifestation of the Triple Goddess) in her hooded robe and mysterious aura. Beside the watching gargoyle, a brilliantly painted bust of Tutankhamun oversees all that transpires in the room. These objects, along with those of the Nature Being faces, which are molded in ceramic leaves holding various wind chimes and wall candleholders, give one the vivid sense that being in my cabin is like being surrounded by dozens of characters and critters, all having a touchable presence and . . . watching eyes. How companionable that is for me. I hope it would be comforting for you, too.

The Catholic Church has always been right.

Seems as though I've had a preponderance of "Catholic" questions and comments from my correspondents. I believe that's most likely because I was raised in that faith and I have a great number of Catholic readers. This particular correspondent agrees with my writings, yet feels a need to defend her religion.

On a personal level I would never denigrate or single out a specific religion, other than to point out observations or reiterate their historical facts. Regarding Catholicism though, many times I find myself in the same position Gandhi found himself in with Hinduism. He loved Hinduism, yet despised its caste system so much that he went on a hunger strike in an effort to effect a change in attitude regarding the treatment of the untouchables. His efforts brought about increased tolerance for the caste. I'm not about to go on a hunger strike for Catholicism, but despite its faults, I still hold some of its facets within my heart. What I do address are questions others have. I didn't make the Church's history.

This correspondent is strongly defending her faith. That's as it should be I suppose, yet faith and devotion cannot alter or change the color of historical events. I accept this woman's comment. While accepting, I also have a question of my own and, in addition, offer a friendly suggestion.

Why did the Catholic Church call Copernicus a heretic and denounce him as anathema for stating that the sun was the center of our solar system? My suggestion is this: spend a little time researching history.

Why is a homosexual's life considered a spiritually wasted one?

For me personally, this is the most important question for me to answer . . . to answer *to*. This is *the* priority response of the entire book. Why? Because it desperately needs correction—clarification.

This questioner's inquiry was, sorry to say, generated from a response that was printed in my previous question-and-answer book, *Daybreak*. That particular book was one in which the responses came from several sources of spirit intelligences (No-Eyes and various Advisors) and also myself. These individual responses were not followed up by a clarification of "who" answered which questions. This is probably something that would've better served as a more informative aspect for the overall work had I clarified them by giving each response a distinction as to who the responder was. I mention this because the answer given by an Advisor in response to the question on homosexuality has caused me much grief since the publication of *Daybreak*. I accept personal responsibility for the heartache this response has caused many of my readers. I accept personal responsibility because, though the response was "given" by one of the spirit Advisors, I had the responsibility for what I wrote. I take this responsibility very seriously, especially after I realized how deeply words can affect readership. Now, having the availability of hindsight and learning an important lesson from the experience, I've grown into the wisdom of closely examining that which I finally pass into the publisher's hand. Regarding the formerly published response of this particular question, I should have looked at it more closely and asked for more detailed clarification and kinder wording. Depending on which Advisor responded to a question in the former book, the answer could appear compassionate, harsh, clipped, or a bit more complex than I personally would've put forth. I could tell which entity was responding by the tone of the answer. Some Advisors' personalities are extremely compassionate, others are "toe-the-line" strict with no gray areas considered. Clearly the formerly published response to this question was given by the strict Advisor, who addressed his response to the specifics of a particular individual rather than addressing the concept as a generality. And . . . I should have censored it by asking for another Advisor to respond to the question. I shoulder the blame for my lack of thought and foresight given to the importance of "filtering" the responses better, and consequently, my shoulders have been bent from the weight of it ever since. I'm so pleased to now have the opportunity to make amends for the Advisor's harshness, and for my own former omission of softening his response and clarifying it as pertaining to the circumstances of a specific individual instead of it relating to an overall concept. In taking this opportunity to reverse the damage that's been done, I'm going to be as open and straight-forward as I can be.

Heterosexuality is not a sin. It is not a sin to be asexual. Bisexuality is not a sin. Homosexuality is not a sin, nor is it a sin to live a sexually celibate life. Sexual behavior is not any type of sin unless it is "forced" on another or involves "children." Those are the spiritual facts. No individual's sexual behavior can "waste" a lifetime incarnation or make it a voided experience. Even behavior as heinous as incest and rape does *not void a lifetime;* however, these two latter sexual acts *will* incur serious karmic debt for the individual's spirit.

Sexuality is inherent. The particular behavioral tendencies are unique to each individual. The variances of sexuality are characteristic features of the individual and are as different as other traits that distinguish one human being from another. Like the delineating characteristics of ethnicity, gender, political views, and religious associations, one's behavioral sexuality appears to be open season for criticism, prejudice, and persecution.

Earthly civilization erroneously holds to what it falsely perceives as a societal norm. That norm is skewed, arrogant, and egotistical. That norm is seen as being white, heterosexual, male, Republican, and Christian. The myth implies "if you are all of these, you *deserve* to be on this planet." Those not possessing these qualities are then viewed as being expendable, or in a servile class, or one of less intelligence, or one who needs to be purged, or should earn less, or . . . well, history proves that this list is endless.

An individual's life is never wasted because of his/her inherent sexuality. What was harshly addressed and rigidly worded in *Daybreak* was a response to a specific and narrowly confined personal situation of a spirit who *required* a *heterosexual* relationship in the current incarnation for the purpose of accomplishing a related goal and didn't manage to carry it out. In that *singular instance* was the spirit's incarnation seen as a failure because it didn't succeed in accomplishing the *"specific"* goal. This was an issue of a "goal-specific" incarnation. This was in no way ever meant to imply that homosexuality, as a whole concept, created a "wasted" life. And I've been completely mortified to know that this is how most people have interpreted the former *Daybreak* response.

I would like to clarify another aspect of this issue. The Bible supposedly opposes homosexual behavior as "unnatural." Know what? Jesus had no problem with it. Much of the ancient written material that the Church's founding fathers sorted through was more or less "sifted" through for the purpose of "choosing" what to include in Scripture as a sanitized version that correlated with the church leaders' own ideologies on spiritual behavior. These ancient-time leaders were as puritanical and prejudicial as those of today who have devised the false "norm" for society. Hence, judgmental and discriminatory biblical statements and "sayings" were falsely attributed to have been voiced from the mouth of Jesus in an attempt to control society through Scripture. Well, wake up, world. Jesus never condemned anyone. Jesus laughed with gay men and danced with lesbian women. He freely did this because he never gave sexual diversity any kind of distinction or made a point of recognizing or noting any differentiation. Jesus traveled through many lands and experienced many cultures along the way. He loved them all. He loved and rejoiced in the brilliant colors of life, the colors of diversity. To

Jesus, life was a never-ending celebration that invites our full participation through which we're given the wonderful opportunity to joyfully savor all the glorious sounds, scents, and images life has to offer. Jesus openly and publicly accepted life's beautiful facets of diversity. And, like Jesus, we must work to rid our world of evil's greatest dark force. This dark force of evil has a name. Its name is Prejudice. And Prejudice can also be quickly recognized by its nicknames of Intolerance, Bigotry, Hatred, and Persecution.

I dreamed I was taking great amounts of an herb—hemlock. What does that mean?

It means that you have lost interest in living. You're severely depressed and don't want to go on living. This dreamscape element is a strong warning to seek help. Receiving assistance from mental health professionals is not a sign that one is crazy. More than anything, it shows that you want to help yourself to bring sunlight back into your life. Note: suicide is never an answer. It is wrong.

We envision and depict angels as having human form. If there's intelligent life on other planets and they have different physiologies, wouldn't their own concept of angels reflect their own, unique bodily characteristics? If so, whose image would be correct?

I found this to be a very interesting question. The key words here are "envision" and "depict," because that's precisely what we tend to do. We make the heavenly entities, including the idea and image of the Divine, in our own image . . . our *human* image. But, you see, that's where the big glitch lies. Our original image was one of the spirit . . . luminous light. It is that light that the Creatrix emitted from her own image. The inception of physical bodies only became a necessity *after* the spirits expressed a desire to experience the physical. So then, whatever form of appearance in which all intelligent beings everywhere *envision* angelic entities to look like would be a correct representation of their *personalized* imagery. Both (or all) versions of these *envisionings* would not be wrong because they're merely imaginings of physiological relatedness made through natural association. However, in reality, both are incorrect because spiritual beings have no bodies. They are of "light." They are pure thought.

If you ever saw the film *Star Man,* you will recall that the Starborn entity entered the woman's cabin in the form of a light . . . intelligent energy. His body was formed through thoughts that assimilated the genetic imprints borrowed from the DNA of her deceased husband's hair strands. Likewise do all spirit beings of light "take on" the physiological appearance of intelligent life forms (people everywhere) they need to relate to. This is solely for the purpose of communication and has consequently resulted in the false idea that all of these beings possess the identical physical form as we do. Angelic beings have no physical form. Angelic beings are of light. They are pure thought.

Is the "Touched by an Angel" television series a good representation of how angels work among us?

No. The series' angels are way too full of platitudes and sugary-sweet personalities. The angelic beings working among us are . . . those among us. Those . . . among . . . us. Think about that for a minute. Glance about you. Who are those among you? Who do you see? A trash collector and maybe a grocery clerk. A street-corner flower vendor. Your handyman. The casino porter or bartender. Those among you have fun, drink, watch TV movies, smoke, have hobbies, raise children, fix your car, and clean house. Those among you are those who you can relate to best.

Angelic beings are not effective if they emit an aura of elevated spiritual status. Nor are they effective if they appear in any way to have some haughty "holier-than-thou" philosophy, behave in a sanctimonious manner, or spout platitudes. They are only effective if they physically present as a down-to-earth human being. Wait a minute. Have you seen the film *Michael,* starring John Travolta? That film amused the heck out of me because *that* was an angelic being! Some religious folks were of the opinion that that movie was disrespectful, but it wasn't. That movie was far more real and representative of how true angelic beings (minus the wings) present themselves in the world than those sanitized angels on the TV series you asked about. Just think about it. How would an angelic being be most effective? How could one best move about in our world in an anonymous manner? The next time you envision some angel on earth, don't add a glowing halo and feathery wings to the picture, because you'd be wrong; and the soft-spoken platitudes you're expecting to hear just may be replaced by an unexpected string of expletives. It appears to be a human trait to have a knee-jerk urge toward spontaneous imagery caused by assumptions based on how we *think* things should be, or appear, or behave. I believe the automatic imagery would be far more accurate if, from the beginning, the complete record of Jesus' humanness and actual day-to-day behavior had been included in Scripture. Jesus didn't live a spiritually sanitized and censored life, neither do those angelic beings who are walking, working, and playing among us. So if you ever happen to come upon a soft-spoken individual whispering platitudes and attempting to project an aura of halo light, it's most likely a human full of self . . . an angel impersonator . . . doing a very bad job of it.

Does renunciation of the flesh set the spirit free?

Flesh. Spirit. Not even on the same plane. One is physical. One is of the spirit. Spirit remains the spirit and is not affected by physical data. Eating meat is giving sustenance to the physical body. Eating meat does not feed or nourish or contaminate the spirit. The spirit does not need air to breathe.

The spirit doesn't need entertainment or recreation. The pure spirit does not have sexual urges that need attending to. The spirit has no cravings or habits to satisfy. So . . . if the spirit is not *of* the flesh, how can the flesh have a hold on it?

Now, if you're dead, that's another thing. If you're dead, that question may apply because you want to speed forward with undue haste, not be drawn back into the heavy atmosphere of the flesh (physical). In that case, I'd definitely say that the spirit is set free by renouncing the flesh (physical). These differentiations of circumstances are necessary to determine whether a statement, saying, or concept is correct or not. Context is very important to take into account for any conceptual consideration.

What is your opinion of the Hindu caste system, which includes the untouchables?

I touched on this in a former response. I'll let the words of Gandhi answer for me. "I regard untouchability as the greatest blot on Hinduism. Hinduism has sinned in giving sanction to untouchability. We are guilty of having suppressed our brethren. We ought to purge ourselves of this pollution."

Is Animism a valid concept?

Animism is the belief that all natural objects have souls, particularly animals. Animals have an etheric life force within them. Animals have personality and emotion. They have emotional responses. They do not possess the same type of Divine-related spirits we do.

Are physical afflictions evidenced at birth karmic?

They can be, yet most often they are not. Even those physical afflictions that occur later in life through accidents, warfare, disease, etc., won't necessarily be a karmic effect from a past-life experience. I think we need to shift the focus from "why" bad things happen to "how" we should *accept* them and continue on in *spite* of them. Looking for the "whys" is frequently a search for a "cause" . . . a scapegoat to blame. When this is done, we do others great harm; consequently, we do ourselves greater harm in the process. Searching for one to blame is not being in Acceptance of what is. Too many times, searching for blame brings God into the picture when God is never to blame for any misfortunes we may experience in life.

The questioner is wondering if karma can shoulder the responsibility (blame) for birth defects. Is "blame" the word we're really looking for? Isn't "causal factor" a better term? It's a better term when we see how medical research has shown that many birth defects are genetically transmitted in the infant's DNA. Chemical ingestion by the mother can cause birth defects. We saw the evidence of that with Thalidomide and, today, HIV and drug dependency are also passed on to the infant. We witness diseases that are gene-related with a direct correlation to ethnicity. And we watch the babies of Third World countries suffer from diseases caused by such geographic factors as viral-vectoring insects and polluted waters, and those caused by societal factors such as scant medical resources or poor hygienic practices. These certainly are not all karmic, but rather give evidence of our earthly conditions, situations, and behavior. What's far more important than looking around for someone or something to blame is living in Acceptance and utilizing that Acceptance by taking that disability forward in a creative manner and making the best of life . . . in spite of it.

Is there such a thing as being born evil?

In essence, yes, but I don't like the wording used here. I prefer this concept to be viewed as "evil choosing to incarnate." This is one of those concepts that can cause havoc among the uninformed because it's too easy to misidentify a normal child's bad or constantly precocious behavior as being evil. With the obsession some religious groups have with

Satan, the accusations of "evil" are far too accessible. It's like having a loaded, hair-trigger magnum called a Satan Seeker at the ready on their hips and, with knee-jerk reaction time, they point it indiscriminately . . . sometimes discharging it.

I'll admit that it's often so difficult to determine bad behavior from evil—it can nearly be like a toss of the coin, but we must never be premature in our judgment and jump to conclusions. Though Hitler would appear to be a prime candidate for the expression of this concept, he was not born evil. He became a heinous, manipulative personality through a developed ego and focus on self. He controlled others through fear. Once that has gained a hold on people, their wills are easily bent and their ideologies reshaped like soft putty.

Yes, a dark spirit can indeed incarnate. Though this is managed without sanction by the Powers of Light, it is still done. However, and this is a big however, most dark spirits will not choose an infant to enter. Why? Because through parental nurturing, love, and spiritual education, they may risk reformation. Hence, most dark entities wishing to enter into the physical will seek out a likely adult form to overtake. A likely individual would be an alcoholic, someone on the verge of suicide, a drug addict, etc. This is an aspect of the "walk-in" concept. Choosing an infant form is a waste of valuable time for a dark spirit who doesn't want to wait to grow up to begin wreaking havoc. The times a dark one enters an infant are so rare as to be practically nil. It is because of the minute percentage for this likelihood to happen that I almost left this question out of the book. I included it solely because I've personally witnessed too many ignorant segments of society who walk among us with their hair-trigger Satan Seekers armed and cocked.

I read that the Shroud of Turin has been carbon dated to the Middle Ages. True?

I believe it's true that you read that. I've read that too. It's written that the ancient burial cloth was kept in the Cathedral of St. John the Baptist in Turin, Italy, since 1578. The Catholic Church calls it the Holy Shroud. Though it is owned by the Vatican, the Archbishop of Turin is responsible for it. The chapel of the Holy Shroud in Turin has been closed to the public since 1990.

Because of controversy over the Shroud's authenticity, the Church commissioned a scientific investigation of the linen cloth in 1988. The results determined that the cloth dated back to the Middle Ages and couldn't possibly be Christ's burial linen. However . . . the small fragment of cloth that was examined was handed over to the researchers by special appointees of the Church. Was a substitute cloth used? And why would that idea even come to mind? Perhaps it comes to mind because the Shroud of Turin not only shows the image of a man who was scourged, stabbed in the side, crowned with thorns, and crucified, it also showed *blood flow stains* from the wounds. And we all know that dead people do not continue to bleed. Only a *beating* heart can continue to circulate the blood through and out of the body. If the Shroud is authentic, it proves the body was still bleeding when taken down from the cross . . . still alive. If the burial linen is not authentic, why not pitch it in the trash barrel, instead of preserving and venerating it as Jesus' image? The Church's *behavior* on this issue is not aligned with its *public* statement. So what does it really believe?

Now, this question necessitates a look at carbon dating. Radioactive carbon 14 (radiocarbon) is naturally created in the atmosphere by the bombardment of cosmic particles and permeates the living organic matter on earth. Organic matter also absorbs carbon 12 (common carbon). Once an organism dies, it no longer takes on carbon 14, which begins to decay at a half-life of 5,700 years. Since the ordinary carbon 12 does *not* decrease over time, the dating is done by calculating the ratio of the radiocarbon to the common carbon of the organism against the current existing proportion. The more carbon 14 found in a test sample, the more recent was its death; a lesser measured amount would indicate an older specimen.

What has to be present to make radiocarbon 14 a valid method of measurement is a *constant*. What I mean by this is a "standard" that never fluctuates or alters. For example, we count years by the standard of 365 days representing one year. We couldn't have an accurate dating system if one year the measure was 365 days and the next was 207 days and the following was 401 days. We'd be in a mess. So 365 days became the standard measure to gauge one year by—a constant that never alters from year to year, the exception being leap years.

Now comes the glitch in radiocarbon dating. Scientists have measured the current ratio of carbon 14 "creation and decay" and have discovered to their great surprise that it is *building up* at a rate *greater* than the decay. The present rate of radiocarbon buildup is 18.4 atoms per gram per minute compared to the formerly measured 13.3 atoms per gram per minute—a buildup that *surpasses* decay by 38 percent! This discovery proved that the atmosphere's bombardment of radiocarbon *fluctuates* and is not the constant they thought it remained over the years. At a time of *greater* bombardment, the organic matter would absorb *more* carbon 14, making the object appear *younger* when, in actuality, it could be of much *greater* age. Conversely, a time of less bombardment could make a sample seem very old when, in fact, it wasn't. This new discovery of the atmosphere's ongoing fluctuations completely shattered the idea of "reliability on a *constant*" with which to accurately measure carbon 14. Consequently, well—think about it—this new scientific discovery not only affects the accurate dating of the Shroud, but also the historical dating we've already received and accepted from archeologists and the paleontologists. In the scientific community, heads are being vigorously scratched and the old, traditional "facts" are seriously being rethought.

The virgin birth of Jesus proves he was the prophesied Messiah.

Key word here is "the" Messiah, because there were many saviors prophesied throughout various cultures hundreds of years before the Christian one came along. Two appeared around 600 B.C., when the virgin Maya birthed Gautama Buddha and, in Syria, Mithra was birthed of a virgin in a stable on December 25th. The virgin Ishtar, who was called "Holy Virgin," birthed the Babylonian god Adonis. Around 1200 B.C., the virgin Devaki birthed Krishna. In Persia, Zoroaster was born of a virgin around 1400 B.C. Dionysus was a Greek god who was birthed by a virgin in a stable. In Tibet, around 700 B.C., Indra was born of a virgin.

Since the beginning of civilization, prophets in different cultures have predicted the "coming of a messiah" for their people. They have predicted that the messiah would be born of a virgin and so there have been many of these events manifesting throughout history. As it happens, Jesus' mother was the *last* of the long list of historical virgin births, not the first as Christianity would have us believe. Who's to say there won't be more as time marches on?

Was Jesus really born on December 25th?

No. Jesus was born on June 12th. There is no record of the date of this birthing; therefore, those formulating dogma for the newborn religion of Christianity found it necessary to pinpoint a birth date. They borrowed that of Mithra's because the religious belief system of Mithraism had become a strong spiritual force in the Roman Empire.

If a time of peace and harmony is coming, what about those who have big karmic debts to work out that might not be harmonious?

My first reaction to this question is to ask one. Why wouldn't the karmic process be harmonious when the basic, underlying purpose of it is to balance out a previous negative with a current positive? It seems to me that anytime someone reverses or neutralizes any negative act with a positive one, that act increases harmony.

Another aspect of this question is location. They say "location is everything," you know. You're leaving out the possibility that karma can be worked out anywhere, on any planet, on any dimensional plane. Karmic debts are strictly associated with one's soul, not necessarily with other specific individuals as popularly believed. This means, for example, that an act of cruelty directed to a person in one life can be effectively balanced out by the performance of a related act of kindness *wherever* the next life is experienced. It is the *act* that needs balancing out rather than the need being contingent on directly correlating it to a specific individual. There seems to be a popular belief that Joe must come back in his next incarnation and gift you with money because he stole money from you in this life. Nope, not so. In Joe's next incarnation he'll have to be generous with his money to make up for the stealth and greed exhibited in this one. See? It's not a person-to-person concept here, it's a private affair within one's own soul.

The payment of karmic debt is a positive event. Neutralizing one's previously committed negatives naturally uplifts the composite state of society. That statement made me think. It made me think because, as I look at society's overall state of being, I am not at all impressed by its current behavior which is generated from a focus on self. And that shows evidence of more karma-*creating* going on than karma-balancing. Wake up, folks. Wake up and boot your ego out the back door before you have your first morning cup of coffee. Tell it to take a hike because you can't go about your business with it hanging around and making a mess of things.

Everything I do lately is wrong. God must hate me.

Well, do you think God hates you for doing everything wrong lately or do you think you're doing everything wrong *because* God hates you? Anyway, the answer doesn't matter one way or the other because God does not hate. God can be displeased, but God does not hate. God is displeased with negative *behavior,* not with people.

You're just in a slump. Everyone gets into those now and then. When these come along, it calls for a time-out period. Take some measures to reduce the stress in your life. Experience a little recreation. Spend some valuable time in contemplation. Do volunteer work. Relax and read for enjoyment. During these times, it's best not to read for research or intensive study, because that can compound your situation. These slumpy periods usually come when one is attempting to "force" a condition, situation, event, or relationship. This is a time for accepting Acceptance and letting things ride for a time. Instead of being swept faster and faster like a downhill racer, get off the skis. Get off the skis, sit beside the run, and look up through the pines. You need to put a halt to the momentum. You need a break. You don't need to bring God into it. God loves you . . . slump and all.

I know a rabbi who claims the Shekinah is not an actual entity but is a term for a concept. This concept means "God's spirit at work in the world."

Exactly, the Divine's *spirit* at work in the world. I agree with this statement. Where the rabbi and I differ is whether this spirit has gender or not. I believe the Shekinah is the Female Aspect of the ideology of God (Goddess) at work in the world. He says the Shekinah has no gender because the term refers to a "concept." This last ideology is a result of the ongoing strongly held opinion that patriarchism has clutched to its chest with a tenacious death grip ever since the end of the first century C.E. Through this endeavor we've witnessed a conscious movement to eradicate the ancient and long-held strong beliefs in the originating Goddesses that every culture once revered. If the ancient Talmudic texts described the Shekinah as God's divine wife or consort, how then could she *not* be a feminine deity? Like the Catholic Church, which denies the historical existence of Pope John (Joan) in the ninth century, religious sects of white America are in denial of their recorded feminine past.

I'm not the least bit inclined to participate in a debate over this issue because history speaks for itself. Let's look at some of it.

Today we've ended up with a multitude of "concepts" that have shed (buried) their feminine deity origination. The "Goddesses" have been conveniently erased from societal memory and, therefore, it is generally assumed that they must've been imaginary characters of fable, myth, and legend. Today many of the actual *names* of these Goddesses have become the very *terms* for the remaining "concepts" that their beautiful personalities strongly represented. We've already noted this about the Shekinah, who is the Female Aspect of the Mother *Goddess* at work in the world. Her beautiful living *persona* has been deplorably reduced to mean a mere *concept* where her very name is now commonly used as the "term" defining this idea.

The Goddess Maat was widely revered in ancient Egypt and perceived as one of that culture's prime deities. Maat was the epitome of truth, justice, and wisdom. She was always depicted with a feather in her hair, which symbolized the "weighing of one's soul by the balance of a feather." Today, in white society, Maat has been stripped of her living persona and has been reduced to a state of anonymity whereby her name has been stolen to represent a *term* for the "concept" of truth, justice, and wisdom. The woman known as Maat, the Goddess, has been dethroned from her lofty position and expunged from memory. Though, in fairness to the Egyptians, I must clarify that, there, she respectfully remains the deity she always was.

The name for the Goddess of Wisdom (Sophia) was adopted by the Greeks. Sophia became the Greek word for wisdom. "Never mind that there is a *real* Goddess Sophia who is 'One of full wisdom and knowing.' We'll just call wisdom by the term of Sophia," says society's revised rendition.

Likewise, the ideology of the moon representing wisdom came about through the extermination of the Moon Goddess Luna and subsequent act of borrowing her name to represent what she symbolizes. Hence, "luna" and "lunar" became the popular term for the moon. This move served as one maneuver among the many that joined forces to create a tyrannical philosophy of spiritual chauvinism. Consequently, the shift to a patriarchal mind-set reduced the long-held matriarchal societies to myth and determined that belief in the original, ancient Goddess ideologies were, henceforth, an act of heresy when women's religion was, overnight, deemed to be a demonic religion. Women honoring the Great Earth Mother Goddess by dancing in the fields and woods in joyful celebration for her fertile soil and harvested bounties were burned as witches who were believed to have fraternized with Satan. From that point on . . . ignorance thrived and Feminine Spirituality was severely persecuted.

Further examples of this eradication of women's spirituality are shown by how the shamrock's symbology has shifted into the popular belief that it represents luck and good fortune when its ancient, *original* meaning was to represent the Triple Goddess. Today the triangle configuration has many meanings. The Church has appropriated it to represent the Holy Trinity of a male God, that of God the Father, God the Son, and God the Holy Spirit. The *original* meaning of the triangle shape was to symbolize the *Feminine Principle of the Female Consciousness,* that of the *Virgin, the Mother, and the Crone.* This was the Divine Feminine Principle, which held that the Consciousness of all women contained an Innocence Within (Child or Virgin), a Nurturer (Mother), and a Wise Elder Woman called the Crone. Corn dolls originally represented the Harvest Mother.

The names of ancient Goddesses have been stolen in the following examples. We've ended up with the word for earth by using the term "terra" when, in fact, the Tibetan Mother Earth was the Goddess Tara. The word "hell" was stolen from the Norse underworld Goddess Hel, who originally symbolized the "sacred womb (place) of rebirth." The month of May came from Maya, the Virgin Goddess of Spring. The word "health" came from the Goddess Hygeia (hygiene). The term "panacea" was borrowed from the Goddess Panacea, who represented a "soothing" personality. And the utterance of "om" from the mouth of the Oriental Great Goddess while birthing the world has been adopted as a meditative chant. If I spent time doing some in-depth research on this issue, I'd end up with an entire book. I think you get the idea, so I'm not going to take up any more of our time debating whether the word "Shekinah" is a real Feminine Deity Aspect or just some term for the concept of the spirit of the male God at work in the world.

Do incarnated angels remember who they are?

A more accurate term for this idea is "angelic beings." No, 99.999 times out of 100 these entities will not have recall of their true identity while working in the physical. This is because they are usually born in infant form and do not enter as adult walk-ins. What gives them the advantage over other incarnated spirits in human form is their compelling sense of purpose. They are usually highly intelligent and one-minded. They possess an inner drive that impels them toward their goal. They are "driven" to search out and connect with their targeted purpose. Their restlessness immediately abates when their destination is satisfied. It is then that they make recognition and settle into their intended mission.

It's important to understand that an angelic being or completed spirit who takes on the task of incarnating into the physical . . . be . . . of . . . the . . . physical. This process of growing up in society imbues the personality with valuable and necessary experiential qualities. Imagine it as being a way of accomplishing a natural measure of human, societal indoctrination for a high spiritual being. Living among the humans, experiencing the variances of society, having human emotions, dealing with problems that daily living presents, and having to educate self in order to support and sustain self. All these factors come into play as a necessary background formulation for an angelic being to be properly prepared and armed for her/his work. It's all related to the requirement of "knowing the society in which you need to work." During this time of physical development, knowing one is an angelic being is a detriment because it prevents true human assimilation of environment. Eventually, after the incarnated angelic beings have succeeded in searching out and reaching their intended, destined goals, enlightenment in regard to their true nature is theirs. And, by this time, it means nothing special to them because, over time, their goal-focused mind-set and determination has eradicated all sense of ego.

How do you envision the Final Battle?

Not like most do. I envision it as intelligence winning the day over ignorance. Spirituality over religion. Love over hate. Tolerance over persecution. The concept of The All over the Ego.

The Southern Baptists publicly made a statement calling for women to give more deference to their husbands. It sounded to me as though they were really making a desperate move to maintain their male dominance. What do you think?

Amen. The Mormons do the same thing. East Indian countries are worse. This statement is an attempt to deny constitutional and basic rights to women. Slavery went out of style and was abolished a long time ago. Suppression of a woman's right to be an individual with a free-thinking mind and free will is pure ignorance and comes from patriarchal manipulation. This is generated from the twisted concept of men being bigger, stronger, and smarter than women. Therefore, women must let the men do the thinking, earn the living, and make all the decisions while she stays home baking bread, washing his clothes, and making babies (preferably a man child) for him to carry on his wonderful name with. This sounds so cynical, but too bad it's not. It sounds so feministic, but so sorry it's reality. So sorry. Yes, in my heart I feel such a great heaviness for the way society behaves toward each other. My spirit sheds tears over all the incredible ignorance humanity exhibits . . . the ego; it never fails to blow up at every opportunity.

More than once I've heard the saying, "God made Eve second because *she* first *practiced* with Adam then *perfected* with Eve." Initially I thought it was funny, but its intent is the same as those Southern Baptists—sexist, prejudicial, demeaning, egotistical, and separatist.

A truly spiritual society is one that is neither patriarchal nor matriarchal. In the attempts to reverse the manipulative patriarchal philosophy, we must not create the same problem we're trying to balance through over-compensation by way of a more heavily weighted matriarchal one. An unbalanced measure of either one is highly destructive. Chauvinistic philosophy must be eradicated by balancing the yin within each male. Sexist women must bring the yang into more balance. We, as the Children of the Divine, were meant to be finely tuned with our balance brought into a precisely calibrated state of being. Men have their unique male characteristics. Women have their own unique feminine qualities. Both have beautiful attributes. None of these include expected or demanded subservience, obedience, slavery, or submission to the other. The wonderful qualities of each gender need to be recognized, respected, and celebrated.

Instead, the sexes are acting like bratty siblings fighting tooth and nail for domination over the other. It's time to grow up. And it's long past time for the patriarchal religious leaders to come out of hiding behind their protective shield of domination and, on equal terms, face the women they've been so fearful of. Come up into the light so you can see that the full utilization and expression of the feminine/human rights, intelligence, independence, and potential won't threaten your own nor will it destroy you. Quite the opposite, as they will greatly enhance your own aspects. What makes you so afraid of women that you can't manage to feel superior unless you're suppressing them? It's time for serious introspection. It's time to see what your true potential is when you're up against a woman's. Real men don't need a psychological whip to feel taller by repressing others. It's time to drop the big sticks and, finally, become the "men" God intended you to be. It's time for each of you to stop playing at being a social and religious tyrant. It's time to grow up and be a man. And please, don't throw that Garden of Eden mythology around. You know, those fabricated words God supposedly said about women, which certain Christian sects love to use as their big sticks to back up their male superiority. After all, men pieced the biblical Scriptures together; it'd naturally be formulated in a manner that served them well over time. Well, God wouldn't curse woman with an eternal punishment of childbirth pain, nor would God condemn men to a life of forever-after labor; those two situations are merely aspects of living in the physical. They are not punishments. God never appointed one gender to be superior over the other, so better watch out for what's going to be revealed in the yet-undiscovered ancient scrolls. A few of them are going to blow those big sticks into a million tiny splinters.

This questioner's comment specifically relates to the state of marriage. In associating the Baptists' philosophy to this institution, we see that it is a detrimental attitude rather than the falsely perceived "ideal" situation it attempts to promote. No partnership can be a synergistically based one if one individual within said partnership claims dominance over the other and expects subjugation. A partnership, whether related to a marriage, business, or other circumstance, only succeeds when both individuals are perceived as being equal in all areas, including intelligence; constitutional, moral and legal rights; decision making; independence; the expression of free will; etc. As adults, these qualities are everyone's inherent rights and any type of partnership, including that of marriage, will not survive without the freedom each of these qualities bestows on each member. Now, how can a marriage be a true partnership if one partner subjugates or attempts to dominate and manipulate the other partner? That's detrimental to a mutual relationship. There are no "senior partners" in a marriage. If love is real, each marriage partner will respect and honor the others individuality, talents, and inherent rights. There will be no jealousy, fear, control, domination tendencies, or ego to bring a metastasizing cancer into the union. In any type of partnership, sexism, racism, or one individual's sense of political or religious superiority has no place, as these incite a natural rebellion within the victimized partner. These are the destructive forces that undermine any partnership, especially marriage. To expect "obedience" or "subjugation" from a partner isn't even logical. It's not a sign of intelligence. It is a clear sign of moral and spiritual backwardness. It is pure ignorance. It exposes a fearful mind and an inner need for superiority. Why? Because only someone *fearful* of another individual threatening to injure their ego will attempt to keep others down (suppressed) in a position perceived as being "below" that of self. Ego and the fear of having it threatened or harmed in any way is the key reason for attempting to create a "safe zone" around self that is, in twisted theory, supposed to insulate that precious ego. The insulating methods are manipulation, subjugation, external posturings of superiority, denigrating and persecuting others. These have no place in our lives. These actions only continue to create and perpetuate further discord in our world, in society, in partnerships, and in marriages.

This Baptist statement associates itself with one of the causes for the growing increase in crimes against women. The physical and psychological abuse women are subjected to within their own home is an atrocity. Most of this abuse is caused from the same skewed philosophy the Baptists and many other so-called "Christian" and Middle Eastern institutions are attempting to promote—"keep the little woman subservient" and "husbands are the masters and king of their home." This *head of the family* concept is the height of egotism. There is no "head" of a partnership or marriage. Any individual who is demeaned, subjugated, mentally or physically abused will eventually *stand up for her human rights*. I've italicized this because it's true.

Too often those holding onto this Baptist philosophy cast the blame on the wives for the discord within the family when, in reality, these suffering women are simply fighting for their human rights. It's not the rebelling women who are to blame, it's the men who suppress them who are to blame. They are the ones causing all the family problems. If a wife wishes to go to college, so be it. If she wants to work and have a career of her own, then she should be able to go for it. If she doesn't want children, then it's her choice because it's her body. If she doesn't want to relocate to another location, then it needs further discussion and compromise. If she wants to have her own bank account, then she should have it. If she doesn't want the same family car that you want, then another compromise is necessary. It's the men's egotistical philosophy that results in the suppression and demeaning of their wives and lovers that *create* societal and marital discord in our world. It is this singular causal factor that fills the hospital emergency rooms and safe houses with battered women. Men, because they can't "control" their women by keeping them submissive, resort to states of rage and violence. Is that how their "strength" is to be measured and remembered? Is that the "power" they want to be identified by? Do they truly believe their superiority is evidenced by how well they can beat a woman into submission? Though I would deeply grieve at such a modern-day state of affairs, it appears that this is so.

Women and men are different. Different does not mean that one is more superior or better than the other. Different does not indicate or infer some type of caste perception that denotes a graduated measure of human status. Both possess redeeming qualities unique to the specific gender. We need to recognize these beautiful qualities and respect them. When the shining qualities of both genders are allowed to be utilized to their fullest in all situations, in all relationships, our world will then approach the threshold of an intellectual, moral, and spiritual evolution.

The papacy is patriarchal because its lineage is directly descended from St. Peter, who was the first disciple Jesus appeared to after his resurrection.

That's how the story goes. That's the party line. That's the prime basis for why the Church is patriarchal and only has male officials, dignitaries, appointees, and priests. This is what its philosophy is based on. So then, how is it the Church has forgotten that, in the garden surrounding the empty sepulcher, Jesus spoke to his favorite disciple *before* he even left the grounds to appear to the disciples who were hiding in the upper room? His favorite disciple was Mary Magdalene. Oops. According to the Church's reasoning then, the papacy should have descended from her, a *woman*. The Church should've been matriarchal! That just wouldn't do, so we'll ignore who Jesus first appeared to, alter the facts a bit, and make the apparition in the upper room be the initial contact made.

This correspondent's purpose in writing was to explain why no women were allowed to participate in any positions of priesthood (priesthood) in the Church. Instead of an explanation, it exposed conspiracy and sexism.

Act of God. God wills catastrophic events? Can you explain this popular concept?

I agree that this commonly used phrase isn't correct. It's a contradiction in terms. Its purpose is to refer to those events that are beyond any means of human ability to control or prevent from happening. Society has made use of this phrase in many areas, including the insurance industry. A more accurate phrase to use would be "act of nature." It's the powerful forces of nature that cause catastrophic events and bring devastation. Nature's force is that which is beyond human control and prevention. To call a killer tornado or monster hurricane an "act of God" is a bit presumptuous, and a false statement. God does not play chess with humans and nature. The Divine does not look down upon us in search of amusement and suddenly decide to wipe out an entire community of people by sending a flash flood ripping through town or etching jagged lines upon the earth to create cracking fissures which run through densely populated cities. These events and those like them are not the "will of God." They are natural events of our planet. They are natural—of nature. It seems to me that people don't necessarily like to admit that they have no control over nature, that nature can make them so completely helpless. Therefore, it's much more acceptable to attribute these situations of powerlessness to the all-powerful Divine.

Did the Virgin Mary have other incarnations?

Many, just like everyone else.

I'm attracted to the utilization of elementals as helpers.

How can this be so, I'm wondering? Cause and effect. Tit for tat. One good turn deserves another. What goes around comes around. "You scratch my back and I'll scratch yours," said the elemental. Everything has its price. Watch what you bring to the table. Life is full of two-edged swords. Many actions exact a payment of high interest. All pipers demand to be paid. The road you're considering taking is one that comes equipped with a tollbooth at its end. You'll not slip past it without paying an exorbitant price for the privilege of traversing its treacherous byway. The way over the top is not always shorter or easier than going around. The straightest route is not always the most direct. And, some helpers are more of a hindrance.

Despite the fact that some people are of the opinion that elementals are merely "thought form" personal slaves, there are no completely mindless, robotic entities out there who await the opportunity to carry out your every bidding. If an entity has the wherewithal to mentally understand a task, it also possesses the capability to want something in return. Elementals are not toys to idle away one's time with. They have cunning . . . usually more than humans do. Nobody likes to be used, ordered about, or toyed with—especially an elemental. If you need amusement or interactive play, try Super Mario. That's not being sarcastic, either. That's just plain good advice.

Look, we accomplish our life goals by our own efforts, applied after careful contemplation and analysis. We know what the goal or objective is. This is in the mind. Next we plan out several methods of reaching this goal. By trial and error we're persistent because we're determined and single-minded. Through our own talents and efforts do we reach for the brass ring and, only after it has been firmly grasped are our hearts full to brimming. The sense of personal accomplishment is a true blessing.

Gosh, I just cannot imagine why anyone would want to delve into the darker shadows where elementals dwell. Why, that's just like *knowingly* opening Pandora's ill-fated box and never being able to close it again. Don't we have enough to deal with in life on a day-to-day basis without attracting additional grief to ourselves? Playing with fire can get one burned. Pushing fate too far by seeing how long you can hold a lit cherry bomb will get your hand blown off. Dealing with an elemental that has a mind and will of its own is like playing with a nuclear toy.

What does returning to God mean?

We were created. We will not be uncreated. We do not uncreate our own children, so why would God? To return into the essence of God simply means that we've gone "home." Once we've melded back into the Divine, we continue to maintain all the unique identity facets of our composite spirit crystal. Everyone we've ever been has blended to create the totality of each individual spirit. This spirit never loses that identity or awareness of self or the ability for intercommunication *within* the essence of God.

The human body comprises thousands of different cells, each belonging to various individualized groupings. These cell groups have cell memory. They have an identity and a recognition that transpires between them. Liver cells regenerate liver cells. Blood cells do the same. White blood cells put out a call to increase their numbers in order to fight infection and T-cells are the infantry that attacks systemic invaders. All bodily cells maintain a strong sense of identity and purpose. They interact with other cells within the mainframe of the body. So, too, is the way of completed spirits who return home to the Divine. It's likened to a family reunion, where every member has returned to the homeland.

I've heard some fear expressed from people regarding this "going back to God" scenario. They seem to think they'll no longer have identity or memory of their own wonderful individuality. That's just not so. We were not created to end up as nonentities. We began as God's children who, through our own efforts, improved ourselves and will ultimately end up as God's companions.

Is book learning necessary and important for our spiritual development?

Development. A broadening of scope. Enhancement. Perhaps, if you will, a "full-bodied" expansion. Book learning increases one's database of traditional knowledge as it is known to current society. Book learning reveals what has been discovered; therefore, this type of endeavor is a form of discovery.

The issue of this subject matter is "spiritual" development; therefore, any type of book learning regarding this subject would be associated with Spirituality. Books related to this category would include the study of world religions, the entire range of philosophy, canon and Gnostic scripture, metaphysics, and the science of physics. One cannot have a strong foundational database of traditional spiritual knowledge without initially obtaining a firm grasp of the subject's full totality. When this research has been accomplished, something happens. The research, studying, and reading suddenly become a box, a trap within which the mind becomes confined. There is a name for this box . . . conceptualization. The more one reads and contemplates that which has been studied, the more one realizes that traditional knowledge is rigid with molded concepts. The more concepts one comes to recognize, the more one feels boxed in by them. The more one is boxed in, the greater the urge to break free of the traditional knowledge that binds and to reach into the Beyond, which beckons with the bright promise of rich refinements of knowledge that comes not as unyielding concepts, but as a gentle and sure Knowing. This, then, is the value of book learning. It provides us with a necessary foundation for that which awaits us beyond the traditional. Book learning, when utilized to its fullest extent, acts as a natural impetus to look beyond that which has been recorded. Book learning provides us with a jumping-off point from the linear to the nonlinear, from form to formless, from the known to the possible. It leads us along the fence lines of traditional conceptual confinements to the gate that is marked with the words: There Is More Through Here. And it is at this point when we leave the square concepts of traditional knowledge behind and walk through the gateway to greater understanding. This understanding is not molded. It has no form. It has no name or separatist term to define or confine it. This understanding cannot be owned by a religion or claimed as a possession by any ethnic group or by any individual. It is beyond naming, past defining, above owning. It is the What Is within the Universal Mind. It is that which our spirits connect with when we ascend beyond the traditional conceptualized knowledge of humankind. It is The Knowing.

The Knowing is recognized by its clarity and simplicity, which are so beautiful that there are no words to write them down with, no images to verbalize to another. The Knowing comes as bright bursts of inspiration, heart-thumping epiphanies, and waves of warm emotion. It comes not as "words," but as a sudden vision displaying *reality* in all its magnificent majesty. It is then that the book learning becomes so simplistic, so mundane.

Spiritual development is derived from the expansion and blend of the intellectual and behavioral facets of self. The *behavioral* aspect is that which *reflects* the spiritual development of the intellect. All the traditional book learning and biblical scripture studying in the world will not bring about spiritual development as it was meant to be evidenced within society unless one's spiritual behavior is experientially aligned with The Way.

This truth is evidenced when ministers are seen to condemn and point fingers at those they personally categorize as "sinners." These so-called clerics may have the ability to quote biblical verse by rote, but what does that prove if their behavior does not reflect the heart of the Supreme Beings? This sort of behavior exhibits a mind strongly steeped in traditional "religion," and not a mind that has made the transforming transcendence into The Knowing of true Spirituality. Unless one reaches the stage of recognizing the confinements of conceptualized book learning and understands that so much more depth of knowledge lies *beyond* its limitations, that individual's mind will forever remain in a spiritually undeveloped state, where behavior is likewise reflected through evidence of the ego holding sway. The actions of this type of individual will be weighted by the ego expressed through self-righteousness. For . . . *The Knowing transcends the ego and the self is suddenly nowhere to be found.*

Taoists believe that children bind one (a parent) to earth for another reincarnation. True?

Sure, it's true. It's true that Taoists *believe* this. They believe that having a child creates an extension of one's genes left in the world after the parent dies. This fact is supposed to imply (or prove) that a portion of self remains behind to interact with. Therefore, if any offspring survive you, you must return to clear out any relationships that required resolution. I suppose that, in theory, it would appear sound, yet it just is not the case. Children do not have any type of "hold" or "binding" effect on the spirit of a parent. What I find interesting about this Taoist concept is the fact that an individual may have hundreds of offspring from former incarnations living in the present one. Think of all the incarnations one has throughout time and all the children those experiential times have produced. A Taoist in this *current* lifetime may now be *sharing* a time when offspring from his *former* incarnation were produced. See? The philosophical concept isn't justified by reason and logic. Having children does not mandate another reincarnated experience for the parent. Gosh, I don't think this planet would be so populated if everyone thought like that. If having children bound one to another cycle of return, I think vasectomies and tubal ligations would be the fashion statements of the day.

Can spiritual maturity be attained without practicing meditation?

Meditation is not a requirement for spiritual maturity. Do we, in fact, know what spiritual maturity is? Spiritual maturity is thought and behavior that reflects the light of the Trinity's Divine Aspects. This means behavior sans ego. This means total acceptance of all others. Perceiving everyone as a spirit—*a child of the Creatrix*—not as a Vietnamese, or a man, or a heterosexual, or a blue blood, or an addict, or a lawyer. *A spirit* is how a spiritually mature individual visually and mentally perceives another person. Period. And associative spiritually mature behavior follows on the heels of that perception. As I've mentioned in a previous response, "different" does not equate to "unequal."

Meditation is a practice, not a prerequisite. Meditation is an optional spiritual event. Like prayer, it is not necessary for the attainment of spiritual maturity. Spiritual maturity is the Ship of the Soul, which carries no weighted collection of barnacles such as Scripture, rosaries, prayer wheels, incense, statues, buildings, circles, novenas, meditation, pipes, etc. Spiritual maturity may belong more to the ascetic hermit living in a remote cave than the jewel-bedecked priest performing intricate ceremonies over a golden altar. The idea of "stuff" being associated with Spirituality has got to go. Stuff includes ceremony and all its varied material trappings. God needs no pipe or incense to bring one's prayers. God does not favor an intricately worded traditional prayer over one that comes spontaneously from one's heart. God does not favor knowledge of Scripture over knowledge of right living—goodness. God has no preference as to which path one takes to spiritual goodness. God favors unifying Spirituality over religions that divide us. God favors naked communication (empty handed) over that which is cluttered with ceremony and "stuff."

Let's get rid of the idea that we need to lug stuff along our spiritual trail. Meditation is wonderful to calm the physical and soothe the mind, but it certainly is not necessary for the attainment of spiritual maturity. That comes with aligning one's behavior with universal, Unconditional Goodness.

Do all out-of-body-experiences evidence the silver cord?

No. It's not uncommon to not see it; in fact, most times it won't be visible. In actuality, the silver cord is more of a conceptualized *visual* (symbol) of the spirit's relatedness to the physical body.

When mass deaths occur, such as plane crashes, do the spirits of the dead congregate as a group at the scene or do they individually speed through the tunnel to the light?

This depends on the individual spirit. Some of this group will congregate while others quickly leave the scene. Eventually they all leave. Disaster locations like the Oklahoma City bombing or sites of historical mass deaths such as Treblinka, Dachau, and Auschwitz give off a haunted aura and people tend to believe these places are inhabited by associated spirits. This "haunted" sensation comes not from the existence of remaining spirits, but from the dark and devastating emotional aura the event *imprinted* upon the space in time

Visiting these places makes for an impressionable experience in that we are able to clearly envision the event at the time of its activity and our senses make a corresponding reactive response to these effects. These sensitized responses include empathy, fear, chills, sorrow and, frequently, psychic visuals and audio replays by way of regressive visions and clairaudient fragments. Due to a spirit's desire to be away from such places of pain and suffering, they do not tarry. They are eager to be comforted by the warmth and love in which the Light engulfs them.

I am sixty-four years old. Am I too old to find a teacher?

Interesting question, because you've probably had several teachers in your life by now. The popular conception of a human spiritual "teacher" is rarely true. The idea of an aged sage or elder from atop the mountain is mythical. It is the box in which society loves to enclose its theory of a wizened one. It is this box that serves to conceal the real teachers who come into your life. Preconceptions are blinding. Preconceptions close the eyes and ears to those who cross paths with the true teacher who subtly whispers the sacred words.

A "teacher" can be your grandchild, your pet, nature, a particular phrase read in a book or article, the verse of a song, something said in a polite comment by a passing stranger. Life is literally loaded with spiritual teachers. They go unnoticed because their appearance is colored by a prescribed designer concept of them which, in turn, closes the eyes and ears to their presence. Is the age of sixty-four too old? It's too old to not have made recognition of a life that was probably full of a wide variety of teachers. It is not too old to open the awareness of them surrounding you now.

Do charms and talismans work if properly constructed?

Regardless of the quality of construction, it is the *faith* in these items that can manifest desired results. Notice that I wrote "can" manifest. Destiny and fate are real. Some vitally important lessons in life will come by way of results *counter* to the intended purpose of a charm or talisman. Wearing a special scarab or crucifix will not necessarily miraculously spare one from a train derailment or automobile accident. These articles of faith do not take the place of personal responsibility and awareness, nor will they negate destiny. They have no effect on the dictates of fate. More often than not, they are symbols of wishful thinking and one's personal sign of hope.

Why aren't the concepts of reincarnation and karmic debt taught to children at a young age?

This is not a societal issue, but a parental one based on personal spiritual philosophy and religious upbringing. I imagine that parents who hold to this spiritual philosophy do teach this concept to their young children. The problem with it not being more publicly widespread lies in religion and the deletion of the concept from the original biblical Scripture when the Council of Constantinople was convened and made canonical revisions. Being "reborn" then became associated with the ceremony of baptism rather than with the concept of reincarnation with which it was originally intended to be equated. The practice of *switching* original concepts to explain Christ's words was a popular activity throughout early Church history.

So today, as in the ancient days of old, society is peopled with those who hold the *letter* of Scripture as concrete truth (those of organized religion) and those who inherently have the inner Knowing of the *spirit* of Christ's true conceptual intent (those sometimes perceived as heretical). The official version of today's Scripture resembles little of Christ's original spiritual philosophy.

Children possess beautiful open minds. Most often they come into this world free of any preconceived notions. Their minds are as a clean slate ready to be written upon and it is the parents who first do this writing. This writing will not include the concept of reincarnation if the true "spirit" of Scripture is not an inherent Knowing or understood as such by the parent. Rather than a pure understanding of the Universal Spirituality, which is present within the Supreme Consciousness of the Divine, the separatist conceptualizations found within "religions" are impressed upon the receiving minds of young children. It's clear that, until certain revealing scrolls are discovered and publicized worldwide, reincarnation will continue to be viewed as a heretical belief among the religious traditionalist communities that hold their scriptural beliefs to be arrogantly superior to and above all other ideological forms of interpretation.

Is attempting to achieve personal goals a form of "creating one's own reality?"

No. *Denying* reality is an attempt to create one's own reality. Having goals, plans, and aspirations for one's life is nothing more than being practical. It's when one places self in the psychological position of being in *denial* of reality that one is attempting to create a "personal reality." The two are completely different situations. Having a goal and working toward that goal is merely traveling upon one's chosen road in life. Creating one's own reality is *opposing* the natural course of life—one's destiny. It's constantly struggling against the current, striking at the boulders that lie in one's way instead of allowing the flow to carry one *around* them in a prescribed manner. An attempt to create one's own reality places one in a state of flux and in constant combat with life. In essence, this activity says of the practitioner: "I will not and do not accept my life. I have no Acceptance. Life will be as I *want* it to be for me." Sounds heavy with the "I," doesn't it? It is an extremely egotistical attitude.

Generally, if an individual has a strong sense of Acceptance in their life, his/her efforts toward achievement are not associated with the "create your own reality" concept. If one is continually bucking life, is frequently angered by circumstances, and finds self engulfed in states of frustration and denial, then that one has no Acceptance and is therefore caught in the web of complexities brought about by attempting to create a false reality and forcing it into a position of being superimposed over the true reality. This superimposed image will never be a stable one, for it is not comprised of a solid foundational substance.

It's important to understand this "create your own reality" concept and realize that it's counterproductive. It means that one is in denial. It means one has not or will not accept

Acceptance for what is. It creates internal and external conflict in one's life. It represents the wearing of the rose-colored glasses. It indicates a juvenile thought process whereby fantasy and personal ideology are desired over reality. It is intellectually immature.

The concept is NOT indicative of simple planning for one's future. It is not associated with the natural desire to achieve goals. It is not related to reasonable or logical plans made in relation to what is. It does not exist where Acceptance dwells. Understand that just because someone plans for the future or has specific goals does not mean that he/she is attempting to create a different reality. Reality changes each hour, each minute. We make tentative plans for the future and accept that which alters those plans. By doing this we remain flexible and make alternate adjustments. By doing this we maintain a wonderful fluid state of being that cushions the unforeseen bumps and bruises we receive along the way. Acceptance keeps us supple. Creating our own reality makes us rigid to a single desired course. One rides the waves of life. The other fights the shifting currents. One bends in a strong wind. The other breaks.

If you could modify, alter, or redo anything in your writings, what changes would you make?

I would've strongly stressed at the outset, perhaps at the end of *Spirit Song,* that the wisdom of my teacher was not compressed or contained within an ethnic box. With the clarity of hindsight, I would have proportionately downplayed her ethnicity in relation to her vast scope of universal knowledge. She, being a woman strongly connected to the Primal Divine Consciousness, was in a state of complete Knowing of reality and all aspects of What Is. Her comprehension of The All was unadulterated by any type of separatist ideologies such as man-made religion, ethnic beliefs, popular psychology, present-day science, and technology, etc. Her knowledge came from far beyond these simplistic, humanistic conceptualities of the day. I neglected to adequately stress her strong connection to the Universal Mind; therefore, in the readership's perceptual view, she was relegated to being an aged Indian woman framed solely within an ethnic box. It reduced her beingness to a "humanistic" level, when, in actuality, her Consciousness was more of the spirit vibration and of a finer dimensional frequency where she interacted with and drew from a truer, more alive reality. Simply stated, I should have played down her ethnicity and overstressed her vast base of universal knowledge, for she was of many worlds, many realities, and we communicated and interacted within most of them.

Regarding one's life purpose, I've tried several different courses of action only to have the projects I thought would be most fulfilling to me either fall completely apart or fall short of completion. What's wrong?

It sounds to me like you're trying to force things here. It sounds as though you've planned a course and attempted to push through associated probabilities related to your path, then bucked the obstacles instead of utilizing them or working them in.

A life purpose isn't something that one necessarily sits down and decides to manifest. A life "purpose" is most often different than one's career. They are not one and the same. For example, one could have a life career as a schoolteacher and a life *purpose* as a volunteer in some helpful capacity. Up here in the rural mountains, our small communities are not large enough to support a full-time, paid fire department, so we have volunteer firepeople who do this aside from their nine-to-five jobs. The nine-to-five job would be the career and the volunteer fire work would be the life purpose. But most often, a life *purpose* is not one that is particularly chosen. I see by the wording of your question that you "chose" projects that would be most "fulfilling to you." That's all right to choose a career, but a life purpose is different. One's purpose is unique and quite specific. It is a project that had been decided upon before ever entering into the physical. Destiny, if you will. Also, a life purpose is not contingent on being personally fulfilling, as a career can be. A life purpose is what you are here to accomplish *aside* from a separate career. This purpose is in no way related to what the "I" *wants* to do, but rather that which the *spirit* predetermined was fruitful to do during this lifetime.

In other words, we don't sit down and think about what sort of purpose might be nice to accomplish. We don't scan the wide variety of purposes and pick one that we believe will be most personally fulfilling. No, no, we don't do that. That's not how it works. If you're looking for something to do that's fulfilling, choose a career that meets that requirement.

Most often we do not even have to think about a life purpose or expend mental effort toward the idea because the intended purpose for an individual will enter one's realm of activity *of its own accord.* Think about this one. What if there were a small child in your neighborhood or living in the locale of your job who will one day grow up to be a great leader or teacher? What if you were out mowing your lawn or walking back to work from lunch and saw that child cross the street and you noticed a car about to run a red light? What if you raced to pull that child out of harm's way? What if that were your sole life purpose? Ah, but we don't think of those kinds of purposes, do we? We would much rather think in terms of greatness. Maybe being a famous teacher, leader, or healer. Our little egos skew the entire concept out of shape. Saving that future leader or teacher when she/he was a small child would be a great purpose, yet people are blind to that which they haven't the foresight to see or know; therefore, their idea of a personal life purpose must be one that is visibly great in his/her *own* eyes from the outset. Wrong.

We are a living strand within the great Web of Life. Our individual lives are as a connecting thread of that Web.

Everything we do and think makes a vibratory movement upon that Web and each singular movement and thought affects the whole. One's purpose may have been fulfilled long ago while, today, that one still seeks the life purpose. It has passed unrecognized. It has manifested without fanfare. This is the reason why I stress the importance of Unconditional Goodness. How do you know what wondrous effect a simple smile will cause another? Perhaps the recipient of that smile was contemplating suicide because of a loss of faith in humanity. What if that one smile saved a life? "Oh, too simplistic," you say. Well, hello? Of course it's simplistic. Who ever said or proclaimed that one's life purpose should be complex? Who ever deemed it to be something to be fretted over and decided upon? A life purpose just is. It . . . just . . . is. Don't waste valuable energy pondering what yours is. Don't become frustrated because it hasn't revealed itself to you (it usually doesn't). Don't buck life attempting to force some imagined purpose to manifest. If you live a life of Unconditional Goodness, you've probably already fulfilled your purpose for being here. Go about spreading that goodness wherever you can, in as many ways as life presents an opportunity to do so. Quit fretting and pacing over your life purpose and . . . live! Live. Little do you know the good that you do. Each hour presents so many beautiful opportunities for us to take hold of. Each hour is a gift, a gift of life. Cherish it.

What was the higher reason for why Princess Diana and Mother Teresa died within days of each other?

Why is it that humanity has a penchant to believe that every event has to have some mysterious "higher reason" associated with it? There exists an ideology called the concept of "synchronicity," which is in no way related to magic or mystical aspects. Life happens as life does. If the destiny of two individuals turns out that they each pass over within a short time of one another, then that's just how their separate paths went. People die every minute of each day; just because two famous people died within days of each other does not indicate that a higher reason was behind the synchronicity of events.

Other correspondents' letters I received following these two events indicated that perhaps the End Times were about to occur and the two famous people were "taken" in order to spare them suffering. It appeared that people thought it was reasonable to assume that all the "good" folks were to be removed from earth before devastation occurred. That's a big assumption, a really big one. Wouldn't it be more reasonable to *keep* the so-called "good" people here on earth during the catastrophic events, so that their special talents could be put to highly effective use during a time when they would be most needed?

Making wild assumptions and endless speculation over the causes for events is fruitless. This is where the quality of Acceptance is so incredibly valuable. Life makes its presentation with a wide variety of events—some good, some not so good—so what? Do we wring our brains in an attempt to squeeze out an acceptable reason for events or do we just accept with grace as a part of life and go on? We need to be productive, both physically and intellectually. Our behavior must reflect right attitude and philosophy. What will prove to be humanity's most valuable asset for the future will be the ability to persevere through Acceptance, to energetically rally with enthusiasm in the face of opposition and adversity. But to sit and make false assumptions for the possible (and most oftentimes improbable) causation of events will not be productive behavior to indulge in.

Everyone, whether through personal experience or through knowledge of ongoing world events, has been witness to ponderable events, events that confound the mind. These events become firmly ensconced in time and remain an unalterable record of our civilization's history. No amount of speculation or question can change that which has passed. And to assume that the event(s) were ominous precursors to a future cataclysm is pure folly generated from a fear-based perspective. The next time the thought of an event being an omen of the future comes to mind, remember synchronicity. It happens all the time and is different from coincidence. Synchronicity.

What would be the best career or job for our sixteen-year-old son to get into for the future?

Whatever he's interested in or drawn to be involved in. Whatever his skills and talents lead him to.

This parent desires to guide the son into a career or job that will be lucrative or beneficial. This parental desire is okay; however, it's best to leave this important life choice to the young individual who follows his/her inner guidance toward such ends. Inspiration, skills, talents, high interest, tendencies, curiosity all gently prompt an individual toward a general direction that eventually leads to a specific subject matter or area of study. This then will point to the career or job-related activity the individual would do best at. Don't push. These things can take time. Allow your son to make his own decision. Take valuable time out to spend in conversational "discovery" with him. Learn what his interests are. What his goals are. Maybe he has none as yet and that's okay too. Don't feel deflated if he says he wants to be a car mechanic. What's wrong with that if he's skilled as such? Don't ever attempt to force a child into a career she/he isn't compelled toward. Don't prioritize careers into status symbols. No career or job is more prestigious than another. Someone does best at what they're best at. Remember that.

I've been bad in this life, so is there any way I can change and do good? I'm afraid I'm a lost cause.

Lost cause? No such animal. I'm perplexed as to why you ask how you can "change and do good." You accomplish the act of doing good by doing good. No esoteric methodology. No secret formula. You know what good is. You recognize an act of goodness when you see it, receive it, or give it. How can you believe that you're a "lost cause" if you "fear" that state of being? The fact that you fear that indicates your inherent inner goodness, which is vitally alive and well. You don't need me to tell you how to be a good person. Everyone alive knows good from bad. They "know" the difference but don't always give proper attention to it. You, on the other hand, *want* to do that. Your own expressed desire to be good and do good is your saving grace. Now . . . put it into action.

Who are the "Watchers?"

The Starborn ones. Our advanced planetary neighbors and ancestors.

Who tells the Starborn what to do and when?

Since you can't hear the inflection or tone of my voice when I answer this, please do not read it as being sarcastic. Who tells *you* what to do and when?

I think your question has come from something I've written in one of my books about the Starborn wanting to move ahead and "being held back." This may have led you to think they are being directed by some higher authority. The fact of the matter is that they themselves—their own reason and logic—is what holds them back. The inherent Knowing of what's right to do and when overrides their own personal desires—just as our own does. Don't you sometimes just want to get into someone's face? Maybe be a little more verbally graphic than your sensitivities allow you to be? Sure you have. We all have. But we squelch that urge and mind our manners. We behave with dignity and do what our conscience dictates instead of tossing it all into the wind with a devil-may-care recklessness. Control. It's controlling self. That is how the Starborn know what to do and when in respect to holding back at "watch" instead of allowing impatience to rule (ruin) the day for us.

How did the Starborn achieve their highly developed technical status?

I believe I went into this in *Daybreak*. To recap the response here, I'll just say that they lacked the ego earthlings cherish. Due to the ego, various ancient civilizations of earth annihilated themselves several times over by their race for superiority and resulting misuse of advanced technology, specifically, through their knowledge of crystal physics and magnetic forces. So, if one civilization keeps misusing technology to repeatedly destroy itself and the other one never misuses it, who will live longer and advance further? Though our science and technology have still not retrieved the knowledge the aforementioned technologies once utilized with gusto . . . we still have something just as powerful. Nuclear power.

Is money the root of all evil?

No, ego is. How could money be the root of all evil when it can be used to feed the hungry, shelter the homeless, come as a lifesaving windfall, bring security, provide funds to charitable organizations, etc? As with all things, the *use* of an object is the prime factor that determines the good or evil aspect of it. Is fire evil? Doesn't that depend on whether it's used by a person to warm a house through the heat of a woodstove or used by an arsonist? Wine can be consumed by family members at a religious dinner ceremony or by a drunk driver while weaving down a busy neighborhood street. Opium can be used in China's opium dens (or anywhere) as a mind-numbing narcotic or it can be used as pain-relieving morphine in a hospital. Marijuana can help people with glaucoma, help sleep disorders, and relieve the terrible nausea from chemotherapy or it can be misused. You see, it's all in *how* a substance is utilized. The *purpose*. A handgun can be used as a noise source to chase away coyotes and bears or it can be used for a robbery or murder. No, money is not the root of all evil. Ego is. Ego determines how money and everything else is used.

It seems that the more I learn and the more spiritual I become, I feel more and more like I'm driving myself to a nervous breakdown or insanity. Can you help me to understand this? Is this expected on my journey?

I'll try, though to "expect" anything would put yourself in Expectation, a negative state we always want to avoid as much as we can.

Simply put, the more spiritually advanced one becomes, the higher the vibrations are raised. The higher the vibrations, the more aware one is to the existence of great contrasts between pure spiritual behavior and that of the heaviness of society. This then frequently gives one the feeling of "not belonging." It exacerbates the presence of a sharp differential that cannot be ignored by the advanced spiritual being, who must continue to interrelate with and work among society's masses. The advanced individual's attained state is not one of aloofness, but rather one of acute awareness. This awareness heightens empathy toward all the less-fortunate individuals of the world. It intensifies recognition of society's negative behavior, and emphasizes the negative attitudes generated from humanity's mass ego. This situation represents one of great clarity, whereby life is seen for what it is, as compared to the general populace, which lacks acute awareness and frequently wears colored glasses or blinders of apathy. For the spiritually developed individual, this clear sight can be overwhelming until it is brought into perspective through Acceptance. This is not to say that Acceptance equates to apathy, but Acceptance is necessary to temper and soften the painful cutting effects of empathy and gross negativity that is now increasingly perceived.

The behavior of society, as recognized by the spiritually advanced individual, can be devastating and appear to be a seemingly hopeless situation. It can cause the individual to feel out of sync with the world, business associates, friends, family. It can initiate a desire for withdrawal from society and into seclusion; however, this will not alleviate or alter the basic situation. Recognizing humanity's ego-centered negativities can even plunge a spiritually aware person into states of dark depression and despair. These possibilities are those that could make one feel as though a nervous breakdown were imminent. Yet, through understanding, this need not be the case. I don't keep harping about Acceptance because I like the sound of the word. I keep repeating it because it is not only a necessary quality for those striving toward spiritual development, it is also a *critical* attribute for survival once that attainment has been achieved. Acceptance is not apathy. It is not wearing blinders and having an attitude of "Oh well," or "So what"; instead, it says something more like this: "This is how it is and, since I can't do a thing to alter it, I accept the reality of it." Having Acceptance is having a very special aspect of grace laced within one's personal perspective and philosophy. Having Acceptance doesn't mean you necessarily *like* what you observe any more than you did before, it just means that you can *deal* with reality much better. The attainment of spiritual development brings new and different facets into one's life, but having Acceptance serves to maintain a beautiful equilibrium and balance to the new and clear perspective that has evidenced itself. I won't go as far as saying that everything will be rosy, because, for a spiritually developed person, that is not reality. You will still experience periods of despondency or melancholy over the state of humanity. You may shed tears of sorrow over society's ignorance and egocentric behavior. You may spend hours in prayer in an attempt to make a difference. Yet despite these occasional states of natural responses, it remains a fact that Acceptance will tip the balance from thoughts of imbalance toward rational understanding. Understanding the reality of a spiritually developed individual living in an ignorant and egotistical society makes all the difference in the world. Understanding that others do not think as you do and do not have the same heightened philosophical perspective as you is paramount to maintaining a strong intellectual and emotional balance. You are as the butterfly living among the younger, immature ones—the caterpillars. Eventually they will grow and develop into that same elevated, higher perspective from which you observe the world. You are not necessarily "better," you're merely different . . . for a time.

Also, beyond the balanced perspective a spiritually aware individual must maintain regarding societal behavior is the issue of reality. By this I mean that a spiritually aware individual will have experienced events of Consciousness that have taken place in other dimensions and on different vibrational frequencies. This person will have come to understand that time is not linear, that it's also vertical, that there is also nontime and nonspace. Balancing these realities with the singular third-dimensional reality in which society places all its belief is not an automatic accomplishment. The attainment of this balance comes over time, but when it does, it is completely comforting in its personal validation. I hope I've helped you with this issue. The psychological aspects that are associated with spiritual attainment are ramifications that are difficult to adequately explain.

Please define "spiritual growth." This phrase is so bantered about nowadays. I thought it meant to find out the truths, practice unconditional love and have Acceptance, grow in knowledge of and about God, to be balanced and grounded with this knowledge. I don't know. Am I close? How do you define it?

It appears that you did a bang-up job of defining it yourself. I wouldn't disagree with your perspective. I'd add the practice of Unconditional Goodness, getting rid of the ego, and perceiving everyone as a child of the Divine Essence rather than viewing them as a categorized individual by way of ethnicity, gender, etc. You did good here.

What does "growing toward God" mean? Is it that we are trying to learn to be a better servant, vessel, or be like God (which is hard for me to swallow), or? . . .

First of all, we are not vessels or servants or little gods and goddesses. We are children of the Supreme Essence and, being these children, we are not servants to the parent, nor are we vessels through which the parent reidentifies self, nor are we characterized as being identical clones of the parent. Growing toward God means that we increase our behavioral and spiritual philosophical attitudes to a raised level that more closely aligns with all aspects of spiritual goodness. Growing toward God means to rid self of ego and all negative behavior, to practice Unconditional Goodness at every available opportunity.

How is it that one person can be completely content in going to church every Sunday and I absolutely don't want any part of it. God, I feel so damned different, like I took a blindfold off and now wish I hadn't. I can't stand religious arrogance.

The answer is that people are different. They're all unique individuals possessing varying philosophies and beliefs. They're all at separate levels of spiritual development and awareness. Some only have traditional learning, while others have attained The Knowing in addition to traditional knowledge. That is how some are perfectly content in going to weekly religious services while others are satisfied with knowing they don't need to.

Now . . . please don't ever wish you still had blinders on. Understanding more of life with crystal clarity comes with

having The Knowing and that wondrous gift is more treasured and precious than the Hope diamond.

About your disgust with religious arrogance, well . . .
that's more like religious ignorance, isn't it? Have patience
with these ones. Have Acceptance of where they're at. One
day their pompous, full-blown balloons will all be deflated.
Let your Knowing be a blessing and a gift cherished. Don't
turn it into a dreaded burden.

Are you close to Jesus? How is that done?

Spiritual reality precludes names and specific historical
individuals. I feel closely connected to the Divine Consciousness. How is that done? By not having hate within your
heart, showing tolerance for the beliefs of others, having respect for their unique individuality, and practicing Unconditional Goodness. You don't even have to possess The
Knowing to accomplish this. It's as easy as aligning oneself to
the Divine Essences of the Trinity.

Oh, Mary, please don't give up on us.

I wouldn't think of it. What do you take me for, a quitter?
To do that would cut my mission short. I may, at times, feel
like giving up on myself and question my effectiveness, but
I'd never give up on my readers. Thanks for the encouragement. We'll ride the rough waters together.

My neighbor has what she terms "the know." The prob-lem is that she believes that she has a "gift" but has not been given instruction or any tools to assist her in learning, using, or understanding this gift. She wants to ask you why she's been given this "know" if she weren't meant to do something with it? And why has she been given "half" the package?

You didn't specify the qualities of this "gift." I don't know
whether it's evidence of mentalism, such as psychometry, or

whether it's something like precognition. At any rate, any such talent doesn't need guidebooks. She already has the whole package within her. Growth is the other half of the package. Utilizing such skills comes naturally. It comes into play when needed. To force practical use or "work" is not an activity aligned with the talent. It's enough that the ability is there to utilize when an opportunity presents itself for service. The entire package is there; it is the "tool" itself. It is whole when it's utilized.

If a numeric numbering system (code) is applied to the Bible, predictions appear. Why can't people see that this type of thing can be applied to any text, even a comic book?

I'd like to respond by saying, "your guess is as good as mine," but it's not a guess. It's ignorance. It's religious wishful thinking. It's looking for the esoteric and mysterious when there is none.

I want to do right by my children. The way I understand it is that we have a prechosen path. If I make a bad choice in my life (marriage, divorce, relocation) can it destroy the children's destiny?

Initially, I'm inclined to wonder why you assume one of these life choices would be bad? Instead of being negative, you should consider the possibility that one or more of those choices *are* associated with your children's destinies. A divorce or family relocation may have been *foreseen* by the spirit of your child before it entered into the physical. You can't question every decision in this associative manner. Life must be lived on an hour-by-hour basis. You make decisions and stand by them. When these decisions affect or include children, usually these have been foreseen and already factored in when associating them with the spirit's intended destiny. On earth, with our limited mental capacity, perception is narrow and shortsighted. The big picture is rarely known, therefore we have a tendency to question much of what we do in relation to purpose and destiny. This shouldn't be so. Hindsight usually proves this to be true. Through hindsight comes understanding. This after-the-fact understanding clarifies many of the hows and whys of behavior and decisions. Live life as it presents itself. Do whatever you have to do according to your conscience. The rest will take care of itself. Make your decisions based on *your* life because you have an individual destiny. This teaches your children to follow their own path when their time comes.

With a brain injury, what do I have to offer others?

The fact that you were able to ask this indicates an ability to effectively communicate your thoughts. How about trying your hand at writing? Or doing some type of clerical or computer volunteer work? I recently enjoyed reading Christopher Reeve's book, titled *Still Me*. It was tremendously inspiring and encouraging for me and I can imagine the wonderfully uplifting effect it would have on anyone who thinks she/he has some type of impairment that prevents that individual from being a viable asset to others. Sometimes it's difficult to see past an impairment because it becomes an overpowering facet in one's life, which frequently consumes all prospects of possibility. When we consciously make a determined effort to minimize the negatives and emphasize the positives, perspective alters and newborn possibilities suddenly blossom on the horizon. An impairment represents an altered course that leads to new options. Many times these new options would not have been considered if the impairment didn't present itself. For example, the late Edwin Carter probably wouldn't have taken the time to write *Living Is Forever* (a predictive vision of our future) if he hadn't experienced a broken leg that provided a forced time of recuperation. He made use of that time. He made a valuable contribution to humanity through the recording of his vivid vision. His accident altered his course so that he could accomplish something important. His "novel" is, in truth, more predicted fact than imagined fiction.

The term "disability" is a misnomer. Disabilities are "re-abilities." They are "re-directions" in one's life. They "re-open" doors that were most likely once closed or formerly passed by and ignored. If perceived correctly and taken advantage of, a disability can be stripped of its surface disguise and be recognized as a shining "possibility." And "impairment" can be transformed into "empowerment." What do you have to offer others? Yourself.

Why are special people taken from us? Princess Di, John and Bobby Kennedy, Jim Henson, John Lennon, and Jacques Cousteau, for example.

I touched on this issue in a previous response. Death is part of the natural order of life. Birth, living, and death. Though the good folks are missed and a void is left in the wake of their passing, the good they accomplished remains behind as a testimonial to their achievements and purpose. For everything and everyone there is a time. The work of these dedicated individuals continues; it has not ended with their crossing. Others have taken up the causes they began. Their achievements continue to develop and become enhanced by those who have taken up the causes. Some individuals have a purpose to "initiate" certain activities, philosophies, or projects. When these are firmly ensconced in the mind of society, their purpose is seen as a successful completion and a job well done. It's not an accurate perspective to perceive these people as being "taken" from society as though they were snatched away by some master hand. A better perspective would be that they succeeded in making great contributions to the world and will always be remembered.

Is there actually an Earth Mother spirit?

Everything has energy mass and is interconnected. The great Web of Life is the grand cohesion that brings all aspects into a coalesced unit. Vibrational energy is sensitive and responsive. It is affected by forces surrounding it. Thoughts are energy as much as physical actions are. The earth possesses an energy field around and within it. It is a living force having its own unique identity. It has vitality that can be enhanced or drained depending on the forces that affect it.

Throughout recorded history, most every culture believed in an Earth Mother Goddess. Though her names varied widely, the concept remained the same. She was the provider and nurturer, fertility for crops, wisdom and compassion. The term "Mother Nature" is common and, when heard, is quickly recognized as a reference to the seasons and all earthly elements of nature and weather. Mother Earth is perceived as providing us with rich minerals, gemstones, fossil fuel energy, life-sustaining water, granite and marble from which our buildings and statues are constructed, precious metals of silver and gold. Freely, as an offering of self, does the Earth Mother gift us with her treasures. As the earth evidences continual movement with each breath the Earth Mother takes, she is also sensitive to all the vibrational influences that actively affect her. Industrial and nautical dumping poison the life her waters support. Manufacturing smokestacks choke and suffocate her by depleting her supply of oxygen with an influx of harmful carbons and poisonous chemicals which, in turn, defile her life-giving rains with acid. A nuclear test . . . So too is she equally sensitive to the thoughts and actions of every human she provides for. She clearly communes and returns our actions with her own response. Haven't you ever noticed the correlation between earthquakes and like types of natural disasters frequently occurring in geographical regions where wars have recently taken place? The Earth Mother is communicating with us. She is responding to humanity's behavior. Is there really an actual Earth Mother spirit? The evidence speaks for itself.

Is it wrong to consult a psychic?

There is no clear-cut "yes" or "no" response to this question, because the answer directly relates to *intent*. It's wrong to consult a psychic when you're not taking personal responsibility for your life or decisions. It's wrong to give the power of the personal responsibility of your life over to another to control. It's wrong to let another individual manipulate your life path. Only *you* can decide where to live, what job offer to accept, which girlfriend is sincere enough for a life commitment, and whose depth of love is great enough to sustain a lasting marriage. One who doesn't want to take personal responsibility for all aspects of his/her life will be the first to cast blame for the outcomes. He or she will be the ones who look about for scapegoats.

Now, those who have misplaced an important document and have personally expended great effort in searching for it will naturally be led to outside assistance, particularly an individual possessing a greater level of insight. Those who are searching for a missing child, a crime perpetrator, etc., have every right to reach into fields that extend beyond their own resource capacity. In these cases, psychic consultation is a natural course of action.

A bona fide psychic has a responsibility to ensure that his/her clients are maintaining full personal responsibility for their lives. Psychic consultants depend on integrity. Accuracy is not nearly as important as integrity. The attained quality of that integrity is evidenced by their willingness to either *manipulate* the lives and decision-making process of the clients or their willingness to help clients empower *themselves* with self-confidence for this decision making.

This integrity *gives* personal decision-making responsibility rather than *taking* it away. To simplify, if a question involves some type of *decision* to be made, a psychic should not be consulted. If a question relates to a search or discovery that remains unobtained after much personal effort has been expended toward solution, then a psychic's assistance can be sought. Now, don't twist this concept about. When I say "search" or "discovery," I emphatically do not mean search for which boyfriend to stick with or a discovery of which job to accept or which city to relocate to. See? Don't fool yourself by shuffling around the terms and trying to make them fit into your own purpose. It's the *subject matter* associated with your *intent* that clearly determines the correct action in this matter. Finding the right girlfriend doesn't fit. Discovering which city to live in or job to take doesn't fit in either. Those are personal decisions that only you can make. Discovering your purpose is a no-no to consult on. The issue of past lives is also no reason to glean from another, because these indications come quite naturally from dreams, meditation, visions, leanings, insights, etc., rather than from a stranger who might end up being completely off base, resulting in a serious situation that leaves you following an unrelated and disconnected trail not associated with the history of your spirit's totality. Psychic consultation can be a blessing for those who have expended all personal resources in searching for lost articles, missing individuals, and perpetrators of crime. Individuals have a responsibility for all thoughts and actions taken in their lives. Those issues outside the realm of decision making can be resolved through the assistance of an insightful psychic. I hope I've finally clarified the technicalities of this issue. Furthermore, I still strongly maintain that these consultations should be shared (given away) as a gift to others. A paycheck from a job or career provides one's living expenses; psychic insight is a spiritual gift that should be shared. Do we ask someone for payment when we give them a gift? Of course not.

I don't know. I'm told I've made myself very unpopular for voicing this specific philosophy. I don't know. Nor do I care. I do know that if I personally possessed the gift to heal or locate a missing child, I certainly would never accept payment for the service. Then again, that's just me.

So much has happened in your life, yet you never allowed personal trauma or persecution to interrupt your writings. How did you manage to keep going?

Without sounding corny . . . a deeply ingrained sense of purpose combined with the hourly support of a very special friend. I was allowed to immerse myself in self-pity by staring at my open wounds and wallowing in my sorrows for only so long before an individual representing reason and reality came to stand before me and, nose-to-nose, get in my face. This served to lift me above physical events into the spiritual realm of my purpose. And it was this dedication that kept me going despite the ongoing earthquakes that continued to shake the ground I stood on. My support no longer needed to be physical. It came by way of the ceaseless encouragement, emotional support, rational intellect, and the love of a destined companion. Without these combined blessings assisting me, I believe I would've felt completely alone and tossed aside, though there are those in my life, including that same friend, who assured me that I would've made it through all on my own. I don't discredit that hypothesis; however, that scenario would've been incredibly more difficult to achieve.

One of the primary spiritual concepts I'm big on is Acceptance; throughout my former life experiences, that singular philosophy was strongest. I kept accepting whatever happened, whether it was the uncharacteristic behavior of others or the appearance of new rumors. Acceptance of reality greatly helped to maintain an equilibrium that never tipped into dangerous waters. When the chips were down, I discovered that I heavily depended on the concept that, in tandem with the aforementioned supporting aspects, served to stabilize the ground beneath me. I became one-minded. Relegating ongoing events to the background, I kept thinking,

"The books, my readers, I have to stay focused. I can't let self get in the way." And so the daily grind at the typewriter spent working on dream symbology became, not only an activity which immersed me in my purpose, but also served as a blessing which managed to dull emotional pain and place more mental distance between me and current personal affairs. My work was good medicine. It became a therapeutic activity that kept me on course.

Is it true that an amethyst crystal can intensify or enhance dreaming?

Yes. All of the Earth Mothers attributes are beneficial in some manner. Even her precious gifts have gifts.

Can objects in the material world absorb immaterial essences such as emotions or mood?

Psychometry would not be a fact if this weren't so. Many locales are falsely assumed to be haunted because they retain the *imprinted* emotionality of a former event. Thoughts as well as actions are things. These "things" possess individual and specific energy patterns that become attached to the locale. I believe the knotty pine walls of my cabin contain a good measure of my personal essence because I stained and varnished each one and, as I did this, expressed great admiration for each piece's unique grain pattern that emerged with the application of the red mahogany stain. I believe that the wonderful sense of deep tranquillity I feel when sitting out on the front porch cypress rockers and viewing the valley below is so great that the entire cabin must also become enveloped and permeated with the aura of that serenity surrounding me. The total and full sense of happiness that overcomes me while watching the deer feed beside the birdbath is so powerful it must radiate out and be received by the cabin structure. The peace here is ingrained in each floorboard I walk over, each windowpane I look through, each pantry door I touch. It can be no other way because, whenever I walk into this cabin after being away for as short a time as just a few hours, its very aura is a touchable sensation that fills my spirit and, in nearly audible words, whispers, "Welcome Home." I'm sure you've had experience with this at some point in your life. Do you recall ever walking into a building or room and having a distinctive feeling come over you? Regardless of how a room is decorated or furnished, it may exude a specific and unique aura. It could even be an empty room devoid of all material objects. Haven't you ever been hit with an unexplainable cold or warm feeling when entering a new place? An eerie feeling? A sense of nervousness or anxiety? Even foreboding? These are evidences of your personal, sensitive receptivity to the imprinted energy that permeates all matter.

Is it possible to know one's destiny?

Although "destiny" is frequently associated with the ideology of "purpose," the two may not necessarily be the same. When a couple, upon being introduced, recognize one another as being old friends or mates in a past life, that meeting can be seen as destiny. They were destined to connect once again. This destined event may have nothing whatsoever to do with each individual's purpose. So, you see, there can be a considerable differentiation between the two words and the conceptual ideologies they represent.

Most often, destiny is not a singular event. It is usually comprised of multiple situations during one's lifetime. When one just seems to "fall into" the perfect job, that is evidence of destiny and will most likely be recognized as same when the individual smiles and says, "It was destiny." Many instances of destiny can manifest in one's life. A chance meeting that occurred because of a missed train, a job that opened up due to another person quitting. These happenings will frequently be the result of "synchronicity," which brings the major players and factors together in unexpected ways. That childhood friend you just happened to bump into at the gas pump will usually be the result of synchronicity. After unsuccessfully searching every shop for one unique item, then finding it at a flea market that a friend dragged you to, is synchronicity at work. This would clearly shout, "Destiny!"

To have the mind-set that destiny is only associated with an "end" type of event or a "culminative" life experience is not accurate, for life is just loaded with destinies at every turn. Destiny is not something that is usually known; rather it is recognized after the fact . . . after prescribed events leading up to it have transpired.

Destiny is most often associated with positive events while fate is usually related to negative ones. The two terms are not synonymous. For example, it was not destiny that the State Patrol car was parked behind a blind when you sped past; it was fate. We frequently hear the term "that fateful day." This indicates a negative event. Rarely do we hear "that destined day." John F. Kennedy was destined to become president; he was not destined to be assassinated—that was fate.

What's going on in your life now?

Busyness. I love working on the cabin and property. In between writing books, I've helped to stain the entire cedar exterior of the cabin, build two sets of railroad tie steps (those things are heavy!), dig in the dirt (redesigning the drive to improve problematical drainage), replant blue spruce trees, gather kindling in the woods, stack the firewood that Sally split, and for leisure, read in the late evening hours. Also, in October of 1997, Sally brought her elderly mother out here from Overland Park, Kansas, to live with us. She needs assisted living and care. Having Mary Belle here with us has been interesting and adds a new dimension to the household. Since she can no longer drive, taking her to the doctors and providing entertainment, such as going out to eat and swimming at the Cripple Creek Beach and Yacht

Club adds to our extra duties. I'm not one to sit idle. I count my high energy level as one of my blessings. Note: For those who've never been to Cripple Creek, which is an old gold mining town nested down in the bowl of a volcanic caldera, the closest thing we have to a "beach" is probably a sandy bank beside a mountain stream and the nearest we can come to a "yacht" would be an old relic of a prairie schooner (covered wagon). Besides all of the above, I've been shown the direction where the "second phase" of my mission is to go: establishing a women's spiritual sanctuary, the Magdalene Abbey—and I've been looking at possible options that will facilitate the manifestation of this purpose.

What about El Niño? This sounds like one of the weather changes you predicted, but are scientists trying to cover up other signs to come?

I don't believe so. I don't know why they would. Scientists usually like to publicize their knowledge. It wouldn't be right to make such an assumption.

Yes, El Niño can be said to be included in those predictions detailed in *Phoenix Rising* as being one foreseen facet of nature which brings altering effects upon the land. El Niño is not a unique phenomenon, though. This event happens frequently; it was just that, this time, it grew larger and more intense, creating more noticeable changes in the weather. More than *new* events occurring, the future will experience greater *intensity* of characteristically common events. By this I mean that the active known geologic elements will increase in intensity of behavior, such as Mt. Pelée finally blowing instead of just evidencing frequent spewing and rumbling. The familiar activities will become more intense. This includes earthquakes, hurricanes, tornados, flooding, microbursts, etc.

I really doubt that the scientists are withholding information. If I were a scientist, I certainly wouldn't want the deaths of thousands on my conscious because I held back information that could've saved them by way of an advance warning and subsequent evacuation. Scientists like to be first to publish, be on the leading edge of discovery, and be recognized for success. I doubt a one of them would hold back valuable information from the public.

I've heard that the Mayan dateline stops at December 23, 2012, so would that date signify the end of the world?

How far would you have them carry out the calendar? We must be careful not to construct assumptions that we were never meant to make. When I formulated the three-year calendar for the *Millennium Memories* journal, I didn't intend to subtly infer that no time would exist beyond the last entry date. This type of thinking creates the perception that society is like small children at a sleepover, where they gather beneath the covers with a flashlight and see who can tell the scariest tale. There appears to be a craving for the mysterious and ominous in society. Everyone seems to be looking for something to ohhh and ahhh over, something that makes them quiver and shiver with whispered secrets and trembling expectation. It's time to perceive with the intellect and not imagination. Assumptions don't keep one grounded in reality. Looking for and thinking you've found mystery in everything perceived will only lead to the disappointment of reality when it hits.

I can't find Whispered Wisdom *in the bookstores. How come?*

You'd have to ask the bookstore folks that one. The book is still being printed and can be ordered directly from the Hampton Roads Publishing Company. Keep in mind that bookstores are presently in a highly competitive situation. Now that technology has elbowed into their retail realm with the Internet book outlets, they can't stock like a techno-warehouse can. The book you're currently holding in your hand is my eighteenth book; to expect a bookstore to carry all eighteen at once isn't reasonable—takes up too much shelf space. You won't experience this type of disappointment if you write Hampton Roads (address in front of book) and ask to be placed on their mailing list, or you can e-mail an order, too. By doing this you'll receive their newsletter/reader catalog, which will keep you apprised of all upcoming books and give you an opportunity to order whichever ones you wish. This is a tremendous service that few publishers offer directly to their readers. I'm sorry you experienced this absence of title on the bookstore shelf; then again, I couldn't find a copy of James Michener's *Centennial* when I wanted to add a hard copy to my home library shelf—had to comb used-book stores for it. My problem is that I used to give away first editions to the local library after I'd bought and read them, then later realized I should've kept certain titles of the hardbacks for my collection. I've since learned to be more selective in what I keep for the bookshelf and those passed onto others. Anyway, write or give Hampton Roads a call at 1-800-766-8009. It'll save you future frustration and the title will come right to your door.

What's your opinion on cloning?

Human organs for medical technology, yes. For complete individuals, no.

I see a great need for organ transplants and witness people of all ages dying because of no availability. I see no problem with genetically harvesting human organs by way of cloning. We shouldn't have to wait for and depend on others dying in order to save a life. Growing skin for grafts has been done for years. Growing organs shouldn't be any different. We do have the technology. Perhaps it could be a way to save endangered species of animals that don't seem to be reproducing. It could be a method to avoid extinction of many beautiful species.

Cloning complete human individuals is a nightmare of technology. It is one of society's worst nightmares. It is a medical nightmare as dangerous and scary as science's nightmare of nuclear power.

Aren't there many different races of Starborn and, if so, are there more than one interacting with us here on earth?

Yes. Five races of peaceful Starborn interacted with us during the singular event of Creation. Throughout history they've continued to interact. In ancient times, an arrogant and manipulative type of Starborn interacted with the South American peoples, who perceived them as gods and created carvings of them. Eventually these "bad influences" were removed from earth by the joint effort of the original five planetary races who were maintaining the position of being Watchers.

I see Dr. Kevorkian as a great humanitarian. How do you view him?

I would personally agree with you. I'm a great believer in death with dignity. Though I'm not an official member of the Hemlock Society based here in Colorado, I agree with its philosophy. The verdict of "terminal" for a patient says it all. Allow the individual to choose her/his own time and circumstance of departing. In keeping with this philosophy, I also live it. I have a living will. I in no way want to become a burden to anyone, kept alive through mechanical means, resuscitated if the heart stops, or kept alive more than forty-eight hours if in a comatose state. If I'm meant to go . . . I want to have the freedom to go without interference or someone hampering the journey. Our spirits choose our physical life *entry* circumstances; our minds should have the equal right to choose our exit circumstance, which allows us to "enter" back into the spiritual life. There are some individuals whose spirits are capable of voluntarily detaching their connection to the physical body, but most can't manage this. On the surface, this act would appear as if the patient had died in his/her sleep from natural causes.

Now no assumptions, please. I'm not implying that I advocate suicide. That's entirely different. We're specifically discussing the issue of "assisted passing" or "chosen passing" as directly associated with *terminal* medical conditions. Suicide is not an acceptable option for a physically and mentally healthy individual.

More and more I hear the phrase "Don't get mad, get even." Is this what the world has come to?

I suppose if you hear this a lot, then that'd be a good conclusion to deduce. Taking vengeance in one' s own hands is pure ignorance. Where is the acceptance and tolerance of another's behavior? Wanting revenge is strong evidence of ego at work. Being vindictive is the behavior of an ignorant, self-centered individual who displays a position of being very low on the hypothetical, spiritual totem pole. I have to admit that I too have heard this comment coming from an extremely smug attitude, as though it represents the absolute epitome of personal cleverness. People who hold this unspiritual attitude have no compunction toward verbalizing slander, gossip, negative insinuations, or active violence. Personally, I cringe when I witness this type of twisted philosophy or behavior. It shows thought patterns steeped in manipulation and control, a belief that one possesses the right to judge, or chastise, another. And whether it's justified or imagined makes no difference to the believer. Acting out "an eye for an eye" severely demeans and diminishes one's integrity. Many times it becomes one's "rule to live by" and that philosophy characterizes a tyrant. It is the opposite of having Acceptance. It tells the world that you cannot "live and let live." Acceptance shows intelligence and wisdom. Revenge shows great stupidity and ignorance.

I am a twenty-eight-year-old, single woman who does not want children, yet some people perceive this as selfishness. What's your opinion?

Initially, I think it would be a little more than interesting to know if these people you speak of have children. That situation would tend to color their statement quite a bit because several people I know who have children are sometimes (frequently) envious of those who don't. It becomes a sour grapes sort of attitude stating, "If I have to have my life complicated with the demands of child rearing, so do you." Or, "If I can't be free to do whatever I want without having to lug children around with me everywhere I go, then you can't either." I've heard all these pathetic statements said in a joking manner, but clearly with seriousness behind them. (Many jokes are a cover-up for true attitudes.) Flippancy usually covers a good measure of truth. Where is it written that women *must* bear a child? Where is it written that women aren't or can't be fulfilled unless they have children? Furthermore, where is it written that a *single* woman *can't* have a child if she so wishes? These concepts and related ideas appear to be extremely antiquated and stuffy. If a single (or married) woman doesn't want to have children, so what? That in no way indicates a selfish perspective. These self-righteous people would rather an unwanted child be born in lieu of not having a child at all. Where's the logic in that? Children do not define a woman's purpose or quality of contribution to society.

In the old days, a childless woman was called "barren" and looked upon with a stigma of being less than whole, one who would never experience a fulfilling life; in some cases, it was even legal grounds for divorce. This primitive attitude is synonymous with saying that women are worthless unless they bear children. We've come a long way, baby. Today it's becoming more common for women to opt for a single life, or single with children (never married and artificially inseminated or going through adoption agencies), or married and choosing to have no children, or staying single and choosing to have no children. These choices have been a woman's right since the beginning of time, yet just recently have stood up to the finger-pointers of society. Women were not created for the sole purpose of being human incubators. Today's woman is highly intelligent and makes astute observations of her world. She sees teen mothers killing their newborns as though they had not a shred of respect for life. She witnesses babies starving in Third World countries. She observes children who are improperly cared for and unwanted. She sees some cultures killing their babies because they were born female. She passes homeless children on the street, and she is aware of the high incident of crimes committed by children. Observing all of these situations, she ponders the wisdom of bringing more children into the world even though she can provide a good home and care. She decides to marry or remain single. She decides to have children or not. Whatever her decision is, it's solely hers to make. I have friends who are single by choice (never married) and love their life. I have single friends who are planning on having a child without becoming involved in a male relationship. And I have married friends who plan to remain childless. All of these women are happy with the surety of their decisions. They are following their conscience and inner promptings associated with their life paths. They have no doubts or moments of question. They are fulfilled. They do not feel they're being selfish in any way.

Every individual's choice is unique. Having a penis doesn't mean that it must be used to fertilize an egg. Likewise, having a uterus doesn't mean that it must contain a viable embryo. Last time I looked, men weren't criticized or demeaned for choosing to not be fathers. Motherhood, like fatherhood is a private choice. That choice is every individual's right to make. There is no moral, social, or religious right or wrong to it, only what coincides with one's path and conscience.

A tornado came through my town and I accept it because it was God's will.

You're accepting a false premise. It was not God's will to have a tornado rip through your town. It was solely the randomness of nature's natural forces. God does not will destruction nor choose a site to have it occur at. God does not flatten your house and decide to spare your neighbor's. How would that be indicative of God's great love and mercy for us? To think a Supreme Being would pick and choose who to devastate and who to spare is . . . well, it's unthinkable. It's ludicrous.

This planet has magnetic force fields surrounding it. It has warm and cold air currents, thunderstorms, winter snow blizzards, moving plates, magma beneath the surface, pressure requiring frequent release, winds, and precipitation. These and more are all natural aspects of the planet and cannot be construed into being forces manipulated by the will of God. For four days in October of 1997, I was completely snowed in by a sudden and unexpected blizzard that also paralyzed Denver. Sally was in Kansas attending to putting her mothers affairs in order to bring her back here. I was alone. I couldn't get out and nobody could get in to me. Though I had plenty of firewood, food, and gas for the generator, I never believed that the situation was God's will. Weather is weather. More accurately . . . weather happens.

Are homosexuals living in sin?

Not unless they all just murdered someone. This issue has been discussed in a previous question and response. An adult individual's inherently inborn (natural) sexual lifestyle is not a spiritual issue at all unless it involves abuse or a child. Jesus loved everyone. Why shouldn't we too love everyone?

I find it increasingly difficult to be around the insincere and phony people in my community. Is it wrong for me to seek solitude?

The spiritual attitude for this would be: Have Acceptance of others while among them, utilize solitude for rejuvenation. The more spiritually aligned you become, the more heightened the awareness of your surroundings and the behavior of others becomes. This situation brings with it an inability to ignore the growing disparity between correct spiritual behavior and that which one observes occurring in society. For a time, as with the correspondent who felt she was approaching a nervous breakdown because of an inability to "deal" with society's primitive behavior, the state of a newly attained spiritual lifestyle or philosophy can be somewhat disturbing and frustrating to balance with the preponderance of unspiritual behavior one is surrounded by. A simple analogy would be like a diamond trying to maintain its brilliance in a dark cave of black coal. But this is not diamonds and coal; this is life. This is the reality of *balancing* the relationship of one's higher philosophy with society's lower one. This is managed through Acceptance, Wisdom, and understanding.

Once an individual grows into the wisdom of higher spiritual philosophy and applies the living of it, he/she is then exposed to greater opportunities to provide an uplifting effect upon others. This acquired Spirituality then becomes a beautiful tool with which to inspire others, through words and behavior. This acquired Spirituality does not have to be a draining detriment to self, but rather, through the utilization of right logic and reasoning applied to your thought process, be utilized as a positive effect. This then is the proper perspective, rather than one that compels the individual to run for protective and insulating cover from the world. Solitude can be a "long spiritual drink" that rejuvenates or it can be a detrimental "clamshell" within which hides one's beautiful spirituality. How will society ever elevate itself if those numbers of people who are reaching the wisdom of spiritual attainment hide behind closed doors or retreat to some remote cave? It's the *interaction* of these people with society that will eventually have an uplifting, positive effect on the overall spiritual state of humanity.

As those who are spiritually aware become not separate individuals, but single facets that grow into a great multitude comprising an entire body of Wisdom, society will discover its increasing inability to maintain its current behavior without, one by one (individual by individual), experiencing embarrassment by its egotistical (unspiritual) thought and behavior. This cannot occur if the spiritually enlightened hide their lights. One example of this in action would be for those who are spiritually aware to attend a Religious Right rally, where the leader is attempting to incite active denunciation and persecution for a selectively targeted group of people, and for the "aware" individuals in the audience to finally stand up for spiritual tolerance by holding placards: "STOP THE HATE!" and "HATE IS EVIL!" My observation is that certain religious leaders have appointed themselves as the Grand Inquisitors and . . . how can that happen so long after the Inquisition has proven to be such a black spot on the Church's history? No, the spiritually aware don't sequester themselves, they get out there and have a face-off with ignorance.

After experiencing much heart pain in my life, friends tell me to forgive and forget. That seems contradictory to me and I think trying to live that kind of philosophy does more harm than good. Am I way off base here?

Not at all. You're right on target. Any event that transpires in one's life becomes a solid aspect of that individual's historical reality. Said aspect cannot be altered, rearranged, nor undone. It is solidly imprinted on the skein of time. It is added to one's memory. And memories are not subject to selective erasure or deletion. Memories are remembered. Perhaps it would be nice and wonderfully convenient to have the ability to differentiate memories between desirable and undesirable, then eradicate the objectionable ones. But that's not how it works. The odious memories remain interspersed among the fragrant ones. They do not go away. They are set in stone. So to say "forgive and *forget*" is to voice an impossibility that represents a clear contradiction in terms.

Now that we've clarified the "forget" part, let's take a look at the "forgive" term. Forgive. This symbolizes a really difficult state to achieve with any measure of lasting stableness associated with it. As a word, as a concept, forgiveness is wildly overrated. That may have struck you as an outrageous statement, but it's true. Think about it. Forgiveness is directly attached to a performed event in one's life. An event actuated by another that was in some way hurtful to the recipient. That event becomes a solid, unalterable fact of reality and is imprinted upon the historical memory base. If it cannot be voluntarily forgotten, then it remains alive with vitality in one's memory. To forgive is to demand neutrality in respect to a hurtful event. The idea of forgiveness presupposes that the damaging or hurtful emotional effects of an event are soothed or diminished, even perhaps completely eradicated. This is just not reasonable to expect. Just as the memory of the event cannot be eradicated, the painful *effects* cannot be erased from one's mind and heart. So "forgiveness" is not the precise word we're intending here. Rather we must reach an effective level of "Acceptance" for hurtful events that have transpired in one's life. Though we still hurt, we can *accept* the ignorant, rude, or unspiritual actions and words of others. Though the memories of these are indelible imprints upon us, we can still accept that which has become part of our historical past. Though the distinction between "forgiveness" and "Acceptance" may not be as clear-cut as you'd like it to be, it's there regardless. Forgiveness can be a nearly impossible state to move self into, but

Acceptance comes much easier and accomplishes the same result. That's why I advocate it so strongly.

The Forgive and Forget ideology is an outstanding contradiction in terms. Life is full of them. A few obvious ones that I've recently taken note of are the following commonly used phrases: Religious Right, White Supremacy, Military Intelligence, National Security, Lord Jesus, Perfect World, Moral Majority, Random Violence, Holy Wars, Dumb Blonde. I could most likely come up with a string of others and fill a few pages, but it'd be too depressing to see how confused society has become.

Do you know that your expressed philosophy over psychics not charging for their services is causing you to have detractors?

Yes, I'm aware of this. My philosophy remains unchanged. I'm also told that the existence of controversy and detractors are marks of popularity. Whatever. My readers know that I don't bend to philosophical trends nor feel any need to color the truth for the sake of maintaining popularity. What good is my work if I compromise it for popularity? What good is sticking to the "party line" if it's not an accurate one? I feel I must either transmit the messages I came to give or get the heck off the planet. There is no in-between state. Controversial concepts are a part of that message. I put it out there and people can take it or leave it. Readers have that choice. If someone doesn't like what I have to say, then he/she shouldn't be reading my material. However, I can't leave this issue without also adding that it's not nice to speak ill of another. Just thought I'd pop that little tidbit in.

My message is specific to the ideology of The Way—the technical concepts of spiritual reality and its many-faceted elements. All my works are associated with these aspects. My sole concern is geared toward sharing knowledge, not gaining popularity.

I've heard various comments that were directed at my

personality, too. Besides being called a flake, savior, goddess, fruitcake, I especially like "eccentric." This last descriptive term came from a local resident who's seen me about town doing errands. Well, I suppose I do dress according to my personality (the mood of the day) and don't give a rat's hat for current dress style or tradition. I wear whatever suits my own individuality. I think this "eccentric" idea came after I was seen wearing OshKosh bib overall shorts with black-and-white-striped tights. I've also taken time out from working on the house and gone into town wearing stain-spattered jeans and a torn, flannel work shirt (one of three sets of grub, work clothes). And I've been seen wearing a gauze, peasant blouse with embroidered vest and long, cotton skirt with knee-high moccasins. Levi's worn with sweatshirt and tennis shoes work well for me too. So I tend to wear a wide variety of styles depending on my mood and what I'm busy doing that day. If variety of style is eccentric, then I suppose that's me. If unusual style is eccentric, then that's me too. If being yourself is eccentric, then that's definitely me. Current fads in fashion statements are societal aspects that pass me by. Well, I guess that's not entirely accurate. When the concept behind the bra-burning era struck, I hung onto that one. So maybe I'm different in more ways than one. That's to be expected; I'm an individual—just like you. It's far better to be despised for what you *are* than loved for what you *are not.*

Most of the predictions chronicled in Phoenix Rising *have come to pass. Anything new from you?*

In *Fireside* I talked about "books becoming like gold" in the future. I also mentioned that the insurance industry would topple and the medical field (HMOs, etc.) would be thrown into confusion. Computers will scramble society and bring it to a halt. Religious persecution will increase. Hate crimes will be rampant. Get yourself a good generator and store gasoline for it. Have a propane camp stove (and full tanks) with your supplies. This will only serve for a limited time though. Collect plastic milk cartons and fill them with water (it's good to freshen them occasionally). Maintain a *minimum* amount of money in the bank, enough in the checking account to cover monthly expenses or better yet, withdraw it all, close the account, and pay your bills with money orders from your cash stash. Keep a healthy, separate cash reserve at home (as large a one as you can afford) and don't go into it for *anything*—you won't want it depleted when you need it most. If you drink or use a lot of milk, store boxes of dried milk. Begin collecting silver and gold (preferably in an easily disposable form such as coins). An alternate form of transportation than a car or truck is a necessity, such as a motorcycle providing increased mileage (store gasoline for it), or a horse, or bicycle, etc. Winter heat from gas or electricity will not be possible for a time; get a woodstove. I don't recommend the pellet stoves because of the type of fuel they take and the unavailability of it in the future. Have a six-month supply of necessities (storage). Most important is the cash stash, because whatever is in investments, stocks, CDs, or savings accounts will be locked or lost completely.

I'm not going to get into geologic or meteorological events because those have been beaten to death by others. We know earth movement is natural. We experience it each day, just as we witness the tornados, flooding, and droughts. These related aspects were detailed in *Phoenix Rising*. The map configuration published in *Daybreak* has not altered. My former information has not changed.

I've been told I have an overscrupulous conscience that is causing my life to be filled with chronic guilt. Can you help me with this?

I'll try. Though an overscrupulous conscience can cause great anguish, I sympathize with the condition. Guilt, especially *false* guilt, can be misery. To live in a constant state of guilt is no way to exist. To think one is always doing or saying the wrong thing is no way to live. Always questioning your every thought, word, and action to weigh it against rightness, or social correctness, or public opinion is not allowing self the right to have a personal perspective or unique attitude. This questioning comes with a fear of being yourself, a fear of hurting others' feelings, a fear of being in the wrong. But you, everyone, has the right to express self, to be free to have a unique opinion, even to be wrong. Being wrong is not a sin. Being wrong teaches us lessons and increases our awareness and knowledge. An overscrupulous conscience is corrected by a simple mental adjustment in philosophy—understanding that you have the right to be the unique individual that you are and the right to express yourself. There is no need to deeply question your every move and word. Where is the freedom in that? Where is the beautiful spontaneity in that? Spontaneity is a beautiful blessing every individual can rejoice in utilizing. It unleashes those unnecessary "holds" we voluntarily restrict ourselves with. Stop questioning self at every turn and . . . live! Stop beating yourself down. Self-flagellation isn't what it's spiritually cracked up to be. The idea went out with the belief in a flat earth. It went out with the old-time saints and their theory of how saintly behavior should be. If you practice goodness in life, you're doing good; you're okay. Quit believing it isn't so. Why bring imagined shadows into a sunny life?

We didn't come from apes, right?

I know I didn't. Unless you're different from the rest of earthly humanity, your ancestors are not apes. Rather than peering through dark jungles for your relatives, look up . . . to the stars. Besides, humanity is a lot older than anthropologists believe. North America was initially peopled with a race other than the Indian one. There is much to be unearthed and discovered. There are brighter lights yet to be shed on earth's history. We've only turned the first page of its history book.

Therapeutic touch practitioners were tested for their ability to perceive human energy and failed. Does that prove this healing to be a sham?

That conclusion would be the result of false logic. It would be the same as saying there's no such thing as electricity because a burned-out light bulb won't turn on. Just because a practitioner can't actually sense or physically feel one's energy course through the aura or over the body surface does not also mean the energy and its paths are not there.

The Chinese have known about the body's energy paths for thousands of years. They call this energy chi, or, more accurately, "qi," meaning "breath." This chi can cause problems when its flow is obstructed. The object of acupuncture, acupressure, and therapeutic touch is to unblock the obstruction and get the energy flow circulating again. The more sensitive practitioners can feel this energy and pinpoint the trouble spots that block the flow; however, it's not an imperative ability to achieve effective results. Frequently, when one of my family members had a severe headache, I could manipulate the aura surrounding the shoulders, neck, and head to successfully alleviate the condition. This was accomplished through "working" the energy flow. I found that the blockage point was most often a tight knot at the base of the skull. Intense pressure held on this spot worked wonders in conjunction with smoothing out the aura and easing the energy current into a stronger rate of flow. Rather than actually "feeling" the energy, it was "sensed" as an inner perception. Generally, it's better if the practitioner can actually feel this energy, but is not a paramount skill to effective healing. The "test" you saw was not an indicator of anything. If this test was conducted to discredit the theory of this healing technique and debunk its effectiveness, it failed to accomplish both objectives.

I see a lot of religious hypocrisy in the world. You probably are even more sensitive to it than I. How do you deal with this situation?

When you can't change a condition, situation, or the behavior of others, all you can do is accept it and pray it will one day change for the better through the gaining of wisdom, reason, or enlightenment.

The Bible-thumpers who interject verbatim Scripture or use the word Jesus in every other sentence and then turn around and ridicule another's religious belief or lifestyle are being hypocritical. The churchgoers who dress in their Sunday best and attend services to be noticed or admired are hypocrites. Or those who attend religious services with hatred within their hearts or place their bodies in church while their minds are on the Sunday picnic or ball game they're planning on attending in a few hours are being hypocritical. Those who consider themselves members of the Religious Right or the Moral Majority and publicly denigrate others are hypocrites. The Southern Baptists, who denounce the rights of women by attempting to subjugate them to their husbands, and boycott Disney because its films are not aligned with their beliefs (and also because Disney perceives all individuals as being equal and employs people other than heterosexuals), are exhibiting behavior counter to the teachings of Jesus and The Way. This behavior is not only extremely hypocritical, but also displays religious egotism. It attempts to alter society according to *their* beliefs. It is evidence of trying to make changes through hatred and superiority rather than love and equality, using false scripture as a swiftly slicing sword. Religious hypocrisy is right up there with the White Supremacists when it comes to egotism and hatred. We, as a society, cannot tolerate hatred of any kind. Hatred is an evil force that will destroy the world unless it is countered by the good people with love in their hearts. Everyone has the right to worship as they please, to live life as their conscience directs, to have constitutional rights and freedoms, to read and view what they choose, to spiritually believe as they may, to love whomever they love. We cannot tolerate the actions of those who think otherwise. We cannot stand mute, turn our heads, and close our eyes and ears, and allow ourselves to be dominated and manipulated by those consumed with intolerance and hatred, ego and hypocrisy.

Due to recent hate crimes against various ethnic individuals in the Denver area, the Denver residents have formed an "anti-hate" organization. They've witnessed enough hatred and intolerance in their area and on the newscasts. They've had all they can stomach of it and have organized Walks Against Hate through the city streets. Every walk gets larger and larger as onlookers are moved to join in.

There're indications that this movement will continue to grow and spread far and wide. There are premonition hints to where this will lead if the idea expands to other cities and becomes a nationwide effort. Can you see it? Can you feel it? The evil of hypocrisy and egotism being opposed by unity and equality? Tolerance rising up to trample intolerance? Love and Acceptance in a face-off against hate and persecution? The Children of Light gearing up to finally silence the Children of Darkness? Yes, it's time. Our planet cannot survive if intolerance and hate do. These *must* be eradicated.

So while there are circumstances where we cannot do anything to change the behavior of others and, in order to "deal" with this, we utilize Acceptance, there are too many other times and situations where we do have alternatives at our disposal. Get involved. Help to organize anti-hate groups in your neighborhood, community, or city. Stage public "walks" to show your determination and solidarity—others will be compelled to join in the effort. Good people are plain tired. They're sick to death of the hatred and hate crimes. We, as a people, are too sick of watching it happen time and time again. It's time for spiritual intelligence to stop being smothered and dominated by the ignorance of spiritual superiority. It's time for those with spiritual wisdom to light up the world and dispel the darkness that is pervading it.

My friend and I were driving home one day when a man ran in front of the vehicle. My friend was driving and couldn't avoid hitting him. He died two days later. It's been difficult dealing with this.

I have great empathy for your experience. Though we can accept the fact that an event was unavoidable, that doesn't necessarily mean we can ignore it. We are left with the emotional pain of the incident. We may feel guilt over being involved in an event that caused a death, even though we understand we weren't at fault; even though our minds know it was an accident, we may still feel deep sorrow with our sense of being responsible. But who *really* was responsible? Who was the real *cause* of this death? The *man* did the running. He *chose* a direction in which to run. He ran in *front* of a vehicle. Your friend was merely driving down the road where *she* was *supposed* to be. There was *no* fault in her actions. Now I know that experiencing a "no-fault" accident won't negate the fact that it happened and that someone was killed, but your friend must understand that she experienced synchronicity. Yes, it was her car that intersected a running man's path at that specific moment in time, but *she* was not the factor that altered a course to create the resulting situation—the *man* was the factor who activated the "altered" aspect of the synchronic event. It was *he* who *caused* the event, not your friend. Understanding this fact may still not help to alleviate the residual emotional effects of the accident; those will fade in time. Time is a great healer. We naturally feel bad when unavoidable events like this happen, but in this particular instance, the driver was not in any way at fault. It does no good to second-guess alternate scenarios, such as, maybe if I'd just taken another street or, perhaps if I'd stopped for coffee the timing would've been different. That type of speculation isn't fruitful to healing. That sort of thinking isn't even valid in this kind of situation because the man could also have done something to delay the timing. You can't view this incident as destiny. The man created an incident of his own fate. Your friend was merely an innocent aspect of that reality. In this event, the *man* was the person who had a directional *choice,* not the driver. He had choice of motion and direction, and was free to make a voluntary, conscious choice for both. The driver, on the other hand, had no such choice to make because her motion (rate of speed) was dictated by the posted speed limit and her direction was determined by the street itself. The man chose the situation, not the driver.

Now I want to move onto a different aspect of this event—the man's spirit. In his new totality of spirit, he knows the driver is not responsible, not to blame for the death of his body. Perhaps he now feels sorrow over the great emotional pain he caused the driver. If your friend agonizes with prayerful apologies to the spirit, this may produce a harmful effect for the spirit. Both driver and spirit are trying to tell the other that they're sorry. I think it would help your friend if she shifted her perception of this (guilt) and let the spirit know that she *accepts* his actions. By doing this, she transfers her focus on *forgiveness of another* rather than personal *guilt of self.* I don't intend to make this seem like a diversionary tactic because, though it may appear to be such, it isn't solely so. By accomplishing this shift of focus, the situation as a whole is handled in a spiritual manner rather than an emotional one. The level on which it is dealt with is raised. Communicating one's apologies to the spirit is not half as effective as communicating acceptance and forgiveness. He'll rest much easier if he sees that your friend doesn't blame herself and is on her way to healing through Acceptance. He knows he caused the event. He can be "held" to the event and driver if she continues in self-deprecating thought and pain. Her pain will "pull" on the spirit and cause him anguish too. He feels her distress and, in turn, it causes him sorrow. Your friend needs to let him know that it's okay. How does she do this? Her *thoughts* are enough. Mental "thought-talk" is heard just as well as if one sought out a medium. And it's one on one—so much more personal and confidential.

A friend of mine is constantly making fun of others: clothing, weight, race, etc. This habit bothers me a lot and is becoming extremely irritating. What can I do?

Clearly, the fact that your friend is free to voice her opinion in front of you shows that you allow it. Why not also allow your own opinion to be shared in a like manner? Since you haven't said anything about it to her, then you've subconsciously let her dominate the conversation or even the entire relationship.

Friends should be friends. That means that they have equal right to express personal perspectives without holding them back in deference to the others. Dominance has no place in friendship. Yes, some personalities are more extroverted than others; yet that shouldn't be a factor that prohibits the expression of self, even for the introverted personality. You're supposed to feel comfortable in a friendship, not restrained. How will a friend ever know the real "who" of you if you don't bring it forward and express it? There should be no wallflower characteristics attached to a true friendship.

Chronic criticism is a mark of egotism and there are many ways it can evidence the false sense of one's superiority. By constantly putting others down, as your friend does, it shows an inner need to stroke one's own ego at every opportunity. Those perceived opportunities are everywhere and usually come in the form of people passing by. Overweight people are not society's clowns to be laughed at. To do this exposes one's own sense of superiority. Criticizing the appearance of others, whether it be physical shape, color of skin, demeanor, perception of social status, type of clothing, or whatever, indicates an ignorant mind, one full of the perceived perfections of self as compared to those of others. These people, like your friend, view self as being the epitome of societal preference—the model human by whom all others are judged. It's an extremely puffed-up attitude, don't you think? Especially when it means that this type of person does not recognize another's *right* to be a unique individual, to have the right to express the unique qualities and characteristics of self.

I notice the smirking side glances people give one another when seeing me dressed in some of my favorite outfits (lace-trimmed calico long skirt with a plaid flannel shirt). So what? Do you think I care about that which ignorance perceives? If I want to wear overall shorts with striped tights that remind others of Raggedy Ann or the witch of Oz, then I'll wear them anyway just because it fits my mood of the day (not that I necessarily feel like Raggedy Ann or a witch that day). If I need to take a break from staining the house and take off to the post office to pick up mail wearing the grubby, torn work clothes, I can do this without being embarrassed. If folks smirk or raise their eyebrows when they see me like this, then that's their problem, isn't it? If I want to wear Levi's with a lace-trimmed camisole top (which is more common than not), then I will. I never cared about an "in" style. I dress to match my own beingness. This gives a comfortable sense of complemented being, which doesn't grate against the aura.

If you have a true friendship with this woman, I suggest you exercise your right to express an opinion, especially a contrary one. You asked me what you should do. Well, nobody can tell you what to do, but I can tell you what I'd do. I'd ask my friend if she realized what she was doing—*doing all the time?* And if she is aware of her constant criticizing, ask her *why* she feels the need to do it? Has she even looked at the reasons behind her behavior? Maybe she hasn't.

Maybe this is exactly what she needs to do without ever having realized it before. Many times people aren't aware of their own behavior and the presentation it displays to others. They can be completely unaware of how they're exposing positive or, in this case, negative qualities and unspiritual attitudes. A discussion about this would definitely be my next move if it were me. Anyway, true friends should feel free to express their irritation with one another's habits or idiosyncrasies. Don't be afraid to say that it bugs you when she criticizes everything about others. Don't be fearful of harming the relationship by expressing self. If you are, then the friendship isn't all that it's cracked up to be . . . it's shallow. You've made it clear that she's always free to express her opinion; now's the time to express yours.

I have a brother-in-law who has to "best" others in a conversation about any subject. His know-it-all demeanor is grating and tiring.

Sometimes this isn't an ego thing. Sometimes this is simply one's way of trying to help others through the sharing of information or wanting to be of assistance. However, the way you described your relative seems to fit the first cause and this is usually generated from the ego as a subconscious attempt to overcompensate for a personally perceived inadequacy of some type. These kinds of individuals need to know and understand that it's okay to *not know* something. It's okay if your knowledge is not currently in an up-to-the-minute state on every issue or subject matter, and that people aren't expecting you to be a walking encyclopedia. A know-it-all attitude frequently is evidence of one's desire to be useful to others and doesn't necessarily indicate an overblown ego. If the situation is bothering you so much, which it obviously is, take your brother-in-law aside and broach the issue. You may find that he's coming from an entirely different place than you and other family members assumed.

Your books have given us so many profound messages and beautiful philosophies to live by. If you had to confine these into only one or two concepts to give us, what would those be?

Love and hate. *Love one another. Stop the hatred.* These are the two most important spiritual concepts, because, when these are followed, all other negatives fall away and fade away into oblivion.

Should parents be held responsible for the crimes that their children commit?

Guilt belongs to the perpetrator. Some segments of society have the false philosophy that parents indirectly perpetrate a crime their child commits because they're responsible for their upbringing and supervision. Well, hold on a minute. Are distilleries and breweries charged as the guilty, perpetrating party when a drunk driver kills someone? Is the registered owner of a stolen gun arrested for a murder if the burglar kills another with it? Individuals know right from wrong. A child knows it's wrong to steal or take a life. A child knows it's wrong to deal drugs just by the nature of the act's need for clandestine transactions. They know it's taboo to carry a weapon to school. The basic elements of society (the newscasts, for example) graphically inform viewers about the existence of right and wrong behavior. Parents instill this concept at home while the child is growing up. What that child *does* with the information is that *child's* decision. A parent needs to earn a living in order to support the family's needs and cannot be a shadow for the child every moment of the day. We chastise parents who *do not* work to support the family, then we want to make them a criminal who is held responsible for the child's activities while the parent *was* away at work. It cannot be both ways. Society is expecting a parent to be in two places at once. Perhaps society needs to hold the film industry, and the toy manufacturers, and the video game designers responsible for the violence the children are influenced by with these. More than a lack of parental supervision, the increase in crime perpetrated by children is more frequently caused by those societal elements that have a high-impact influence on their lives at every turn. Cartoons and computer games are loaded with violence. Certain societal *attitudes* are highly detrimental to the forming philosophy of impressionable children. What am I talking about? One example is what I've personally overheard a hunter say. What kind of message does a young boy get when hearing a hunter extol the high excitement of the hunt and revel in what he ecstatically calls, "the thrill of the kill?" The *thrill* of the *kill?* It's thrilling to kill? Killing is thrilling? Good grief, no wonder children are losing the respect for life. It's not only *parental* example children learn from, it's also *society's* example. *Society* becomes the ultimate perpetrator. From the fat roll of big bills the drug dealer flaunts, to the hunter extolling the thrill of the kill, from the perceived "power" of gangs, to the increasing insensitivity toward life brought on by the continual bombardment of television newscasts. Television broadcasts the widespread incidents in increasing numbers on a daily basis. The more children see, the more nonchalant and desensitized they can become. From playing cowboys and Indians to acting out war games and Rambo characters, children emulate life.

Also, there is a philosophical ideology called the "age of reason," whereby an individual becomes officially responsible for his/her actions in life. I'm sure different religions have their own criteria about the exact age that qualifies a child for this concept, but the Catholic Church uses the age of seven. After turning seven, the Catholic child becomes responsible for his/her actions and is ever after subject to "sins" caused by transgressions perpetrated against religious dogma. This "age of reason" concept is not confined to religion, but is generally accepted by society as a viable, societal tenet. So then, who is society? The adults comprise society.

Ergo, can all adults be held responsible for the state of their world and how their children perceive that world and respond in kind to it? Singling out parents shifts the need to take a look at self and accept personal responsibility. No, parents are not responsible for the crimes of their children; the child is directly responsible due to its age of reason and will; society is indirectly culpable because of its influence of violence upon the child.

Another element of this to consider is how siblings raised in one household and being exposed to identical child-rearing methods are shown to each turn out differently. Upon reaching adulthood, one child may keep a spotless apartment while her sibling will be sloppy and dirty. One sibling may be eccentric while the other strongly holds to the traditional mores. One may have a deep respect for life while the other enters a life of crime and murder. What does this prove? Doesn't it prove that like upbringing does not produce like adult behavior and philosophy? Doesn't it prove that the effect of parental guidance has *minimal* effect on the individuality of the child? Especially when he/she reaches adulthood? Or attains the age of reason and responsibility? It's also a fact that children disobey parents. Are parents to be held responsible if the child blatantly disobeys them? The child made the choice to disobey, not the parent who taught them differently. Society needs to get straight on this.

I recently heard a new book publicized on television that sounded as though it addressed this very issue. I can't recall the title, but I do recall thinking that it was about time that someone pointed out that parental upbringing didn't necessarily have the strong effect on children that society thought it did. I've observed that most parents do their utmost best by their children. I've seen parents agonize over what they should've done or shouldn't have done. I've seen a tendency for society to blame the mothers for how the children turned out. I've seen enough blame and searching for scapegoats to turn my spiritual stomach—if my spirit had one.

I am so disappointed in my best friend who is in a terrible state of anger because her mother didn't leave her anything in her will but personal mementos. Can you help me come to terms with this upsetting situation?

Hmmm, where is it written that one must profit from another's death? You know, I've witnessed so much greed in this world that, at times, it appears to be a vicious insidiousness. Me, me, me. We're supposed to love and respect our parents, not think of them as a source of a future windfall upon their deaths. To my way of thinking, the most precious and valuable inheritance would be receiving one personal item that was special to the parent, maybe a piece of jewelry the mother or father favored and wore. This singular *item* in tandem with *memories* should be more than enough to inherit. To equate parents to net worth is ignorant, cruel, and selfish. It's disrespectful and insensitive. To "expect" to inherit money or property from a parent is pure greed.

People make wills to ensure that their *wishes* are followed. Contesting that will shows a great lack of respect for the deceased. As individuals with free wills, we all have the right to gift others with the physical possessions we leave behind upon our deaths. Those recipients honor and respect said right by abiding by the deceased's wishes. To contest (or grumble) is to dishonor and disrespect. To contest is to be dishonorable and greedy.

I'm sorry your friend is in such a deplorable state over her mother's will. Perhaps you could attempt to help enlighten her regarding this issue. Help her to see that people need to love and respect their parents for who they are (were), not for their money and possessions that offspring "expect" to one day obtain. *Inheritance is not a "right."* It is a gift. Inheritance is whatever *gift* is received from the deceased. The *living* rarely appreciate the *value* of that which a deceased individual has chosen to leave them. Personally, I wouldn't expect a thing from my mother's estate after her death, but I sure would be tickled to have some memento that she wore, like a scarf or ring or whatever. This type of object carries her essence, which, to me, is far more valuable than any other form of inheritance I can think of.

And what of *memories* children have of their parents? Aren't those more precious than any physical "thing"? All the care the parent gave the child throughout childhood? All the nights a mother sat up with a sick child and all the meals she cooked? The homework she helped with? Yes, this is what a mother does, but that doesn't mean it shouldn't be appreciated and fondly remembered. Memories can be the greatest treasure we have. I wonder why more people don't recognize that?

We think we know others but we don't. We think we know a friend or relative until something like your experience pops up. Then the "hidden" person jumps out and exposes his/her real self to the world. Clearly, due to your recent experience with your friend, you never witnessed any evidence of a greedy attitude from her or you wouldn't have been so shocked by it now. Death can do strange things to the living. All rationale can fly out the door. Death is one of those events that can expose the darker side of those it touches. It can also reveal the "light" side. I never understood relatives who bickered over the possessions left by a deceased family member. That behavior is the height of greed and . . . disrespect. You know, there is a clause that can be put in a will that treats any beneficiary who contests it to be treated as though that individual had *predeceased* the will-maker. I'm glad Nivea, my own attorney, is one sharp lady.

Do you date? Do you think you'll ever marry again?

The decision to include this question in the book was one that took considerable time to come to. I went ahead because it had been asked so frequently.

Date? Marry again? No to both questions. Besides, some women just have this strong sense that there was only one man meant for them to have a relationship with in this life. Also, I've survived experiences that, regrettably, served to instill a great lack of trust. Experiencing the two close relationships with the immediate familial men in my life, father and husband, I've twice personally witnessed the strong male obsessive desire for greener grass, where the concept of fidelity becomes meaningless. The manners in which this attitude shattered love and destroyed family life when I was both a youngster and an adult is not something I ever wish to be a part of again. I have two sisters who experienced the same with their mates. Today, as proven out by the publicized evidence of the widespread practice of this infidelity (the President and his constituents' comments affirming the commonality of his type of behavior voiced by male interviewees) attests to the fact that, generally, men cannot love their wives enough to remain faithful to them. As a result, though I have good men friends in my life, prior experience negates any *personal* relationship that would even get as far as accepting an invitation out to dinner with one or letting one buy me a cup of espresso. I've been left with a whole new perspective that I'm completely comfortable living with. I've found a lifestyle niche that is spiritually peaceful and without emotional conflict. The work of my mission is paramount. I've come to realize that I'm very capable of living as a completely independent individual. My life is busy and full. I have my three wonderful daughters. I go out with friends. I occupy my time with construction projects on the cabin and grounds between reading for leisure, writing the last of my books, and working on the planning stage of the abbey. I have an elder living with me now who requires daily, monitored care. I also have wonderful companionship that provides strong encouragement, makes an intellectual sounding board for my philosophical ideas, maintains a stalwart supportive position on behalf of the mission, and is my emotional mainstay. And, not to leave out the many furry people of the cabin, my joyful little puppies fill my heart with their unbounded, unconditional love. My life couldn't be more full . . . or peaceful . . . or balanced.

What's up with women these days? Every time I attempt to extend a courtesy like offering help with grocery bags, they respond with rudeness. They act like Ms. Independent.

No, it's more like they're acting like Ms. Wisdom. Don't take offense. Don't take it personal. You need to read a book called *The Gift of Fear,* by Gavin de Becker. This man has a consulting firm that advises the world's most prominent media figures, corporations, and law enforcement agencies on the subject of predicting violence and recognizing potential perpetrators of crime against one's person. He teaches methods of avoiding abuse through heightened awareness of another's behavior, and informs women of the importance of strongly attending to the voice of their inner self (intuitive insights). Carrying a lady's groceries was one of his prime examples of how men gain access into a woman's car or apartment. You picked a bad example to extend your kindness through.

Today's reality presents us with an ugly picture of increasing crimes against women. Every few seconds a woman gets raped, abused and battered, even murdered. And you wonder why they prefer to carry their own grocery bags? Mr. de Becker tries to make women understand that it's far better to be rude to a stranger than be hurt or end up dead. Women, in general, do not wish to be rude to a stranger. This fact is what the perpetrator counts on so he can be as pushy and forward as he likes or needs to be in order to manipulate his victim into the ideal situation, which perfectly accommodates his intent. Once he gains entry into her car or apartment, he's already manifested half his goal.

You need to be aware of society's reality out there. Put yourself in the woman's place. I know you know she has nothing to fear from you, but she doesn't know that. She's not merely exercising her independence, she's also behaving in a manner that will best serve her safety. Get a clue here. Why do women need to do this? Could it be because men are abusing, raping, and murdering them at a greater rate than ever before? It's the men who are causing this "rude" behavior from women. This is no longer the fifties, where the ideologies and behavior of the Cleaver family rule the day. The next time you feel the urge to assist a lady loaded down with grocery bags, reverse perspective. Put yourself in her position and look at you through her eyes. You are a complete stranger. Does she see a gentleman or a rapist fronting his ulterior motives with a kind smile and honey-coated voice? Mr. de Becker advises her to err on the side of "life" and see a rapist. The state of our society is not one to be proud of. It's happening because so many men can't control their testosterone and prefer to let it rule their intellect and control their actions. Don't take it personal, it's just the way it is. This isn't just some cynical, feministic attitude I've taken; it's proven every day on the six o'clock news. If you're not seeing it, then it's because you don't wish to—you're voluntarily in denial. Sexual crimes have increased a thousand fold, and now . . . enter Viagra.

My church emphasizes the concept of it being a "woman's duty" to bear children and I'm having a problem with that. Would you have any comments on this?

You bet. Please refer to a prior question and response regarding this issue, but there's more to say on it. Listen, a women, like everyone, is an individual whose *spiritual "duty"* is to follow her own *spiritual* path. If children are not a part of that purpose, then *nobody* can tell her it is. Churches depend on tithing for income. The more members the *fold* includes, the more money the church will collect in the future. See? The hidden philosophy is to make as many followers as possible by increasing the head-count of the fold. Fill the world with believers and make us rich! That's not being crass; it's being real and honest. Reality often behaves in a cynical manner and so it is seen as being such. Religions have deemed birth control to be a "sin" because the utilization of same prevents more faithful from being brought into the fold. Control. They want more people to control. It's *your* unique path to follow, *your* free will, *your* decision, and your *body*. How is it the Church's right to tell you what you can and cannot do with your own body? Whether to have children or not? Just because you're a woman doesn't mean you're a uterus with legs and nothing more—no mind. Having a womb doesn't designate one's life purpose. Jeez, Louise, these preachers are getting desperate. With golden voices the priests expound the concept from the pulpit while they don't have to personally support the large families they sometimes produce (at least not publicly). Hypocrisy. Ulterior motives to so-called spiritual dogma. Patriarchal dogma is more like it. Dear reader, I would advise you to follow your own conscience on this and all other philosophies. Use your insights and instincts. That's what they've been gifted to you for. You are a beautiful individual. Accept and appreciate that fact. *Exercise* that fact.

Isn't artwork an extension of one's soul?

Soul? Not precisely. It's more an *expression* of one's personality, philosophy, or current perspective on life. The *already-formed* totality of one's soul doesn't alter with time passing through a current life, but attitude, personality, and perspective can. This is why the quality, or style, or subject matter of an artist's work frequently changes. When folks view a piece of art and exclaim that "it has so much soul," they're really not referring to the artist's true soul, but rather his/her sensitivity, the artist's emotional mood that has been successfully transferred from beingness to canvas. Evidence of the state of one's actual, composite totality of soul manifests through behavior effected by attained Wisdom.

Is it true that aging is brought about by the mental?

I believe that question is best answered by looking at the wrinkled skin and long, white beards of the yogis and elders of Tibetan monasteries who have reached the highest stage of enlightened attainment. Gray hair does not equate with an unskilled mentality or unattained spirituality. In fact, the opposite is more accurate because one who is spiritually advanced wouldn't think of wasting mental energy on the preservation of something so spiritually shallow and insignificant as youth. What a fleeting and frivolous goal to have. Wouldn't that be evidence of a purpose that served self?

Now if you're thinking that a mind that has experienced great grief and tribulation in life can cause various effects of aging, then, sure, life wears on the body. That type of mental influence can certainly affect the body's physiology. Gosh, just look at me—all that silver hair that recently appeared in the last year is a prime example. But hey, so what? I kind of enjoy seeing the face of the Crone easing forward.

Are the Five Races indirectly associated in any way with the five Starborn ones?

No. Directly.

Why do men make war?

Is it a desire to be strongest and best? Maybe biggest? Control? Domination? Love of war games? I don't know. Wars . . . how ignorant and hideously primitive they are. When you spend a little time contemplating the separate reasons for the multitude of wars that have filled the world's historic past, you'll discover that they all stemmed from ego. It's ego to want another's land; it's ego to want to rule another country; it's ego to want to be ruler of others and dominate them; and it's ego to want the most destructive weapon. All wars are caused by ego. Well, you might think, what about wars that we engage in for the purpose of defending and protecting another country that is being attacked? That'd be the reason for *our* involvement in a war *caused* by the *ego* of another country wanting to take over the country we're trying to assist. See? It still can be reduced down and traced back to the ego as being the primary cause. Ego rules this planet. It is the Planet of the Ego (Apes?). The humans of this planet haven't originated from apes, so why are they acting as if they were? Just because the ape concept seems to be the most widely held one doesn't mean people have to fit themselves into it and act like them .

Drinking alcohol, smoking, and gambling are against God's laws. They are unspiritual acts inspired by the devil.

Really? Let's take a closer look at this. Initially, I see this ideology as being highly selective where circumstances are brought into play regarding the rightness or supposed wrongness of the concept. The correspondent has made a dogmatic statement that is extremely broad and all-inclusive. Can this statement be correct?

Scripture has Jesus turning water into wine at the wedding at Cana. If Jesus provided the attendees at a wedding celebration with wine (alcohol) for the purpose of imbibing same for enjoyment and celebratory reasons, how then can it be wrong to drink alcohol? Many religions use wine for their communion rites during each service, whereby each member of the congregation is offered a sip to ingest the symbolic blood of Christ. During Jesus' lifetime, he participated in many celebrations and festivities where he ate heartily and drank as much as the rest of the revelers. Don't religions encourage the faithful to follow Christ's example? Or not? Which is it? And if the drinking of alcohol is now supposed to be an act with which Satan has tempted folks, did Satan also cause Jesus to provide the wedding party with wine? Isn't this concept loaded with contradictory and selective messages?

Likewise, Jesus was known to occasionally smoke from a pipe; he also joined in spontaneous games of chance with those he passed by. He laughed when a player made a bad move and gave congratulations when a smart play was made. Life. Jesus loved life. The trouble with Scripture is that it has been so narrowly confined and whitewashed. If an ancient-time scribe had followed on the heels of Jesus for just one week and recorded all he said and did, Scripture would present a completely different portrait of Jesus—one far more complete and accurate. But that didn't happen. Even if it did, it would've been heavily censored and red-lined by those who gathered to pick and choose which statements would be included in the official, canonical record called the Bible. Therefore, Jesus was sanitized according to the God-like ideology that the early Church forefathers saw fit to present him as. The beautiful qualities which clearly exemplified his humanness and great love of life was deleted, all human aspects of his character and life were thrown out with the bathwater. What remains . . . is the skeleton of scripture. Because of this insidious, historical act of expunging and hiding the actual character of Jesus, I'm strongly compelled to one day expose this conspiratorial cover-up.

Is the Bible truly the word of God?

A book *written* by God as sole author *without* any human intervention (as opposed to being channeled, or co-authored, for instance) could possibly be evidence of God's handiwork. The Bible, on the other hand, merely represents *hearsay* and *secondhand* concepts and quotes. It's loaded with people saying, "God told me this," and "The Lord said that," without *God* ever saying, *"I say this."* See the difference? If we really stretched it, I mean, really made a stretch, we could look at the Ten Commandments as being more in line with God's actual words. Yet, in reality, those laws were imprinted in stone by a laser. Does God use lasers? The

Watchers do. And throughout history they've also used holograms to present "appearances" of multicultural, religious images manifesting as visions. They've used brilliant beams and orbs of light (one such orb was interpreted as the sun dancing in the sky).

So religions (and witnesses) interpret what they see through the colored lenses of their dogma-specific glasses. This is done by way of society's desire for miracles and magic rather than the mind being focused on the *reality* of an event. The esoteric, the mysterious, miracles of religion, all overshadow the intellect of reality. This is so. This is evidenced whenever television newscasts televise a report of thousands of believers making a sudden pilgrimage to a glass office building that has cast a shadow of a hooded form. "Oh, the *Virgin* has appeared to us!" And soon lighted votive candles are covering the building's lawn and people are kneeling in self-created ecstasy. The enormous desire for miracles and the signs of them have exposed humanity's primitive mind and brought home the fact that it prevents clear-sighted perception of our true reality. Many of the so-termed "miracles" that Jesus performed in his lifetime were nothing more than a precise utilization of physics, yet were misinterpreted as "miraculous feats" because the people of the time didn't know any better. They didn't know about the forces of antigravity, magnetic fields, the ability to generate mass hypnosis, and like technicalities of the naturally occurring realities of physics. But today we do. And today people still flock to the shadows on a building wall. Maybe this is so because Scripture is packed with religious ideologies, dreams, and grossly extrapolated events instead of realities. Maybe this is so because people have not been given an accurate picture of Jesus' true character, activities, and life. Maybe this is true because, from the outset, people have been misled by religious conspiracy that preprogrammed them to perceive and misinterpret reality as evidence of the miraculous.

I've been told by religious leaders and teachers that I cannot personally commune with God, that only they have that right and authority. Help!

Okay, I can help. You know that stuff you pick up after your dog's been outside? Yeah, you know. Well, that's what those religious folks are talking.

Excuse me, but . . . being a so-called "religious leader" or "teacher" does not put a red phone in those guys' hot little hands nor does it put a holy bug in their ear. We are *all* connected to the Divine Minds. We are all related. The Great Web of Life, remember? The energy of everything is interconnected to the energy of every thing, including every *who*. If you didn't have a personal, direct line to the Divine, how would she/he hear prayers? What, do the Supreme Aspects of the Trinity speak in booming, thundering voices to those leaders and teachers? What? How are they more special or better than anyone else? Come on teachers and leaders, your ego is hanging out. You're exposing your arrogance. You're no higher on the Mighty scale than your followers. Dear correspondent, what these people are claiming is a crock of what you pick up after your dog's been outside. Poo! Don't let anyone shatter the fact that you can commune with the Divine Minds. You can mentally talk to them, pray, or audibly speak to them, or whisper, or sing to them. And . . . that's a fact.

Responding to this issue brings to mind a related aspect. It occurs to me that for someone to tell you that you cannot commune with God is blasphemous, like something Satan would say. It's a devilish idea, for sure. And, as you all know, I'm certainly not one to go around blaming the devil for everything, but this one sure fits the bill, don't you think?

It seems to me that the late night talk show hosts are ignorant. Their idea of humor at the expense of our president, Ellen DeGeneres, the attorney general, and other public personalities is despicable. And if the brunt of the joke doesn't relate to a specific person, it's about sex. What's happening to society?

Open season. Sodom and Gomorrah's past repeating itself. A disrespect for others. A ballooning obsession with sex. No common decency.

I frequently watch the late night talk shows and have also shaken my head at the subjects they've chosen to poke fun at. It is ignorant. There's no other way to define it. And, what's worse, the audience cracks up over it. They're just as stupid as the host. More than once I've commented to others that my own sense of humor must be getting stoic because I don't find the current type of humor funny. I sit with a poker face while everyone around me or an audience is rolling in the aisles. Laughing at others is not my idea of humor or amusement. It is morally and spiritually wrong, unless who you're laughing at is a dressed-up clown or mime.

It's impossible not to notice the way sex bombards society from every front. Television commercials use it to sell things, newspaper and magazine ads are full of sexual visuals and innuendos. Television serial programs use it to keep the viewers tuned in. Newscasts put sex stories at the top of their programming and use it as a promotional "hook" to make sure you stay tuned. Sex and murder are the top, most popular subjects of interest. The two dominate the airwaves and pages of print. Sex and Violence. Look at the James Bond films and how they *used* buxom women in them. What I can't understand is why these actresses don't have more self-respect and see the light? They too use their sexuality; their ego uses it. Add society's top choice of entertainment to the incredibly increased rate of rape, child sexual abuse, and battery of women and you see a connection. Personally I foresee an attitude of the general public that will finally expose and publicize their strong feelings of being fed up with smut.

It seems that sex, violence, and poking fun of others is society's main interest in life. What a sad state of affairs that is.

I recently saw a television ad for a video viewers could order. This video was touted as being "special"! It showed the *entire* violence sequence of various incidents that television newscasts respectfully edited for public viewing. This videotape included vehicle accidents, police incidents, shootings, suicides caught on tape, etc. The premise blew my mind (spirit) away. The advertising focused on being able to "see it all." What the hell is so entertaining about seeing someone blow their brains out all over the pavement? What's so attractive about watching a pedestrian be crushed by a truck? Wake up, people! What's so titillating about human suffering? Where is your head? Stop sitting on it! What are you doing? Wake up and smell the gore you're enjoying. Take a look at yourself, your behavior, your motives. Wake up and see what you're doing to your world. Making fun of others is not loving one another. Obsessions with the physical (sex, food, violence, etc.) serve to keep one anchored and weighted to an unbalanced state of negative emotional and intellectual heaviness. You are not only what you eat, but more accurately, what you *think*. If you think in a manner where enjoyment and entertainment comes from violence, sex, and making fun of others, then you are wallowing in negativity and ignorance. How can you ever expect society to elevate itself when it *enjoys* rolling around in the muck, smut, and heinous horrors of life? When it enjoys digging around in another's dirt and exposing the skeletons in their closets? Jeez, get a clue! No wonder the Watchers are pacing with impatience. No wonder the archangels are crying.

Does everyone have a Little Self?

No. The "letter" of your question is wrong, but the "spirit" of it is right. *Little Self* is the name of one, specific individual—the unique name that my own Child Within's Consciousness calls herself. You are not pointedly referring to her, but to the *concept* of the Child Within. Your question was generated from my mention of this issue in *Fireside*.

Now that we have that straightened out, yes, everyone has a Child Within. Yet I revealed this aspect of my total Consciousness in relation to the concept of the Feminine Principle—the simultaneous indwelling existence of the Child/Mother/Crone Consciousness within every woman. Throughout most cultures of the world, since the beginning of time, this feminine concept has been a strong belief and spiritual tradition. Its reality has not withered on the vine of time. Today it is just as viable as it was in ancient times.

This is a feminine issue. Men have a Child Within, but do not have the multiple Consciousness associated with this concept, whereby it would have to be altered to Child/Father/Elder. Historically and culturally, no such ideology is in evidence.

Your Child Within is associated with innocence, open-mindedness, connectedness to the spiritual realm, and individuality (expressing self freely). Most adults have smothered this facet of self. They've hidden it behind their burgeoning ego and are, therefore, fearful to expose its beautiful qualities. "Unless you become as little children, the gates of heaven will not be open to you." This translates to mean that people need to maintain the innocence of a child, not allow the dark vulgarities of life and resulting attitudes to harden and desensitize their perspectives, not to let it close their minds to the vast expanse of possibilities, not to crush Spirituality with strictures and qualifiers with which religion whittles it down. The Child Within represents "childlike" qualities, attitudes, and behavior. This doesn't equate to being "childishly immature"; that's different. You can be childlike without being immature.

Those who have succeeded in maintaining the vitality of their Child Within will evidence this through experiencing an exuberant love of life and a deep appreciation for nature. They will find joy in subtle sights and sounds, find great pleasure in simplicity, and deeply appreciate the smallest gifts. They recognize blessings everywhere. They are strongly connected to the Great Web of Life and are wide open to spiritual insights and intuition. Rather than finding fault with others, they notice people's commendable qualities. They speak their mind regardless of popular opinion. They're nonjudgmental, and have a sparkling sense of freedom that gives them luminous joy in being "free to be." These are just some of the qualities evidenced by those who have graciously allowed the beautiful Consciousness of their Child Within to thrive and, well . . . be free to be. Sure, everyone has a Child Within who Jesus frequently advised people to acknowledge and give free expression to.

Have you ever restrained an urge to go into a toy store without having any child in mind to buy for? Maybe that child was the one within you. Next time this compulsion shows itself, go into the store and let yourself enjoy roaming about. Buy yourself whatever attracts your interest. You think this sounds silly? Try it, you might like it. I used to find great relaxation in using colored pencils to bring intricate Celtic designs and stained-glass illustrations to life. Today, whenever I go into a bookstore, the children's section is never ignored. I have a bookcase in the dormer corner of my bedroom filled with the titles I loved as a child. Atop the bookcase are a few unique old-fashioned dolls. Raggedy Ann sits in a miniature, antique sleigh beside an antique doll a correspondent sent me. In the rocker are two teddy bears. These items are as much a part of my Consciousness' totality as my science and physics books. Fairies. From the time I could walk, I was strongly attracted to fairies; now my cabin is peopled by all sorts of them in cubbies, peering out from vines, sitting on window ledges, grouped in conversation with Yodas, and I even have a small fairy fountain on my typewriter table beside the computer desk. The interest in fairies began at an early age, when I "knew" such beings were real. When I was a teenager this was verified when I saw a fairylike being standing in the grass staring up at me. Ever since then I've had a greater, validating affinity with the Little Ones and having representations of them all over the cabin is like inviting them into my home to share my life and beingness. Silly? Eccentric? Mental? Whatever your opinion is, it's me. I like being free to be me. Let your Child Within out and see if you don't love the new freedom you feel.

Won't the Internet diminish the need for psychic consultation?

That would depend on the reason for the consult. Generally though, I understand where you're going with this. Yes, the wider and longer the Information Highway becomes, the more resources individuals have at their personal disposal without having the need to seek out others for this same information. Yes, you're right. The most obvious issue that comes to mind is that of geological predictions. At people's fingertips are Internet sites that detail the earth's geology. Having this information provides a clear display of the geologic hazard regions of the world and people can pretty well determine which regions are most likely to experience catastrophic events in the future. Folks can now deduce these for themselves rather than depending on others to point them out. A look at a map showing elevation reveals those regions that hold the best probability for future flooding. Likewise, faults are detailed, volcanos are shown, etc. The latest papers written by geologists and the most up-to-date findings by meteorologists are obtainable with the touch of a finger. With the instant availability of this type of information, published predictions can become outdated and quickly become old news before the ink is even dry on the report or newsletter. It no longer takes a psychic or prognosticator for individuals to maintain an up-to-the-second, leading-edge position of changing situations or events. Yes, information is yours for the taking. Information is as easy as the press of a button, but only if you take personal responsibility and initiative for your own intelligence and resource opportunities. Through the great mass of information

available, you can deduce the same conclusions as a prognosticator can.

Don't you think that dogs make even better friends than people do?

Though I frequently express my love and deep appreciation for my own little furry people (dogs), they are not at all
the same as human companionship. Yes, dogs provide the
unconditional love we all want to experience, but the intellectual and emotional companionship of a human friend has
no equal. Having someone in your life who loves you despite
the intellectual awareness of your faults is greater than a pet's
love, which comes from an *unawareness* of your faults. See
the difference? It's the difference between one being *capable*
of judgment (and *not* doing it) and one not judging because
it's intellectually incapable of it. The love of a dog is comforting, but the love of another human is more precious than
pure gold.

Although I don't agree with your statement, I understand
the emotion that generated it. Life is rife with tragedy and
mistreatment. People can be viciously cruel, selfish, and
rude. Dogs don't exhibit these attitudes toward their owners.
All they do is love. They exist for their owner. People don't
exist for others; they tend to exist solely for self. Dogs don't
cause emotional heartache (unless they're hurt or die); people do. Oh yes, I certainly understand how you're thinking,
but having a human companion who also loves without judgment, or doesn't say cruel and hurtful things, or never criticizes, or wouldn't think of turning against you is the most
wonderful and fulfilling relationship one can experience. It
comes down to having intellect and choice of behavior. The
human consciously *chooses* to love without causing pain. I
deeply love my little pups, but that love is not greater than
the love I have for my human friends who accept and love me
for who I am . . . just the way I am.

How old is God?

Which one? The Trinity of Divine Beings includes Mother/Father/Holy Spirit. Immeasurably ageless.

In Fireside *you talked about your lack of interest in keeping up with electronic technology, aren't you going to be missing out on a lot?*

One doesn't miss out on something that at some point in the future won't be operational for extended periods of time—maybe for years. Read *Living Is Forever* by J. Edwin Carter, published by Hampton Roads. This is my answer to your question. Am I saying that his book was insightfully written as a predictive depiction of our future? Sometimes the passing of time has a clever way of turning fiction into nonfiction. Some novels are only nonfiction until time converges them with reality. This then proves the author to have been a true visionary whom few initially recognized. He did not voluntarily sit down one day and decide to write this book for the purpose of a good read; he was *compelled* to write it. There was a very important *reason* for it. A Higher Power was involved in directing the story's events. It was inspired.

The scenario detailed in Carter's book pinpoints those aspects of life that will be valuable in the future. If electricity is not a viable facet then, how can e-mail, the Internet, computers, etc., be something one will miss? Think about how the world will be without electricity—even for a short time. Seriously, think about it. And what if heavy cloud cover made solar power ineffective? Refrigeration wouldn't work. Heating homes would be difficult without woodstoves because natural gas couldn't be pumped through the transfer stations and propane couldn't be delivered because the trucks bringing it couldn't get the gasoline up out of the gas pumps without electricity. Eventually batteries will run down without a way to recharge them. All types of vehicles will be useless.

I could go on and on, but you can take this further through your own thought process. The domino effect of having no electricity reduces society to a bare-bones existence. And you wonder why I'm not involving myself in keeping up with technology? Because if the future is going to be anything like what Carter and I envision, focusing on technology will prove to be a major waste of time that needed to be applied to far more useful issues. I see the obsession with technology as being a type of mental diversion that is serving to woo people away from thoughts associated with the high probability that our world is going to change drastically. I keep suggesting to friends and relatives that they should be socking away a cash reserve whenever possible and picking up storage supplies every time they go grocery shopping, but I don't see any evidence of anyone actually doing these things. "Stuff" (electronic stuff) seems more important to spend the extra cash on. To these friends I'm not saying any more. I'm not a nag. But I do feel satisfied with the situation a few of those friends have manifested by keeping a keen eye on the future probabilities and making preparations right now for them, friends who are right on top of things with their windmill, generator with stored gasoline and oil, their chicken coops and duck pens (for eggs only), their fishing gear, woodstove, and chainsaw, windup radio and flashlights, and storage supplies. Their situation is encouraging to me. It's comforting because they've not done it solely because of what I've written regarding the future; they've done it by way of their own initiative because they're intelligent and intuitive enough to see society's growing signs and read the writing on the wall. I respectfully tip my hat to Sindy and Pam.

Technology and the fascination with same is fine if it is used as leisure entertainment and not the primary focus of one's life. I know folks who absolutely live for their computer, and the Internet has become as a dark sorcerer compelling them to stare into his face and discover what magic he has to mesmerize them with. Information and knowledge is good. It's wonderful. So is rationale. But there's something even greater . . . the wisdom of foresight.

Is Lucifer the same entity as Satan?

Taking into account the widespread popular belief that Satan and Lucifer are one and the same, I find this question extremely insightful. People believe that Lucifer goes by a multitude of names: Beelzebub, Belial, Satan, Asmodeus, Abaddon, Azazel, Old Nick, Moloch, Mephistopheles to name a few, however, those are the many names of Satan, not Lucifer. Lucifer is just Lucifer.

In *Fireside* I made a comment about Satan getting a bum rap. I used the term Satan because society views him as being the same as Lucifer. Now that this perceptive question has come up, I need to distinguish between the two entities. In *Fireside* I was specifically referring to Lucifer. *Lucifer* got a bum rap right from the beginning because the Creation story in Scripture is but a redesigned fragment of the actual event.

We need to step back a pace here. The Mother Goddess (Sophia) created two other deities, one male and one female. The male one became extremely arrogant and demanding. He claimed he was the *only* God in existence, then was chastised for his arrogance by Sophia. After all the multidimensional creations were manifested, God forbade Adam and Eve to eat of the Tree of Knowledge because he didn't want them to have his knowledge and understanding. He wanted to keep them ignorant. Enter Lucifer, who saw this as being unfair to the new human creatures. Lucifer's suggestion to Eve to partake of the Tree of Knowledge was a *gift,* an asset that was her right to utilize in life. He saw these newly created humans as being given life but not the "tools" to adequately live that life. Therefore he never "tempted," but endeavored to "help." When the male God discovered this, his anger was great, for lesser beings were not supposed to have rationale, reason, and knowledge. Lucifer, along with

Adam and Eve, then felt the earth-shaking ire of God. You know how the rest of the tale has been told.

Lucifer remains the angel he's always been. But because of his act against the arrogant attitude of God, he has been equated with evil ever since. The real evil one is *another* spiritual being who desired to be as God himself, having dominion over those who followed him and manipulating the newly created humans into behavior counter to the principles of the Mother Goddess and the Holy Spirit (Shekinah). This "other" spirit goes by the name of Satan plus all those many descriptive terms people commonly, but mistakenly, attribute to Lucifer.

This questioner exhibited a highly intelligent thought process to come up with this inquiry. Few people would've gone as far as she did in her thinking. Because of this rarity of thought, I'd not delved into making the distinction between Lucifer and Satan in my previous writings because folks perceived the two entities as being one and the same. But clearly, now is the time to be more technically precise.

Are the writings of the Dead Sea Scrolls found at Qumran and The Gnostic Scriptures *found at Nag Hammadi all true?*

Great question. The key word in this inquiry is "all." Just because writings are ancient doesn't mean they are also accurate. After reading through varied ancient documents and then spending a great deal of time studying them, it becomes clear that the scrolls and codex pages written at a later time than the earlier ones were "colored" by the changing attitudes of the newborn Christian Church. The earlier ones were the unaltered recordings of truth, and were later deemed heretical. I repeat: the *earlier* ones (which the Church tried to eradicate and called heretical) contain more of the *real* and *accurate* accountings of spiritual history. The distinction for the reader comes with clarity after much time is spent in a thorough study of them. For instance, from the

Nag Hammadi site of discovery comes the text called *The Thunder, Perfect Mind.* "Thunder" means "feminine" in Greek. This text is true and what an incredible text it is! The scholar who did the translating concluded that the complete text is the work of the feminine deity of Shekinah who, because she is the Holy Spirit persona of the Mother Aspect of the Trinity (Sophia), is also frequently called the "Lower Sophia." To clarify, the Mother Aspect of the Trinity is Pistis Sophia and her alter-Aspect is called the Lower Sophia also known as the Holy Spirit and Shekinah. *The Thunder, Perfect Mind* is Shekinah speaking of how the perception of the deity persona of the Mother Goddess Aspect of the Trinity, Sophia, (specifically her feminism) is so paradoxically treated in the *human* world as contrasted to her *true* nature. The Shekinah is the essence of the Divine Mother at work among humanity. She is the embodiment of the Spiritual Feminine Principle and a mirrored reflection of the Mother Goddess, which is why she is referred to as the Lower Sophia. Though *The Thunder, Perfect Mind* reads as being entirely paradoxical in content, it is a *comparative* text, defining not only the true duality of the nature of Sophia's true self, but also that same nature, as opposed to that which the societal, patriarchal shift had chosen to relegate and downgrade all feminine deity personalities to at the time. The entire text presents truth as contrasted to the falsehoods attributed to her by men. As a text example, the Shekinah defines Sophia's true nature as Life, but she is *perceived* as Death by men. More than any other "discovered" text, this one brings tears to my eyes. I see this text as being the Shekinah's communication revealing Sophia's deep sorrow over how she'd been so cruelly and sacrilegiously mistreated when the patriarchal religious leaders greatly influenced society's attitude toward its perception of women and their deities. All female deities were deemed heretical and worship banned, while the women themselves became synonymous with Satan's advocate—temptresses, weak, ignorant yet diabolically clever, unclean, of a lower status than men—unmarried women were either virgins or whores, their bodies were deemed sinful and required coverings so that men wouldn't be tempted by them (clearly men weren't held responsible for controlling themselves), and on and on.

So too were the ancient beliefs in the traditional (true) Goddesses degraded and decreed heretical to worship. The Goddesses were completely stripped of their validity and cast into the ashes. All deities save the "one, male God" were forbidden. And the strength of this patriarchal Goddess-cide has held its death grip on society for more than two millennia. But the living Aspects of Pistis Sophia and the Shekinah have returned to reestablish their validity and that of Feminine Spirituality by bringing the world back into balance. The human qualities of their incarnation will not include the arrogance and ego of the male God's Aspect. Oh no, gentleness and love will be their way. The way of Truth. The bringing of Light to eyes that have been blind for thousands of years. Women of society will be filled with their spirits. So will the men be unable to deny the effects of their presence. The Nag Hammadi text of *The Thunder, Perfect Mind* is true. Remember, the Trinity is not comprised of three male Aspects, but is, in actuality, two female and one male.

To recap the response to this question, no, not all of the ancient text discoveries are truth. Be discerning when reading them because, just as today, all texts do not represent true facts. A hint for discernment lies in the text's slant. By this I mean, if it sounds heretical to present-day dogma, then there's a real good chance that it's truth. That alone is a fact that bemoans our current state of spiritual affairs.

Do you have a prediction associated with religion?

To be sure, it will be shaken to its core and shatter to the ground in broken shards. The Age of the Divine Mother is dawning. The truth of her nature will light up the world like seven suns. And the patriarchal religions will bend their knees in acknowledgment.

Why haven't I ever mentioned this before? Isn't it clear that it wasn't yet time? A teacher works within the confining framework and understanding of the pupil. A messenger does likewise. Calculus isn't taught in the first grade. And so, even in the pages of this very book, I've previously given fragments of truths leading up to the revelations regarding this subject matter. Some of the messages I'm here to impart have been too monumental to comprehend if the receiver hasn't been properly prepared and eased into them by way of a graduated method of revelation. The Pistis Sophia (Mother Goddess) is real. The feminine Deity of Shekinah (Holy Spirit) is real. The patriarchal slow waltz is over. Get ready everyone, the big party you've been waiting for is about to begin. It's now time for the Sons of Darkness and the Daughters of Light to . . . rock 'n' roll!

Do we have full control of our nuclear weapons?

No, we never have. That's a little fact that our military and government sectors don't want the people to know, and *they* have the nerve to claim they guard national security! There have been instances of launched missile tests over the Pacific where the missile just . . . disappeared. Lights of some type of crafts in the sky were observed at the same time. The book I frequently recommend is *Above Top Secret: The Worldwide UFO Cover-Up* by Timothy Good. The ISBN is 0-688-07860-5. The book was published in 1988, but still holds true today. I don't know if the author has written anything on the subject since then, but you could ask any bookstore clerk to check their *Books in Print* volume for you. The Internet may have some recent information on this also.

Will the IRS ever go away?

I think an affirmative answer to that would be a prediction everyone would love to see happen. Gosh, if folks are like me (tax poor), then they'll be happy to know that this institution's days are weakening in strength. Laws to diminish its heavy-handed tactics are now in effect. The burden of proof is now theirs instead of being the responsibility of the taxpayer. For the ordinary citizen of this country, nothing brings dread and shaking in the boots more than receiving a notice from the IRS. This won't always be so though. One day there will be no such animal as a personal income tax.

Don't you think that the breakthroughs women are making in society are something to celebrate?

No, because they only emphasize the *need* for breakthroughs. The "first woman to be a fighter pilot" or the "first woman to become a Supreme Court justice" or . . . only exaggerates the sorry state of affairs women have been relegated to in society. Why is this? Why haven't women been perceived as equally skilled or intelligent all along? See what I mean? These so-called advancements are nothing more than what women *should've* been recognized for all along. No, they are nothing to celebrate. The same goes with black Americans. You hear "the first black to hold this or that position," when, in reality, it is saying, "After two hundred years as a country, we're finally acknowledging that a black individual may be more qualified for the job than a white person." Rather than broadcasting these "firsts" on the news and celebrating them, we should be recognizing the ignorance society's been in for so long. I don't know about you, but when I see these types of announcements on television, I cringe with societal embarrassment.

Women in society have been perceived as "objects of possession and domination" by men for thousands of years. I've just finished reading a book by a former congresswoman from Colorado, Pat Schroeder, called *24 Years of House Work . . . and the Place Is Still a Mess,* published by Andrews McMeel Publishing, ISBN 0-8362-3 707-2. The many prejudicial incidents recounted in her memoirs of being in the

Congress, with its male superiority and chauvinism, were deplorable. And this is current stuff! Our government is one of the worst offenders because of its "patriarchal palace" mentality. Women in society, what an issue.

The Muslim countries, including Africa, commit inhumane atrocities against women in the form of forcing them to hide themselves behind veils, denying them freedoms equal to those their men enjoy and take for granted, and worst of all—the very worst atrocity of all is the physical mutilation of little girls' genitals for the sole purpose of ensuring their future husbands that they're virgins and assuring their fathers of gaining his allotment of marriage camels. This mutilation is known as FGM (Female Genital Mutilation), but in a move to make it sound less barbaric, it's commonly called female circumcision and consists of the barbaric removal of the clitoris along with the minor and major labia. The "removal" is performed by a designated woman who performs the operation as a profession. The operation is done out in the bush with a dirty razor blade when the child is around five years old. No anesthesia, no sterilization. After her remaining skin is sewn back together, a tiny hole is left—so tiny that her urine can only come out a drop at a time. The little girl's legs are then bound together and she is left to lie alone out in the bush for two weeks when she is, it is hoped, on her way to healing without massive infection. Her new "opening" will either be forced open on her wedding night by intercourse or by the husband cutting it bigger. All this horrendous mutilation of little girls is just for the sake of their father getting his count of camels for the bride price and for the husband being assured he's getting a virgin.

This came to my attention after I bought and read a book by a famous New York model who was born and raised in Somalia. Please read *Desert Flower—The Extraordinary Journey of a Desert Nomad* by Waris Dirie, published by Morrow, ISBN 0-688-15823-4.

What causes Alzheimer's disease?

It appears that the 3A's may be the cause: artificial food ingredients, aluminum, and alpha blockers in the brain. Years ago we didn't see the dementia that is so prevalent in our elderly people today because more natural ingredients were used and folks didn't reach for the roll of aluminum foil to cook and bake with. Back then, foodstuffs weren't packaged in aluminum. Watch out for aluminum combined with carbonation and acidic substances such as tomato sauce. The elements of packaging and cooking materials can transfer into the foods that they contain. Too much of any mineral can negatively affect the human physiology. An example of this is fluoride. The region in which I live has historically yielded up tons of gold. Wherever there's gold, there is an overabundance of fluoride also naturally occurring in the ground. The children in my area are getting so much fluoride in the drinking water (which comes directly from the ground wells) that their teeth are turning gray. What's scary is that that is only one noticeable result. Who knows what other effects this excessive fluoride is causing within the body. So to counter this excess, I personally have to make adjustments. Ever try looking at the shelves of toothpastes in Wal-Mart and picking out the one that doesn't have fluoride? Nada. Even the "natural" Tom's brand has put fluoride in its flavors of toothpaste. What a disappointment that was to discover. So it's off to the local health food store for a couple of tubes of Desert Essence Tea Tree Oil and Neem. I also keep a small box of baking soda in the medicine cabinet with the toothpaste. Combining these two on the toothbrush makes a wonderful way to get teeth really clean.

Advertising has a great deal to do with our lifestyle habits. One teeth-cleaning product will come out with the addition of fluoride and, before you can blink, they all have it. More is not better. Try going to the dentist and telling the hygienist that you *don't* want the fluoride treatment. That's when you witness the ugly sight of a hygienist having a nervous breakdown. You have to argue until you're blue in the face. Well . . . but . . . she's just not doing her job if she doesn't treat your teeth with fluoride. Notice how many toothpastes now have baking soda in them? Well, hello? Why not just coat your brush with the real stuff and brush? It's a heck of a lot cheaper.

Getting back to the issue: it's been proven that an excess of any mineral or element taken within the bodily system will cause some type of adverse reaction. Also, recent gene research has shown that some people are lacking an ability for the brain to maintain a path between cells that is clear of Alpha congestion. Alpha blockers are lacking. This is a rudimentary explanation of this condition and you may want to do your own research and look into it for a more technical explanation and clearer understanding. I don't know what's available on the subject yet because it's just recently been discovered.

As a footnote, aluminum has value. There are a great many uses for the foil; just don't use it to cook your food with *all* the time. I still use it for baked potatoes and I line the oven rack with it when baking something that could possibly overflow the baking dish. Remember . . . it's the *excessive* use that's the issue here.

Don't authors like Anne Rice poison society with Satan-inspired stories?

Folklore is wildly entertaining. I personally believe that her books will be classics on the subject of vampires. Many years ago I read *Interview with the Vampire* and was impressed by her descriptive writing style. The novel section of my bookshelf contains a few of her titles, including her latest, *Pandora*. Look, this is leisure reading and has great entertainment value. It's a journey into fiction and imagination. It's in no way, shape, or form associated with Satan "inspiring" her work. That's plain silly and ignorant. Just because she created a book about the devil, *Memnoch the Devil*, doesn't mean she's in cahoots with him. Actually, I found that book held more than a few interesting concepts that, in the first section of the book, actually defined Lucifer more accurately than Scripture or religious dogma does. However, when you read toward the middle, Lucifer's qualities shifted to those of Satan. All in all, though, it was an interesting book.

I write of Lucifer and Satan. And although some misguided readers think I've been chosen as the devil's advocate, the idea couldn't be further from the truth. This is America. Our constitution has gifted us all with the freedom of speech. That includes whatever we choose to write about, whatever opinions we want to express, whatever ideas we want to share with others. Anne's book *The Feast of All Saints* is about the "freed coloreds" and Creoles of New Orleans. Being rash and jumping to erroneous conclusions that are assumptions is judgmental behavior. You cannot form an intelligent overall opinion about an author unless you've read every book in his/her entire body of work. After reading one book you may have a personal opinion as to whether or not you liked it, but to make a blanket statement like the *author* herself being devil-inspired is ludicrous and doesn't show intelligence or rational thought; in fact, it verges on libel. There are authors I've read who I thought were really off-the-wall, but that doesn't mean the *author* is, just the story was. Anne Rice is a talented authoress. She has the range to be concise with a story or s-t-r-e-t-c-h it w-a-y out. She alters format and style. She is creative and skilled. Let's not associate book subject matter with the author's own identity or that of her personal muse.

What sort of ramifications are connected to the millennium bug?

This questioner is referring to the fact that computers will recognize the year 2000 as 1900. You don't need me to explain the chaos this will cause if it's not corrected in time. All you have to do is think about it for a bit. Any . . . ANY computer that uses a date will be down. Banking will be thrown into confusion and stop. Computerized cash registers won't work. Maybe gas pumps won't either. Jobs utilizing computers may come to a standstill. ATMs will be out of service. The trails one can take this down are endless. Get that stash of cash going because it may be all you'll have access to for a while. Even our local hospitals are stocking up on supplies . . . and reserve funds.

Is there a difference between God the Father and God the Creator? Two entities?

This question shows deep thought. Yes, there is a big difference between the two, yet the difference is not precisely what you had in mind. This question holds two separate concepts—that of the possibility of two male Gods and that of one being Creator. Let's look at this and sort it out. There is but one God the Father. He was Creator of *physical* aspects. There is God the Mother, the Mother Goddess Pistis Sophia who was the Creatrix of *spiritual* or nonphysical aspects. Since she emanated out of the Divine Prime Silence and created the other deities, she is the Divine Creatrix above all others. *God* created all the *physical.* The *Goddess* was the Creatrix of all *spiritual;* she breathed life into the inanimate creations of the God.

What does the world need now?

The world needs a spiritual transformation, a transcendence out of ignorance and into Acceptance and Love. The world needs to shed the ego and become selfless. People need to reopen the shut and locked doors of their minds to become as little children who are not filled with prejudice, persecution, and narrow-mindedness, but joyful with the amazing wonders of reality they then perceive with pure hearts.

The urge to "get even" is frequently a strong desire. How come this is discouraged, when the Bible says, "an eye for an eye"?

It also says, "turn the other cheek," and "'vengeance is mine,' sayeth the Lord." This is another prime example of the many inconsistencies and contradictions contained in Scripture. Even the recorded words of Christ represent inconsistencies. How about when Jesus appeared in the upper room to the apostles and told them not to touch him . . . then supposedly invited Thomas to put his hand in his side?

The spiritual concept of Acceptance rules out the "get even" idea of revenge. Revenge says: "Look at me! I can be just as unspiritual as you are! Blam! Take that!" Now isn't that something to be proud of? Revenge doesn't belong in the physical at all. Revenge is directed by self at the unspiritual actions of *self* by way of enacting the balancing of bad karma.

It could be said that we take revenge upon ourselves while neutralizing all our unspiritual acts that were committed throughout every incarnated life. To take revenge on another in the physical ensures the need to undo that act in the next life. Taking revenge only makes more karmic work for oneself down the road. Who would want to do that? So instead of looking through Scripture for valid verification to back up your wrong deeds, try looking to your own conscience.

Everyone knows the difference between right and wrong; the problem is . . . they just don't give a damn anymore. That's evidence of an all-consuming ego. It exposes the prioritized attitude and love of me, me, me. Wake up and notice that the sun doesn't rise just to shine on you alone. Vengeance? Get some smarts; that's for little people with tiny minds full of self.

Scripture says that women must be submissive to their husbands. Don't women need to get back where they belong?

This is the third way this question has been asked, so I'm going to respond in a third way. Men wrote down what they wanted and then *called* it Scripture. Men put words in the mouth of Jesus in order to give validity to their own desired position in society. It was *men* who chose the words that would comprise the official, canonical Scripture.

In response to the second half of the statement, well, women are getting back to where they belong . . . on equal footing . . . back to where they were *before* men maligned and outlawed their beautiful belief and worship of the Mother Goddess. *The Goddess has returned.* The Second Coming is not what you have envisioned it would be. You think that sounds heretical, but humanity can only be turned around through the love and gentleness of the Mother. There is nothing that can break down the hard shell covering soft human emotion and attitudes more than a mother's love. Quietly, treading on whispered footfalls, is she now walking through your world. Look right and left, and over your shoulder, before acting out an unspiritual deed. Watch your back . . . she may be standing there . . . watching you.

The response to this question takes various trails. It's taken us to the Second Coming, so I need to go into it more.

How will the Second Coming be evidenced?

Generally accepted religious belief places Jesus in the center-field position of being the focus of the First Coming. That's the "religious party line." He was supposed to represent an aspect of God (God the Son?). His appearance on earth was marked by teachings, miracles, a retinue of followers, and a highly visible *physical* presentation of self. In the spiritual realm, this event was ultimately seen with hindsight as ending up being counterproductive because of the way humanity altered and sorted out the Word of his messages and work for their own ends and formed religions from them.

Therefore, because of this human reaction, it was decided by those on the spiritual plane that the next time would have to be different. Next time, the time of the so-called Second Coming, would be manifested by the Holy Spirit (Shekinah). There would be no more miracles performed, no retinue of followers to misconstrue spoken words, no physical presentation declaring deityship, no proclamations of ego. No "I am the Goddess!" type of thing. The *Second* Coming was not going to involve the appearance of a *physical* Divine Being, but rather her *spiritual* presence. Quiet. Gentle. Like the air we breathe, clean and fresh . . . renewing. Why no miracles? Because they force belief. They are egotistical in that they demand the attention and adoration of the people. They say: "Look at me! Look what I can do! I am greatest among you!" No, no more of that this time. This time recognition must come from *within* self, not through that which is manifested without and is seeable, touchable. This time the *Spirit* will move among you, beside you, within you. Instead of "splash," it's a deep undercurrent. Instead of flashy miracles forcing belief, it is the gifting of Truth, which aware people will recognize. Instead of a retinue of inner circle followers, it is the whole of humanity who is silently and quietly touched. Instead of religions being established, *Spirituality* becomes a *living* belief and way of life. Instead of worshiping her name, truth is cherished. Instead of ego, it is love. Instead of the future . . . it is now.

All this sounds quite wonderful, yet as evidenced by the appearance and work of Jesus, segments of humanity will violently kick and buck. Detractors and skeptics filled with hatred and jealousy will abound. Religious leaders will scoff and decry while their followers become self-appointed holy vigilantes and take up the sword against the truth that the Spirit instills. Terrible false rumors will be associated with her. She will experience persecution. Patriarchal adherents will be white-knuckled with their attempt to hold firm their death grip. The ego of ethnic, gender, and social superiority will fight tooth and nail to maintain its long-held position. But despite all of these, Truth cannot be eliminated with a gun. The *Spirit* cannot be killed. The Second Coming, like Armageddon, has been grievously misconstrued. When an anticipated event has been misinterpreted as being literal instead of symbolic, no other possible scenario enters into the human Consciousness as being a probability. This, therefore, sets the mind up for a future shock when Expectation has blinded the mind to reality. As a result, the active manifestation of the expected event is not readily recognized. The mind has been preconditioned to look for signs and markers that have been misinterpreted at the outset, leaving the true aspects to manifest without note. For example, if a generally accepted facet of the Second Coming were originally misinterpreted as the Deity wearing a red robe and coming out of the sky in a blazing chariot led by legions of angels, who would recognize that same Deity who came in a purple shirt and quietly walked among you? It is the people's own preconceived notions regarding an event which allows the event to creep up and manifest without people being the wiser. I keep envisioning a cartoon that looks something like this: A massive crowd of people is looking up into a clear, blue sky. The "returned" Goddess, dressed no differently from them, taps an individual on the shoulder and asks what everyone is so excited about. The shocked person turns and says, "Why, haven't you heard? We're watching for the Second Coming!"

Is there a difference between angels and angelic beings?

This is a highly perceptual question. Angels are a spirit species separate from angelic beings. The angelic beings are those Spirits of Light who never desired to initially experience the physical after Creation. They are beings of pure spirit who are delegated to perform specific missions involving physical incarnations. Thomas, the apostle who was wrongly dubbed "Doubting" was an angelic being along with Mary Magdalene. They came as Jesus' assistant and confidante, respectively. Thomas was not a doubter, but was Jesus' advocate in that he "played" the questioner role in order to ensure the apostles' clarity of understanding whenever Jesus presented more complex concepts. Angelic beings frequently incarnate as "support" and to work in tandem with another's physical mission. The angelic beings enter the physical for spiritual purposes; the angels work on the nonphysical level. This important differentiation is why popular television programs depicting "angel" interaction with humans on earth are so misleading. They only serve to promote humanity's misconception of the true aspects of spiritual reality and the intricate working technicalities of same.

Angels work on the spiritual level. Angelic beings work in both the spiritual and physical plane. Angels do not incarnate. Angelic beings do.

A recent television movie was based on a woman who could move her Consciousness into her computer's virtual reality scenes. Is your concept of the virtual aspect of Quantum Meditation like that?

Yes, but with the exception of the "scenes" being *real* places in other actual, *existing* dimensions, where interaction is done with real people. Another correspondent likened the virtual experience of Quantum Meditation to dreaming, but it's nothing like dreaming or what some call the Dreamtime. No facets or details of the scene are skewed or illogical. Nothing is purely symbolic as a dreamscape most often presents. The meanings of events, objects, people, and conversations don't have to be analyzed as they do with dreams. In Virtual Meditation, everything is as orderly, sequential, and clear as here in the third dimension. Its position is in the cross hairs of both linear and vertical time, because it's participating in the real time of a different dimension.

Our Consciousnesses are marvels. Neuroscientists are baffled by them because they are still in the neophyte stage of trying to understand the mind's full potential. They have entire conferences devoted to the speculation of what a Consciousness is. They're still struggling over a clear and definitive definition of it. *Consciousness is the intelligent energy of the spirit.* This is why it has limitless mobility and vitality. Mobility to shift through other dimensions. Vitality of eternal life. Our little biological bodies are merely temporary casings for the spirit's Consciousness. The mechanical brain of that body houses the Consciousness of the mind. Therefore, it appears that this fact binds Consciousness to the third dimension in a highly limiting manner—not so. It's not so because Consciousness is not *dependent* on a perfectly performing brain . . . nor does it even need a body to exist within. For an example, a case in point for the first half of that statement would be an individual in a coma. This person appears to be mentally unresponsive, yet because Consciousness is the intelligent energy of the spirit, that Consciousness is vitally alive and functional on some level other than the third dimension, where the physical body lies in restful repose. The identical event happens during deep meditation, where the body rests and Consciousness is elsewhere. An example of the second half of the statement is when folks die and the spirit's Consciousness takes off to continue its existence in another vibrationary field. Consciousness is the eternal life within us. Consciousness is the individual's eternal mind. The body can be killed, but not the living mind, which is one's indestructible spirit.

It's important to not confuse Consciousness with consciousness. By this I mean the misinterpretation of Consciousness (the intelligent spirit mind energy) as being the same as consciousness (being mentally awake and aware). I believe the problem understanding this issue came when the term "unconscious" was originally used to define a state of mental unawareness. This led to the idea that "being unconscious" (such as during sleep or a coma) meant to define a state where one's Consciousness was not viable. This just isn't so. What it does mean is that when one is in a state of being unconscious, they are simply not mentally "aware" or "awake." This meaning of unconscious should've, from the outset, been given a separate term that more accurately defined the condition of being *un-awake*. An unconscious individual is simply *unawake* to the third-dimensional present. That same Consciousness may be vitally awake and alive in another dimension that is finer than the tactile third one. Evidence of this is proven out through out-of-body experiences manifested during surgical procedures. The surgical team will swear that the patient is "unconscious," but, in reality, the individual's perceptive mind is clearly conscious on another dimension while it watches, hears, and smells everything transpiring in the operating theater. So you see, the individual was not unconscious at all. He/she was simply physically unawake. *Physically* "unawake" in the third dimension— *spiritually* "awake" in the third dimension. Activity of the Consciousness is not dependent on being physically awake. The activity of Consciousness is not dependent on a mechanized brain.

Okay. Going back to the main issue of this question, we can now understand how Consciousness can enter various dimensions of Quantum Meditation and have virtual experiences there while the body rests comfortably on the soft futon in the family room. To another individual walking into that same living room, the reclining person will only appear to be unconscious, but oh no. Oh no, not at all. The resting person is only *unawake* to the new visitor in the *physical* because his/her *aware/awake* consciousness is elsewhere. The Consciousness is our ticket to everywhere. It is what empowers and facilitates our exploration of reality . . . all of reality.

When I wrote about this issue in *Fireside,* I received countless letters asking if I were going to write a book about future visits with No-Eyes through the virtual experiences of Quantum Meditation, as I did before with her. Readers were requesting that I share these with them. I gave this a great deal of thought and, although I did consider doing this at one time I'm more inclined to leave it alone. The concept of one's Consciousness having "real" and "actual" experiences in other dimensions is too new to people. And although these experiences are just as real and bona fide as events experienced here in the third dimension, I was not comfortable enough with society's comprehension to publicly detail these. You have to understand that, generally, people's mind-set is too linear, too bound to the "touchable" aspects of their world. It's extremely difficult for folks to fathom that the aspects of all other dimensional realities are just as touchable to one's Consciousness, just as *real*. It is the unlimited capabilities of the spirit's intelligent Consciousness that make it so.

What are spiritual gifts or talents?

Contrary to general perception, spiritual gifts have nothing to do with abilities associated with the "New Age" genre of concepts. Spiritual gifts and talents are innate qualities of a developed spirit, which include compassion, selflessness, helpfulness, empathy, clear perception and comprehension, insightfulness, the quality of unconditionality (nonjudgment) associated with attitudes and actions, having the inner Knowing, gentleness, tolerance, Acceptance, etc.

When the phrase "spiritual gifts" is heard, most folks automatically think of the workings of mentalism, such as psychokinesis or precognition, yet true gifts of the spirit are behavioral spiritual graces. They are spiritual attitudes, thought, behavior, and perception. Few view these as gifts. Even fewer count them among their daily blessings.

I've heard all sorts of different stories regarding your husband's death. I'm sure this is a painful subject, but maybe you could, just this once, set the record straight.

In deference to my daughters, I've purposely avoided addressing this issue. I, too, have heard all manner of stories, some quite outlandish, and have anguished over whether it was wiser to let the stories go or, like you say, "set the record straight." As with all rumors, the more they are allowed to wander about, the more preposterous they grow. So be it, because I've decided to respect the memory of my daughters' father by not writing any more about him. It's time the issue was put to rest.

I'm confused about the coexistence of our guides and power animals.

First of all, you don't want to equate spiritual guides with power animals. One has intelligence, while the other produces an "influence" from its inherent energy. There is a huge difference between the two. I understand that your intent wasn't to exactly equate them, but you were coming from the angle of them possibly being counterproductive to each other. The spiritual guide is a spirit *intelligence* like a guardian angel or angelic being who assists you while you travel along your life journey. A power animal is nothing more than a life form that emanates specific *influences* upon other living organisms, including receptive humans. So the difference between the two is that of intelligence vs. influencing energies.

It's important to understand the priority here. Power animals can be perceived as being what some people from many different cultures call totems, yet every living force upon this planet has its own particular influential aspect that can affect other living forces. This fact is directly associated with the nature of the Great Web of Life. All the different species of trees and flowers emit their own unique influences upon life. Gems, rocks, and minerals do too. Not only animals send off this special energy, but birds and fish do the same. We are all connected by the living Consciousness of the Universal Mind. And because of this Great Web of Life that we're all a part of, we are affected by all aspects of that life. If you want to focus on power animals, focus on self. Humans are the greatest power animals walking upon this planet. We have the powerful energy to change the entire world through spiritual thought and behavior. Our influence can be more effective than any other life form on earth. To center on only an animal as having this influencing power is being incredibly narrow-minded. The tiniest alpine flower growing deep in the sun-dappled forest floor sends out an aura of energy. Let's not ignore the fragile yet powerful influences that abound in our world in deference to the few that are "chosen" or have been singled out as being commonly preferred. Look around you. Everywhere, everywhere there are powerful influences waiting to be recognized, utilized, and cherished.

Is it wrong to seek out help or answers to everyday questions and problems from a power animal?

Rather you enjoy and benefit from their natural *influences* while leaving life's answers to that which dwells within self.

What religion do you belong to?

The Divine Trinity's. What "religion" is that? Remember, all religions have been conceived by human minds; so why would I follow human-generated dogma when everyone is already connected to the Divine? When one is open to the Knowing of the Divine, human religion is then clearly perceived as being extremely gray in color . . . sullied, if you will. It's as a shell of dogma containing emptiness, no beautiful divine life and fullness. It lacks the purity of the Truth. It is adulterated with modifications, perceptual alterations, deletions, and self-serving dogma—even egotistical and judgmental. The totality of the Trinity's conceptual spirituality is none of these. Religion is not within my realm of personal interest . . . Spirituality is.

People give their churches money to assist in maintaining their ministries, so why wouldn't it be right to give people money who help through the use of their psychic gifts?

Well, let's get down to the nitty-gritty then. Churches claim to do God's work. But what is God's work? Isn't it practicing Unconditional Goodness? Being nonjudgmental? Living in Acceptance of others? Following the tenets of the Ten Commandments? For this we need churches? If one of the deities of the Holy Trinity manifested in the physical, do you really believe she or he would need your money? What would be expected of you would be *spiritual* gifts (offerings) of spiritual behavior directed toward your sisters and brothers. The Divine Aspects of the Trinity need no money! What would they do with your worthless money? Yet these little people creating and heading up churches in God's name continually preach the "spiritual rightness" of your weekly contributions; in fact some of them get so bold as to demand them and are arrogant enough to threaten the faithful with hellfire and damnation if they don't comply by doing their monetary duty toward their church. When Jesus walked this earth, he did not build a building and call it a church. He did not preach in a building and demand (or even request) money. Yet without these, look what his ministry accomplished. Money is in no way an associated element of spreading the "Word." If Jesus could do it without money, why can't all these preachers? And did Jesus charge people for the healings he performed? The "insights" he freely shared? What was his fee for raising Lazarus from the dead? What did he charge the bride and groom for changing water into wine at their wedding? Jeez, people, go a little deeper with your thinking. You keep trying to justify your actions with false logic. When in doubt, just ask yourself, "What would Jesus do?"

Now I can hear some of you think that I'm sitting here being the pot calling the kettle black. Huh? But wait a minute, the books I write are an expense for my publisher to make. Any book published has created an expense attached with it because it is a physical *product*. It is that product that has been bought because the buyer chose to. Now . . . when I *talk* to folks who come to a book signing, I do not charge them for talking to them. I do not ask a fee for meeting with someone. In my daily life I am frequently asked questions by local folks who recognize me in the market or on the street and I freely give conversation. One correspondent made a sarcastic comment about this issue in one of her letters. It seemed that she assumed that an author who had seventeen books published was rolling in dough. But that's not good logic when you know that only bestsellers bring in the big bucks. I could have a hundred books published and unless they (at least one) get on the *New York Times* bestsellers list, then it's no different from being like everyone else who has to tightly budget in order to stretch the money. So back to the beginning . . . a *physical product* that takes money to create requires money to purchase it, and a *spiritual gift* requires *nothing* in return . . . not even a thank you. A spiritual gift is not truly spiritual if *anything* is expected in return for it. If a preacher has a calling to preach, let him support himself with a nine-to-five outside job; then he's free to preach all he wants on Sunday, or Saturday, or whenever he has free time. Nobody paid to hear Jesus preach; why should a mere human expect more? I'm sure it's not because he thinks his words are worth more.

Another rationale I hear regarding the money thing is that "I deserve it." I hear "I have this God-given talent," "I spend my time helping others," "I deserve to be compensated." Am I mistaken or were there an awful lot of "I's" in those statements? Sounded extremely egocentric to me. And what is this "I *deserve"* baloney? What makes people think they're so great, or wonderful, or talented that they deserve something? We were all created equal, remember? We all have unique skills. Those are divine *gifts* for heaven's sake, gifts! Since when are we so high-and-mighty *deserving* of something special just because we've been given a gift? Since when does receiving a gift make people puffed up with egomaniacal self-worth instead of simply feeling . . . grateful? Hello? Last time I looked, spiritual gifts were given for the express *purpose* of being *shared.* Final word on this . . . it's not *giving* if payment is expected. It's not *spiritual* work if physical recompense is demanded. *All* God's creation "deserves" to freely benefit from divine gifts . . . not the giver.

Do human spirits ever get reincarnated into animal bodies?

Nope. However, your human Consciousness can *experience* the Consciousness of any animal it chooses to visit.

I don't understand why the belief in reincarnation isn't more widespread when it's been accepted by so many cultures and as far back in time as the ancient Egyptians?

Although your question didn't directly specify the Egyptian's belief in this concept, the rest of your letter did. I need to point out that the Egyptians did not believe in reincarnation. They believed in *resurrection* and the immortality of the soul. This is why they built pyramids containing the deceased's personal possessions and material goods such as foodstuffs, writings from the *Book of the Dead* engraved on the tomb walls, boats, beds, statues of Selket (the protector), furniture, boxes of jewelry, etc. Their belief was that you could take it all with you, and their tombs bore this ideology out. Although the concept of reincarnation has indeed been around since ancient times, the Egyptians were one culture that had a varied perspective of the afterlife.

As to why the concept of reincarnation isn't more widely accepted, you have to consider that the religion of North America is predominately Judeo/Christian. You most likely wouldn't even think to ask this question if you lived in India, where the concept is an inherently accepted way of life. What's important here is not why people believe or disbelieve in a particular afterlife scenario, but to have Acceptance of the great diversity of spiritual beliefs. If we're comfortable in what we personally believe, then it doesn't matter who else accepts that specific concept. When our lives are devoid of this beautiful Acceptance, we experience spiritual negativity invading our world in the way of judgments, condemnations, and persecutions such as society witnesses coming from the Christian fundamentalists and Religious Right groups. When a religious sect has no acceptance of another's belief (or fails to recognize the *right* to believe as one wishes) then we observe this sect attempting to dominate and control society through various means, such as affecting government laws, boycotting businesses, exposing the private affairs of individuals, destroying lives and people's right to privacy and constitutional freedoms. Spiritual beliefs are sacred to every individual. They are too sacred and beautifully precious to be dirtied by turning them into a tyrannical force used to harm others. Spiritual respect, tolerance, and Acceptance are what please God. Anything else is spiritual arrogance and superiority.

You once said that Jesus was on earth as a child. If he's still here, once he's an adult will he manifest the miracles of ancient times and teach like before?

Miracles are not a facet of this modern-day event. Faith is. Presently Jesus is not in the physical.

Your conversation in Fireside *regarding Consciousness was fascinating and caused me to think that past-life aspects can be found within the individual's own subconscious.*

Well sure, it's all there because the Consciousness is the same as one's spirit totality. Normally the only door open is that of *present-day* awareness. How could we mentally function properly if we had a continual awareness of all our lives since Creation? Past-life regression does not send us back through time, but deeply into the "within" of our Consciousness, where all experiences remain in eternal memory. I'm pleased that you understood this concept from the book's conversation. Consciousness is wildly fascinating. It's like physically journeying through the Internet or, to put it more accurately, carrying around your own set of ancient, historical records. Everyone you once were is up there in your Consciousness. This is why I coined the "carry-over soul" concept. It's the soul's (consciousness) *memory* of other lives that can bleed through, or carry over, into this present experiential state of current awareness. Who you are today can be an actual composite of all the who's you ever were. Your likes and dislikes, attitudes you've no explanation for, the type of receptivity you sense when meeting strangers, etc., are all effects directly resulting from your composite life experiences.

Who am I?

You are a splendorous, luminous spirit borrowing the shell of a physical body for a very small measure of time.

Who are you really?

I am a splendorous, luminous spirit borrowing the shell of a physical body for a very small measure of time.

Will you ever travel about the country and speak?

As I stated earlier, I've just a couple more books planned before I wrap up the "messenger" phase of my mission, then I begin my "physical" mission of the Magdalene Abbey (a women's spiritual sanctuary and safe house for women escaping domestic abuse) and other types of work. Writing down the messages was only the first part of my work and, when those are done . . . I won't be. Then I'll have work in the physical to attend to. As to traveling about the country, that depends on how the second phase of my purpose unfolds.

Do you foresee a women's religion manifesting in the future?

In the future? It's already here. It's been here for a long time, only its not a religion, it's a Feminine Spirituality. What I do foresee happening is that it will blossom up out of the underground and openly flourish in the future. I see it reviving the strength of the whole Trinity, in which the forgotten and ignored Goddesses of Mother Sophia and Shekinah (the Holy Spirit) will regain their rightful, sacred status and be just as revered as the singled-out male God has been. It will be a woman's faith of the soul, not a religion. The current man-made, gender-selective spiritual ideologies and their ultimate manifestations of multiple forms of patriarchal religions with their male deities and resulting dogmas designed for the manipulation and suppression of women have finally run their antiquated courses and will no longer remain the collective, dominating spiritual force in the enlightened millenniums. This definitive shift has been silently building and gaining strength in the last decades, while women have been silently returning to the worship of the Mother Goddess Aspect of the Trinity. However, many of these women have not completely understood their strong attraction toward this inherent devotion to a feminine deity and have, therefore, manifested it through a benign and religiously acceptable manner by worshipping Mother Mary. But Mary will not be women's future deity focus for the expression of Feminine Spirituality. The choice will be for the Female Aspects of the true Trinity—Pistis Sophia, the Goddess of Faith and Wisdom; and Shekinah, the Goddess of Living Spirituality.

What I also foresee regarding this developing Feminine Spirituality is a manifestation of *true* worship. By this I mean a purely *spiritual* one that is devoid of physical icons, statues, and the other religious accouterments with which the current religions are overflowing with. A true spiritual belief is one of the *spirit,* where the image of the deity will be different for everyone and held within self, while her essence is externally evidenced through the living of Acceptance, Unconditional Goodness, and tolerance. Places of worship will be meditative sanctuaries offering spiritual respite, where the faithful can quietly reflect and contemplate. They will be places where the faithful don't necessarily "worship" in the usual sense, but rather "touch" and spiritually "connect" with the deity in a highly personal manner. These will not be as the churches of today, for they will not have ministers, priests, priestesses, or spiritual leaders of any kind. There will be no dogma formulated nor services held. There will be no women teachers nor human representatives of the Goddesses. The faithful of Feminine Spirituality will enter a sanctuary whenever they wish and, in complete silence, allow the serenity of its tranquil and loving aura to permeate their beingness. There will be no special prayers to repeat verbatim, no prescribed ceremonies, no songs, no ritual objects, nor obligations of monetary tithing. The Feminine Spirituality of the new millennium will finally be one of pure spirit.

The difference between the two gender spiritualities is that men are drawn to the strictures of formulated *dogma* and confinements of the letter of the law, while women are moved by the *inspiration* of the spirit of the law felt within themselves. Today's religions were all generated by men who defined and outlined the specific tenets of the belief systems they created. This situation left women confined within constrictive barriers that kept the full-blown expression of their innate spirituality in a tightly bound wrap of written texts, manipulative tenets, and controlling dogma. Like the torturous Asian custom of binding women's feet to make them misshapened into tiny, lotus-like forms that pleased men but pained and hobbled the woman, today's patriarchal religions hobble the feminine spirit within their *spiritual* bindings. But the reality of this state of affairs is that we've now approached a time of developmental growth, when Spirituality has moved along a cusp of transition to mature into a more personal and individualized relationship with the Divine. We're seeing that, being separate children of God, we all have unique and separate relationships with the Divine Mother and Father; therefore, our expression of that bond is different for everyone and cannot be confined to defined laws of worship or behavior. Every child shows love and appreciation of his/her parent in manners that are uniquely characteristic to the innate behavioral elements—the expression of that emotional sensitivity is not the same for each sibling. So too have we reached a time when women are coming to realize that the expressively constrictive religions of men are not fulfilling their inherent need to communicate with the Divine on a more personal manner which is aligned with their feminine nature—a gentle and sensitive manner. The days of *faith* being *fear*-generated from the patriarchy's manipulative use of fire-and-brimstone threats are waning and being replaced with faith being generated from spirits being filled with divine love. From fear . . . to love. It is the difference of "faith through control" and a "faith through Spirit indwelling." It is the difference between showing faith because of fear versus the expression faith out of love. One is a forced faith; the other is natural and voluntary. That is the prime difference between the *religion* of men and the *spirituality* of women. Our current position on the cusp of spiritual transition serves to awaken women to the rightness of their own inherent nature for spiritual expression and fulfillment.

Was Selket an Egyptian Goddess or just an idealized symbol of protection?

Selket is indeed a real Goddess whose purpose is directed toward protecting and guiding the newly dead's spirit journey into the afterlife by way of maintaining the *order* and *custom* of same. Above the Trinity is the Primal Divine Source; beneath the Trinity are lesser divinities. All of mythology is not myth.

It was a kick to see you'd written an entry on Hampton Roads' website. Welcome to technology!

Ah, that was way back on the first of August, 1998, and I'm not really using the Internet—a friend of mine showed me Hampton Roads' site and asked if I wanted to write something. After hesitating a bit, I sat down and made an entry. Guess I blew away a lot of people by sticking my finger through the techno black hole for a nanosecond. Sorry if that misled you into thinking I've taken a fancy to cyberspace . . . I haven't. My only experience with a computer is being barely savvy enough to open up my manuscript file, write what I want to say, save it, print it, close the file, and shut down the computer . . . *after* Sally has done all the file creation and formatted set-up work for the manuscript. What I've observed about the Internet and its message boards is that unscrupulous people have their egos empowered and energized through anonymity. They say whatever cruel thing they want and don't have to take one iota of responsibility for it. They can pretend to be one person or post as twenty people. I saw this happen after I posted on Hampton Roads' message board a couple of times and then some people got on and began saying really hateful things about me—even about Bill's death—even about my readers. Because of this, I felt that, by my participation, I'd ruined the site for my readers, who were doing such a great job in sharing ideas and growing by tossing spiritual concepts back and forth. After the personal attacks began, I then posted that I'd not be posting any more. Then someone posted as Sally and then as Mary Summer Rain. I suggested to my readers that they practice the Wisdom of Silence and not be drawn to "engage" these meanspirited individuals. To my surprise, the message board regulars found out that, though they desperately wanted to vent their anger at the perpetrators, they utilized Wisdom and remained off the board. They felt the power of Silence. The hate messages got so bad that Hampton Roads had to begin deleting all the vindictive entries. Slowly the board returned to normal after the hate-filled individual could find no victims to hook. I perceive this electronic communication as being a much-favored venue for human monsters to use because they can vent their vindictiveness and cruelty with impunity—having no identifying face to present to their listeners, they sit behind their mask of anonymity and wallow in the fact that they don't have to shoulder one speck of personal responsibility for what they write or for whatever false identity or name they borrow. I'm really not into this venue for communication because it's shown to be full-to-bursting with unscrupulous individuals.

What do you think about the controversy over prayers in schools?

Not much. There is supposed to be a concept called the "separation of church and state," which I currently observe society attempting to cloud through a multitude of ways. School is academics. Church is religion. This idea of incorporating religion in public schools in the form of prayer is one that can only lead to further societal discord. Haven't we experienced enough mudslinging and judgmental actions from the Moral Majority and Religious Right in our society? Do they even have to invade our children's right to experience an education without their influence?

World-over, beliefs in deities are widely varied. A certain percentage of the population has no such belief. By attempting to interject prayer in schools, we completely ignore the sensitivities of atheistic children. Religion belongs in churches, synagogues, mosques, etc., because true Spirituality is a highly personal matter that dwells within each individual's being. It doesn't have to be publicized nor verbalized in a mandatory manner to maintain its validity.

There is another side to this coin. Attending a Catholic school from grades one through eleven, I was expected to join the class in reciting prayers at the beginning of each morning and afternoon session. This became routine and rote, mouthing words while thinking of other things like your next hour's test, your girlfriend, or the upcoming dance. Prayer is supposed to be prayer, a sincere expression of the heart—not routine and thoughtless rote. Prayer in schools will not uplift mood nor improve behavior. It will amount to nothing more meaningful to children than reciting the Pledge of Allegiance or the multiplication tables.

I've attended quite a few forums to hear authors speak and have felt no compunction about paying the attendance fee. Why do you feel this still isn't right for you?

I guess I'm not in their league, because it remains a fact that it still strongly goes against my grain. In all good conscience I can't and will not bring myself to do that. Why in the world would I expect anyone to pay to hear *me* talk? Who am I that folks should pay to hear? Besides, I doubt that many people would attend. I have no official credentials. I'm not a Ph.D. whose credentials could demand an honorarium or any sort of recompense.

Just recently I heard a business associate tell me that because of the technicalities involved in putting on major events, the main organization that invited the various speakers have to charge the attendees in order to meet expenses. The organizers get a portion of the fee and the speakers get a portion. Well I understand the need for the organizers to meet expenses, but why do the speakers need to make money too? This business associate also told me that, by having the attendees pay to hear a speaker, they're, in essence "investing in that speaker's career and continued works." Well I have a big problem with that because I believe that if a speaker's worth his/her salt, why the need for others to invest in that individual? I don't want people investing in me or my work. What for? Maybe I'm just being dense, but I really don't see how attendees' fees are an *investment* or *help* for the speaker's work.

My view of this entire issue is a panoramic one—seeing it not as a small segment of "singular speaking engagements," but these being only a small fragment of the *big picture*. Whenever my perspective appears to be at hard odds with society's general viewpoint, I always fall back on asking myself, "What would Jesus do?" So regarding this issue, I see the big picture as symbolizing the behavioral difference between the temple priests and that of Jesus. There is no room to invent rationalized reasons for being paid for the sharing of spiritual concepts/philosophies or the teaching of methodologies that develop same. Think about this: would the work and words of Jesus have been more valuable to the world if his followers had "invested" money or more of their time in him? Get real.

If a soul, through past memories, feels that commandments have been violated in many earthly lives, can it be a completed spirit?

Yes, as long as those violations were balanced out through karmic experiences. Don't forget, transgressions can be balanced in any dimension, in any vibrational frequency of existence.

In Daybreak *you were asked if a man was a completed soul even though he did nothing "special" in his life. Can you elaborate on what makes a completed soul?*

I believe the question you're referring to was from a man who felt his friend never actualized any big accomplishments in his life and my response was that this friend had made his *entire* life one big accomplishment through the continual works of Unconditional Goodness. My point was to not be selective about that which you term an accomplishment, but rather make one's whole life a spiritual accomplishment.

To elaborate on what a completed soul is would turn the simplistic concept into a complexity of too many unnecessary words and trailing ideas. Let's keep this simple, okay? *A completed spirit is one that has balanced out all negative behavior.* If you envision the soul as being a "scale," then a completed spirit would be a scale in perfect balance, without being tipped down on the negative side.

How does one concentrate on one's purpose for returning?

This is another way of asking how one identifies purpose. Generally, spirits incarnate *for the purpose of balancing out negative actions performed in previous lives.* Most often, that singular reason is why one takes on another life experience. *That* is their purpose. What concentration does that need?

It is the human ego that turns the simplicity of "purpose" into complexity. The ego refuses to believe a purpose can be as simple as being a good person, but rather is of the opinion that one needs to attain some type of "greatness" in life. Phooey! The problem is humankind's incredibly skewed idea of "greatness." Just as people don't know what real power is, true greatness is overlooked in favor of an overblown perception of what a true "accomplishment" is. Generally, folks think the intent of purpose means being a great teacher, stateswoman, leader, or healer. That's baloney. Spiritual purpose has nothing at all to do with society's perception of greatness because society's definition is far different than the Divine's. The Trinity's idea of greatness has no ego associated with it. The individual who gives of oneself in a completely selfless manner is exhibiting greatness. The individual who practices Unconditional Goodness is actively carrying out her/his purpose in life. Make your entire life your "purpose" rather than throwing away valuable time looking for it. One's purpose is like a mist that envelops self rather than a singular mystical pool one must discover.

Can you elaborate on the meaning of "go within?"

There is no elaborating with this because it simply means to *think for self*. You have the answers within your own Consciousness because that Consciousness is, in reality, the totality of your spirit. By mentally going within, you activate connections to pathways leading to the accumulated information your spirit holds—knowledge gained not only from former incarnations, but most importantly, knowledge from experiential times spent in all other dimensions and vibrational fields. *You* hold The Knowing.

How to make these connections? Through quiet time. You don't even need to meditate, just get away from the noise and hectic pace of life and get some precious solitude so you can hear yourself think, so you can hear the whispers of your spirit's Consciousness that flow back to you in clear communication. If you're searching for *spiritual* knowledge and truths, you have to look to the *spirit* of self rather than within the material world.

Some can't quiet their thoughts enough to meditate. If you can't meditate in the conventional way, how else can you get in touch with God?

Where is it written that meditation is the singular way to the Divine? There is no specific "term" of communication methodology. Even if it were written down somewhere, it would be wrong. Meditation is only one of a multitude of ways. How about prayer? How about just "talking" to God? How about just *thinking* of the Divine? How about getting some solitude by sitting in an empty church or park, by going fishing, or putting on headphones and playing soft music or nature sounds? Meditation is great, but it is not "the" great connector to the Divine Minds in lieu of the many other methods.

Why is it so complicated to understand dream symbols? Why not clearer messages from the spirit?

Symbols are images. Images are more readily recalled upon awakening than precise words comprising long messages. If you've ever been given a specific word or name in a dream, you've also probably had a difficult time remembering it when you woke up. Think how frustrating it would be to have to recall entire messages of specific wording. The symbols are not that hard to understand. Once you know that "water" is associated with "spiritual" aspects, then dreams involving water will naturally be directly connected to the spiritual facet of your life. All it takes is a bit of overall associative study to get the general picture of how these symbols work.

What is your current relationship with your daughters?

Though they've not come right out and requested that I not talk about them any more in the books, I personally want to respect their complete privacy from now on. Our relationship is good. They are leading busy, productive lives.

What did Jesus mean when he said, "The way to the Father is through me?"

Jesus used the word "Father" because the religions of his time had turned patriarchal and equated their God to a male entity—father. Most of Jesus' messages were meant to be taken by the "spirit" of his word, not the letter. When he said, "through *me*," he didn't literally mean through his persona of Jesus, but through the "spirit" of what he represented—*The Way*. His statement means this: the way to the Divine is through spiritual behavior.

Jesus said, "In my Father's house are many mansions." Is he referring to the many spiritual levels?

Yes.

Did Jesus fulfill the messiah prophesy mentioned in Genesis?

For some inexplicable reason, the life of Jesus appears to be the only one present-day religions care to recognize and equate to the messiah of Scripture when, throughout multicultural history, many such individuals *preceded* him and fulfilled ancient, messianic prophecies by living spiritual lives and exhibiting the same experiential events of virgin births, performance of miracles, spiritual teachings, persecution, crucifixion, and resurrection. Jesus was only one of many who could be said to have fulfilled the prophesied elements of Scripture's messiah.

St. Paul said, "Salvation by faith alone apart from works." Define the faith he is referring to.

You folks are wrongly perceiving me as a biblical scholar; however, you must keep in mind that all quotations in the Bible aren't necessarily accurate. Some are "misquotes" and some were never even said by the individual attributed to saying them. In other words, words were put into the mouths of apostles and others when canonical Scripture was assembled by the newborn Christianity's founding fathers. This is so important to keep in mind because it appears that the Bible is perceived as the ultimate word carved in stone. Well yes, that is the perception, but carved by *whom?*

Now that we have that aspect said, let's return to the quotation that's been attributed to St. Paul. What "faith" is he referring to? Belief. Trust. Confidence. Staying away from the temptation of doubt.

In the Scriptures, John the Baptist baptized Jesus. What was the point? Was it relevant to that time only?

During that ancient time, the ceremony of baptism was utilized as a symbol of *following* the spiritual Way that Jesus brought to the people. What it represented was one's desire to "accept" the Way of Jesus' messages. Today the acceptance of that Way within our hearts is not the same as the ceremonial intent of baptism (erasing Original Sin). We accept the spiritual Way. In reality, no one needs a ceremony in order to validate Acceptance.

What did the scriptures mean when stating, "Jesus ascended to Heaven?"

I don't know because nobody actually saw him ascend anywhere. It was assumed that he did. Some *said* they witnessed this, but they didn't. After all, how else could his vanished corpse be explained? Be careful. Scripture is loaded with like assumptions and rationales devised to "fix" inconsistencies.

If we question Christianity, will we be damned?

Wait a minute. Exactly what precise "term" did Jesus confine his messages within? Where in scripture did Jesus specifically call his teachings "Christianity"? He didn't, did he? He put no term, no religious name on his messages—men did. After all, Jesus was Jewish! Men created Christianity. Jesus brought the *Word of The Way,* not Christianity. We are to follow the *Spirit* Word and The Way, not the letter of man-made laws and dogma. We are to follow *his* example, not man-made ceremonial rites and self-created tenets. See the big difference? There's Christianity and then there's christianity. One equates with the *behavioral* example of Jesus; the other represents men's idea of a religion. What makes you think that following the example of Jesus' life and words will damn one if they also don't also follow man-made laws and strictures of a religion? It doesn't make sense because, in practice, one is in clear opposition to the other.

If Christianity is false, why has it endured for two thousand years?

This question is asked under a premise of false logic. Endurance doesn't prove Truth. Satanism has existed since recorded history. So has atheism. What of Islam? Judaism? The theory of evolution? According to your basic premise, we should still be believing that the world is flat because that ideology was a firm belief ever since people first gave a considered thought to the shape of their world.

If Christianity remained true to Jesus' intent to follow the *spirit* of his messages and living example, then it would never have become a religion in the first place. But it was men's *egos* that bastardized the beautiful and gentle messages of Jesus into a conglomerate of unyielding dogmas and church rules, all neatly boxed in by the threat of damnation. Christianity is a religion, not The Way of Spirituality that Jesus endeavored to bring to the world.

Is there an "angel" of the Virgin Mary?

No.

You've stated that one's spiritual Advisor could be either male or female. When an Advisor represents the opposite sex of our earthly body, could that influence sexual preference? For example, homosexuality?

Nada. Nyet. Nope. This question combines two concepts. Let's take one at a time.

Spiritual Advisors are, first and foremost, spirits. Being such, they are, in reality, hermaphroditic in their essence of beingness because they are a *composite* vibration of their experiential dual-gender manifestations. Gender-wise, they are neutral. They do not influence a human toward any type of gender-specific sexual behavior in any way. They are *spiritual* guides. The sole reason people have to attach a specific gender with their guide is for the sake of deepening the sense of personal relatedness. Therefore, the Advisor can present a mental or emotional sense of gender to the individual. For this purpose, some Advisors will find it advantageous to present as males, others as female.

Now, homosexuality. I already addressed this issue in a former question. You may want to go back if you missed it in the first reading (page 88). To recap the essence of this issue, sexual preference or lifestyle has no bearing whatsoever on one's level of spirituality or acceptance by the Divine Trinity unless an individual is sexually abusive to another or involved with children. Jesus loved everyone. Love is love. Love . . . is . . . Love. That's what he taught. The current society loves to persecute others and has an obsession with finger pointing. It loves to judge others in order to elevate self. Ego is ruling lives here. Ego is causing the chaos.

Why did Jesus rebuke Martha and praise Mary Magdalene during the famous biblical meal?

The famous biblical meal? There were many biblical meals, some famous and many others that were never included in Scripture. You may be referring to the meal in which Jesus offered bread and wine with the words "This is my body and blood," and Mary snickered. He then rebuked Martha for being offended and aghast at Mary's seemingly disrespectful reaction. The reality of this particular situation is that Magdalene was the confidante of Jesus and knew that a great deal of his actions and words were symbology. Jesus had confided to her that the simplicity of the people's minds required symbols in order to attain understanding. The true intended meaning of the "body and blood" statement was not to copy the *ceremony,* but to *take unto self* the "spirit" of his life example and messages. He never meant to literally drink his blood in the form of wine or eat his body in the form of bread. Mary knew this and, at times, was embarrassed by how Jesus' messages had to be so simplistically conveyed. Jesus thoroughly understood Mary's knee-jerk reaction to such childish symbology because she was a highly intelligent individual who needed no such images or symbols to comprehend his messages. So then, Jesus ended up rebuking Martha, who misunderstood Mary's reaction.

Another famous dinner this questioner may have been referring to was when Jesus was invited to dine at the house of the sisters Martha and Mary of *Bethany.* Mary felt Martha was being rude by shooting question after question at their honored guest and Mary chastised Martha for acting in such a disrespectful manner. In turn, Martha snapped back at Mary. It was then that Jesus rebuked Martha for not understanding Mary's point of view. I've brought this specific dinner into the response because Scripture has a tendency to intermix the identities of Mary Magdalene with that of Mary of Bethany (the prostitute). Whenever the name of Mary is referred to in the Bible, many readers assume the identity is that of Magdalene. Mary of Bethany was the prostitute, not Magdalene. Mary of Bethany had a sister, Martha. Magdalene was an only child.

Jesus drove demons out of a man and into sheep, which then went over a cliff. How did one individual acquire so many demons?

I suppose by leaving self open for such. What is a demon anyway? I see their activity manifesting in a multitude of ways in society. The act of voluntarily suppressing spiritual truths can be caused by a demon. Intolerance can be caused by a demon. Ego, too. Look about and be aware. Observe the high level of negativity evidenced in the world. Hatred. War. The finger pointing of religious leaders. Desire for supremacy. Elitist attitudes. Sanctimonious behavior. The world is rife with it.

How did the demons recognize Jesus and his authority?

Demons are spirits, are they not? Don't you think they could recognize a highly developed spirit? Don't you think the aura of Jesus would be blinding to them?

What happened to the demons after the sheep died?

Well their existence was forced out of the three-dimensional reality for a time. If the physical bodies they inhabited were no longer viable, they look about for others to manifest in. It would be like moving from one house to another—more like the activity of squatters.

If these demons knew who Jesus was, why didn't they convert to God's side?

I'd like to say "stupidity." Clearly they believe they have great power in their purpose, which is to draw people away from God. With that purpose in mind, we can see why they don't convert. They obviously believe their strength is at least equal to God's, if not actually stronger.

Lazarus was raised by Jesus after days of being dead and was never publicly accorded special status because of his resurrection. Is Jesus the source of worship because he rose from the dead?

You can't compare the two instances and conceptualize them as being equal. Lazarus was raised from the dead through the influence of *another*—Jesus. Jesus allegedly rose *himself* from the dead. At least that's the party line on it.

Yes, Christianity, particularly the Catholic religion, is

based on the foundational premise of Jesus' resurrection. However, as I've outlined in previous responses, there have been many spiritual individuals throughout ancient history whose lives have included a virgin birth, spiritual teachings, perception and reception as the prophesied messiah; endured persecution and a crucifixion; and manifested a resurrection. Jesus was the *last* individual in a long line of predecessors to do the same. Most religions have a "savior" behind them.

Do you feel a need to debunk Christianity and conventional religion?

I find your choice of words revealing. "Debunk" as opposed to "expose" facts. The only "need" I feel compelled to satisfy is that of carrying out my mission to bring some measure of reality back into Spirituality. I have no vendetta against organized religion and certainly don't feel compelled to waste my time debunking man-made religions, because, upon observation of their precepts and the behavior of their faithful, they debunk themselves far better than I ever could. Jesus taught Acceptance. They teach and display intolerance. Jesus taught unity. They teach supremacy and elitism. Jesus taught equality, while their dogma is separatist. Jesus taught love, while they exhibit judgment, criticism, persecution, and condemnation. I could continue this for ten more pages, but don't want to. You get the point. Religions debunk themselves by not being completely aligned with The Way Jesus came to show.

We have a concern for your well-being because you antagonize religion. Why do you place yourself in harm's way by doing so?

Mmm, what did your question just reveal to you? Why or how could religion and its spiritual faithful be a *threat* to anyone? Are judgment, and retaliation, and intolerance, and persecution "religious" attitudes? Where is religion's love? Where is its acceptance of others as Jesus taught? Mmmm? Where is its "turn the other cheek" behavior? Is religion so unsure of itself that it must resort to defensive, retaliatory measures to ensure its validity and solid ground? If a religion is true, nothing can threaten it. So where's the harm for me? Identify the source of this harm you speak of. Since when does *The Way of Jesus' Spirituality* cause another harm or instill the sense of threat? It DOESN'T! Therefore, what "way" are religions following? Remember those demons we just communicated about? Their favorite cloak to wear is that made of "the cloth." Again, I remind you to return to the most trusted behavioral check of all—ask yourself how Jesus would act in any given situation.

The greatest threat to untruth . . . is Truth. The greatest proof of Truth is time. Messengers are of the physical and can be silenced and killed. Truth is of the Spirit and . . . Truth cannot be killed. The very persona of Jesus threatened the religious beliefs of his time. Though the people got rid of him, what survived? Truth cannot be threatened nor can it be intimidated . . . nor killed.

In The Visitation you mentioned that the Archangel presented an impression of wings when it first manifested. Do they have them or don't they?

That depends on whether you're talking about angels or angelic beings. There's a difference.

Do you have any wisdom on how to help our children who are having such problems now (from one mother to another)?

This lady was referring to her adult children. Since every individual is responsible for his/her own choices and behavior in life, it's difficult for a mother to restrain her inherent compulsion to interfere. Every individual learns valuable lessons through those personal choices. A parent's most valuable gifts to a child are . . . unconditional love and acceptance. Individually, these two qualities are powerful tools, combined they create the potential for miracles.

With what forms of Christianity do you agree?

What *forms?* Why is it that Christianity has more than one form? As I already stated, Christianity is a man-made religion. I am aligned with The Way Jesus attempted to establish through his behavior and words. Jesus brought Spirituality. Men devised religions of every shape and size. There is no confining shape, nor size, nor religious "term" to Jesus' message or spiritual intent.

Are the laws that create karma set in stone?

Perhaps you misunderstand the concept because there is no law, per se, only the definition of karma. Karma is the negating of a spirit's negative aspects through the balancing effect of positive factors. That's it. That's all there is. If you want to call that definition a "law," then okay, but don't complicate it. It's simple.

Jesus represents a perfect soul. Is it futile for us to strive to be perfect based on his example? Are we asking too much of ourselves?

Perfect? Do we even know what "perfect" is? The only real thing we know of this is that we *think* we know. Jesus displayed great anger at various times in his life. He was also consumed with doubts regarding his own identity and mission. Does that make him less than perfect? Does that mean he was not the perfect individual society has idealized him to be? And anyway, what is this fascination with perfection? If you're a good person and are accepting and tolerant of others, what's the deal with allowing the ego to expect or demand perfection? Even God himself displayed the negative attitude of jealousy for which he was rebuked by Sophia. Perfection is an illusion.

Is there an asteroid or comet collision in our earth's future? If so, can it be avoided in any way?

Well yes, the potential for this event is always there; however, I wonder at the concern over such a future event when one's mind should be focused on today. Society is so full of fears. Well, I'm not unaware of the popular movie scenarios that feed on these sensationalistic plots, but I've yet to see one where the earth is *spared* by *Starborn* intervention. Perhaps that probability hasn't entered men's minds.

Was Original Sin created by the spirits' desire to have sex with the created physical animals?

You need to shift the attention away from the sex part and focus on the "desire" aspect. Supposedly, Original Sin was created by the *desire* to leave God's spiritual domain and experience the physical. That spirits *preferred* a *physical* experience over the *spiritual* is more to the point.

Does the act of baptism erase Original Sin as Christianity says it does?

Is that logical? Spirits are of spirit. Baptism is a man-made *physical* ceremony. Why in heaven's name would a spirit be required to journey to a physical place to have its spirit cleansed by some human being? It makes no sense. The *spirit* of the concept of baptism has been completely lost. The Catholic Church has this concept of varied forms of valid baptisms. One is called the Baptism of Desire. This means that one doesn't have to go through an actual ceremony to make the cleansing effective; all one needs to do is want it—desire it, and . . . it's done! So then, if this is so, why wouldn't a spirit just *want* to be cleansed of Original Sin and be done with it? Why would it go through the hassle of getting into a physical body so a physical man can perform a ceremony to cleanse the spirit? Doesn't the irony of that tell you something? Besides, as I said before, our spirits are a composite of every life we've ever lived. Why would *every* life have to include a baptism to neutralize a one-time Original Sin? That'd be like saying you need to get a new car loan every time you got into your vehicle. Hey, wouldn't once be enough? How many spirits do the churches think one individual has? If an individual's spirit was baptized for the Original Sin back in ancient times, why go through it over and over again. Isn't that overkill?

Has anyone noticed that the hieroglyphics in the Egyptian tombs are "as smooth as a baby's butt," indicating the possibility that they were not cut by hand?

Oh, they've noticed, but you know, those Egyptians were master stonecutters and carvers. Denial, my friend, pure denial.

What is the purpose of reincarnation when we don't remember why we're back and the problems we should be resolving to be a completed soul? Don't we just spin our wheels trying to live a better life, and in the process, keep making the same mistakes?

The success of karma doesn't hinge on memory. Remember, karma is the balancing of negativity with positive aspects. This doesn't mean that the balancing is linear. By linear I mean, for example, if in a past life you slandered Joe, so, in this life, you need to rectify that with the current representation of that past Joe. No, that's not what karma demands. Karma only asks that we do more good than harm in life. That we practice goodness as often as we can so that past misdeeds will be outweighed by them. We are never spinning our wheels by being tolerant of others, by accepting life on a day-to-day basis, by loving and respecting the rights of others, and by practicing Unconditional Goodness at every opportunity. This is all one needs to know about actively making karma a success. You never have to concern yourself with the "why of your karma" if you just remember: *In life, do no harm.*

Was there an angel named Moroni?

The name is right; the entity's recorded presentation is not.

If incarnated souls from the Great White Brotherhood can live lives of frustration and pain, what chance do the rest of us have?

Your question exposes a misunderstanding about the technicalities of a physical mission's designated spirits. These spirits don't reincarnate with any types of special abilities or protective powers that shield them from elements of the human condition. The human condition is exactly what they enter into. That human condition is vitally important for the purpose of their work. They need to be totally equal to those they are attempting to work among and, being open to all human experience is a part of that. This technical fact is why I keep telling folks that returned completed spirits working here on earth (and elsewhere) are no different than the rest of us. These spirits have the same emotions as everyone else. They have to work for a living and make ends meet just like everyone else. Nothing is given to them on a platter or supplied for them through magical means. Though their connection to the Divine Consciousness is usually more active and easily accessed than others, they must remain focused on their mission and keep a continual one-minded centeredness on this. Because they must experience the human condition in order to effectively work within it, they are also aware of the potential of slipping out of sync with their alignment by letting the ego of self smother their purpose.

So don't fall into a muddled pool of some myth that claims completed spirits have any less difficult a time on earth than everyone else. They experience family problems, job layoffs and financial difficulties; pay taxes, fix broken plumbing; pick up dog doo; and are just as susceptible to all the viruses floating around in the air as everyone else. Yet unlike everyone else, they have this incredible burden of maintaining a fine balance between the spiritual plane and the physical. Their thoughts are processed and filtered through the delicate and subtle connectedness to that of the Source while, at the same time, they must effectively utilize that knowledge through the simplistic, confining language and understanding of the current times they must work within. It can be terribly frustrating to mentally be "way up there" while the body is trapped "way down here." It's sort of like being expected to swim through quicksand or—ever dream you were running in slow motion and not getting anywhere? That's what it's like most of the time. There is a fine balance that has to be constantly maintained so that the incredible heaviness of a weighted earthly existence doesn't drag down the light and airy spiritual Consciousness. Other than that . . . they're no different than you.

Why is it so difficult to get an explanation of what a twin flame is?

Probably because, on the spiritual plane, there is no such term or concept. Please be cautious and use discernment with new misconceptions that are quick to appear on the scene and become fads and catch phrases.

Are caves good to live in for future survival locations?

I've had several correspondents who are planning on living in caves in order to wait out future earth changes, but I don't suggest the plan. When earth movement occurs, you definitely don't want to be caught beneath tons of collapsing dirt and rock. Shelters above ground are still the best survival places. Access to immediate, spur-of-the-moment demands for mobility is paramount; living down under the ground hampers that split-second imperative.

It appears that most people are in some sort of financial trouble these days and they've no extra money to spend on survival supplies. My friends think I'm nuts to continue to build mine up whenever I get extra money.

I agree with you about the increasing number of people getting in debt over their heads and I believe that the situation is largely due to the credit companies that keep sending people cards and extending greater amounts of credit lines. It's just too easy to keep accepting them and pulling out the plastic to pay for purchases instead of waiting for stuff until you have the money for it. There is this demand I see happening with folks, an "I want it *now*" sort of mind-set. But getting it now with plastic means they have to pay for it next month when the bill comes due. Rather they had bought storage supplies with the plastic instead of electronics or toys. However, this probably wouldn't happen, either, because I've also observed a growing complacency regarding the future. As each year passes and no earth-shattering event occurs, people are tending to shift their priorities into the immediate present instead of planning for future probabilities. If the Y2K computer problem isn't solved in 1999, then when the year 2000 arrives most aspects of society will be thrown in confusion when everything depending on a computer chip for its functioning will no longer work. Everything from computerized gas pumps to banking facilities will be useless. This is why I've been seriously suggesting to people that they begin to set cash aside right now, to have a reserve of cash-stash in the home or safely buried in the yard. Take just a moment here. Think about how your situation would be if you woke up this morning and couldn't use an

ATM machine, or credit card, and your bank was closed for an indefinite amount of time. What money would you have available to you at that moment? The bills in your wallet and the change in your pocket. That's all the money you would have in the world for a while. So, as a word of warning, don't get too hung up on that "stuff" you think you need right now. Put the buying off for a later time and, instead, stash the cash for it in a safe place. Then, if the Y2K is fixed in time, you have the cash saved up for your stuff. If it isn't fixed by then, you've placed yourself in a more comfortable position to deal with the situation until it is. Foresight and planning can go a long way. If the computer glitch is solved in time, your cash-stash wasn't futile, because, in the end, it provided you with an extra reserve of money that you most likely otherwise would've spent on stuff. If we could knock the Y2K element out of the picture altogether, we're still left with the very real probability that future events involved with the Changes will necessitate a need for a healthy cash reserve. So either way, put some money into your sock.

I heard you weren't growing your own food for survival, how come?

First of all, if I had, I would've left my gardens behind for those who bought the last couple of houses I've moved out of. Secondly, ever try growing a garden at 10,000 feet in elevation? Even my petunias get shredded by sudden hail storms, and what the hail doesn't beat down, the chipmunks and deer eat down to nubs. A protective greenhouse is a must at this altitude, yet the growing season here is barely three months. The leaves on the aspen don't peek their heads out until the last days of May, and it's not uncommon for a blizzard to hit the first of October. My location is why I don't grow my own food. Instead, I store it.

As an aside to this issue, don't forget the vitamins. Add them to your supplies, because eating from storage supplies probably won't give you the complete nutritional nourishment the body needs and you'll need supplements to ensure this necessity. You may not eat well for a while, but at least your body will be getting its vital minerals and vitamins requirements. You don't want to end up with scurvy just because you forgot to store vitamins or canned fruit.

Is it the destiny of every spiritual entity to eventually become one with God?

This depends on what you mean by "one with God." Most spirits' goal is to return to the Beingness of the Divine. These are those spirits who are journeying through the cycles of rebirth for the purpose of balancing out their negative aspects. These ones will *return to the Divine Beingness.*

Now if, by "one with God," you mean *spiritually aligned,* then there are those higher spirits who already meet that criterion. You see, the act of Creation manifested various categories of spirits, i.e., angels, angelic beings, etc., and these do not return to the Beingness of the Divine, but rather are spiritually aligned with the Divine Minds. Generally, people here in the physical are working their way back to the Beingness.

Are heredity, environment, and will equal factors in aiding or retarding an entity's development?

No, not all of them. Will is the prime factor in spiritual development. It is the will that has the power to override subliminal aspects such as heredity, social class, environment, etc. It's through the strength of will and its choices in life that all negative factors can be ultimately conquered.

How come there are a few discrepancies between some of the statements you and Cayce have made regarding the time of Jesus?

Cayce's living philosophy was spiritually associated with a strong bond to Scripture, therefore his perspective was somewhat tinted by the written word of same. I can't imagine the Great White Brotherhood transmitting information that conforms to the patriarchal party line of Christianity rather than giving the totality of the universal truths. However, that's what seems to have transpired.

Will you be traveling to Europe in the future?

No, I've too much to do right here. My plate is already overflowing and traveling would take me away from my destined projects. The way I see it, as long as folks the world over can read my words, seeing me in the physical won't make those words any more real. Remember, it's the *message* that's important, not the messenger.

Can I help you achieve your spiritual goals by sending you a monetary donation?

This is an interesting question. A great portion of my message is to practice Unconditional Goodness. This means recognizing every opportunity that presents itself to help others. If you took that money you wanted to donate to me and, instead, gave it to help support a women's safe house, or donate it to an organization working to alleviate world hunger, or some other such charity, then, you see, you'd be directly putting my message into action! Helping me to achieve the goals of my messages is naturally manifested through people actualizing them in the world. What greater gift could I receive than to see such wondrous results as that? By helping others, you help me. By helping others, you become living proof that my messages have been taken to heart and have not fallen on deaf ears. You've no conception of how much that means to me.

I keep sensing that the year 2004 holds great meaning. Why won't you give dates?

Many times over I've said that it's futile to give prediction dates because of the many probabilities that come into play to alter those foreseen dates. However, I also see the year 2004 as being significant in some manner. Let's wait and see if currently manifesting probabilities alter it.

You're going to be left way behind if you don't get a website and an e-mail address.

Left way behind what? My existence is not dependent on nor defined by any form of human technology. Regardless of technology . . . I am. You need to reevaluate what it is that correctly defines one's existence.

Do you think it's impossible for people to communicate with God?

Since the world is full of folks walking around saying God talks to them, who knows? Seriously, everyone can communicate with the Divine Consciousness, especially through prayer.

Did the astrological lady with the scales come from the Egyptian Goddess, Maat?

Yes, the astrological lady you're referring to is Libra. Originally (Libera) was a Goddess of Carthage believed to be the Queen of the Stars. She represented balance and matriarchal justice.

Why isn't the entire Creation story recounted in the Bible?

Probably because biblical Scripture was formulated to conform to a set of beliefs that were determined by the newly formed religion's (Christianity's) founding fathers. Any matriarchal aspects having to do with the age-old Goddesses or women holding high ranks of authority were thrown out.

Did Jesus love? You know what I mean.

Yes, I do. You mean to ask if Jesus participated in performing any physical expression of love. And yes, he did. He was as much a man as those he roamed among and taught. He found great joy in participating in festivities and gaiety because he could be wildly happy. Then there were times when he was deeply despondent, when he turned to the privacy of his consort, who gave him solace, comfort, and understanding.

Are you still being guided by your Advisors?

We are all being guided in one way or another. Actual channeling happened only when that experience was necessary for another individual in my life's verification and solace. Since I've been on my own and trust my higher instincts, which, as always, have come as strong "Knowings," there has been no need for that kind of contact manifestation. As long as I'm on the right course and continue to listen to my spiritual instincts, guidance has been more of spiritual *companionship* than a guidance.

I feel a weightedness building. Things are closing in, aren't they?

Yes, they are. This correspondent is referring to the Changes and how aspects of it are manifesting in the world in an escalating manner to create a heaviness felt upon the spirit. This is precisely why the first phase of my mission is drawing to a close and my priorities have shifted to the physical aspect of my purpose. While I spend a portion of my days putting the last of my books on computer, the rest of the day is spent attending to projects involved in survival preparations. The writing is on the wall. In our journey through life, we have advanced to the curve . . . the Cusp of Change.

There is only one God.

I agree that there is one male God, but "religiously" speaking, which one do you mean? Currently there are many male gods who separate religious worship and are each proclaimed as "the" one God. There is the God of Abraham, there is the God of Jesus, there is the God of Mohammed, there is Buddha. . . .

If the choir of angels called Principalities are entrusted with the purpose of protecting religious leaders and guiding their paths, what happened?

What happened is "man" decided what purpose the angels had; it isn't true in reality. If it were, those angels certainly have been mucking it up, haven't they?

It seems to me that if the Great White Brotherhood communicated through someone, they wouldn't be referring to any man-made gospels in Scripture.

Perhaps only to stress a point, they'd repeat a true quotation of Jesus, but to use Scripture as a teaching tool would be far beneath them. Why would members of the highest and most enlightened spiritual intelligence stoop to gospels that were written by man? Scripture is not the word of God. There are no "writings" of Jesus, no scrolls of his, from which Scripture was formulated. Scripture is comprised of secondhand stories and hearsay. That's why the gospels vary so much from one to the other. Those of the Great White Brotherhood are aware of this and, when communicating the truths of spiritual reality, speak in plain language with simplicity about the truths. They need no references to writings by ancient-time storytellers.

This Bible thing is quite an enigma. Folks swear that it is the end-all, definitive word of God. Yet a Muslim will also swear that the Koran is the end-all, definitive word of God.

The Jewish people believe in the Torah; they only accept the first section of the Bible—the Old Testament. And what of the Book of Mormon? All of these books have content that greatly varies, so how can they all be the definitive spiritual word? Just common sense reveals that that's not logical. Whenever there is a trace of the human mind and hand upon that which is supposed to be the "written" word of God, doesn't that defile it from the outset? No, those of the spiritual hierarchy are far above referencing little human storybooks with false content.

After reading the book Living Is Forever, *I had the distinct impression that it was an actual preview of our future and your role in it.*

I read the book many years ago and never made any personal connection with the story's characters, yet quite a few of my readers have expressed the very same idea you have. It would be presumptuous to make assumptions. As far as my direction is concerned, I'm finishing up the message phase (the books) and have experienced a strong priority shift from the "message" to "preparations." I believe this Magdalene Abbey concept that has come to the fore of my Knowing is, in actuality, meant to serve multipurpose functions connected to the future: some type of base, a women's spiritual center, and perhaps also providing a safe house for abused women. When I envision it, I sometimes see it as some sort of "hub" bustling with activity; other times I see it as being as quiet and tranquil as a monastery sanctuary, filled with the feel of sacredness. I believe this difference is due to viewing it at different hours of the same future day. As with all things, I take one day at a time to see what each moment unfurls as an offering, opportunity, or revelation. Equating the content of Carter's book to any aspect of my own future is really stretching it.

Did angels ever have to balance themselves through physical lifetimes as we do?

No, angels have remained of the spirit and have not desired to experience the physical plane; therefore, they've nothing to balance out.

Is the Final Battle physical or spiritual?

Spiritual. It is currently being fought within society, within each of us. It has been ongoing for many years; all the while, unaware people full of the narrow concerns of self have been living in fear of its approach.

Are you contradicting yourself by now saying that "the heart should be where the home is," when before you've said to always "follow the heart to be wherever one is led to be"?

I'm not sure how you perceived those two statements as contradictory. Sure, you still need to follow the heart to be wherever you're led to be, no matter where that destination is. However, you still should make wherever you are your "home" (where your heart is), because that's how you effectively *remain within the now* and can manage to live and experience life to the fullest. Rather than the two statements being contradictory, they're complementary.

I know you don't believe in animal testing labs, but it's the only way to experiment with new drugs that could help or save human life.

The only way? I'm for turning rapists into societal assets. Perhaps if the legal penalty for rape was for the rapist to replace a testing lab cat, chimp, rat, or dog, maybe women would finally have the same right to feel as safe walking the streets as men do.

In **Fireside** *you sounded as though the Million Man March was somehow subversive. It seems to me that it was a good event that united people for a common cause.*

What common cause is that? There was a surface cause and an underlying agenda cause. Recently there was another gathering by this group and its speakers called for greater empowerment and show of "black power." Their speeches were antiwhite and anti-Semitic. They were attempting to incite racial *intolerance* and presenting the idea that the black people should receive retribution for historical slavery. This type of thing in this day and age is counter to the unifying ideology that should be society's spiritual perspective by now. If you observe with acuity, you'll see all types of counterproductive movements currently active throughout the world. Instead of tolerance for the individuality and beautiful, unique differentness of people, we're now witnessing a deevolutionary process that turns back the clock to the fifties and sixties. Instead of a societal perception of *all* people being seen as *human beings,* the racial separatism is being more heavily emphasized. When this happens, society cannot grow into an ideology that strives for what's best for the whole, but rather is divided, separated, and embroiled in discord and hatred for the purpose of specific ethnic races to present a show of powerful strength to others. This is not ethnic pride. This is not intellectual or spiritual advancement. This is ethnic egotism. And ethnic egotism will be a perspective that will not survive in our future world. Demanding retribution for the mistakes of our ancestors exhibits childish and immature thought. This is looking backward instead of to the future. This is holding on instead of letting go. This is throwing a societal tantrum instead of having acceptance of the past and looking to the future. Whenever any ethnic group violently speaks out against other races, society, as a whole, has a serious developing problem. Intolerance cannot be tolerated any more. If we're to move forward and become any kind of developed, peaceful society, we've got to first intellectually and spiritually gain acceptance and tolerance. The Promise Keepers are another separatist group that appears to foster intolerance of women's individuality and equal rights. Every incident, event, or ideology that fosters the slightest hint of intolerance of others or superiority of self deevolutionizes our entire civilization.

Were our physical bodies really created to last forever?

What do you mean by "really"? It sounds as though you've heard this idea somewhere, but it's not even sound logic, is it? Think what your neighborhood would be like if it were filled with people who were born before the pharaohs and still going strong. That'd be a mite overcrowded, yes? And what about the Cycle of Rebirth? The next time you hear something like this, apply a bit of logical thought to it before accepting on a surface level.

Why can't people just believe in a Supreme Being and let that be enough?

I think they can't do that because experiencing the Essence of the Divine Consciousness within themselves is not enough. They can't "feel" that warm fulfillment within, so they need to add their own man-made elements in order to have a touchable and seeable religion. They need to have ceremonial robes, rites, prayers, and song. They need to have egotistical input added to the ideology of a deity and create additional dogma, rules, and have group meetings to bolster and support their beliefs. An internalized relationship with a Supreme Being is not enough for them.

Male (patriarchal) religions seem to all be founded on and maintained by fear. Comment?

Yes, this certainly seems to be the case. The hell-fire-and-brimstone sermons, the threats of excommunication, the focus on Satan, all point to manipulation and control through fear. Patriarchal beliefs are linear, whereas the matriarchal spirituality is holistic and circular. The ancient Mother Goddess spirituality was centered on love, respect, and nurture. It's returning.

Why do so many lesbians act like guys if they don't like guys?

I get the gist of your question, but your wording shows a lack of understanding of the concept you're attempting to question. Two of your words within the question give clear evidence of this. Let's look at them.

The first word in error is "act." Homosexuals don't "act," they just *are*. They have *beingness*. That beingness is the inherent "who" of them. There is no put-on affectation, no act. Their mannerisms and mode of dress are natural. Okay, so we've established that there is no acting involved here.

The second word in error is "like." You said they "don't like" guys. That wording and the meaning it implies is not accurate, so let's fix it to make it right. Just because a lesbian isn't *sexually* attracted to guys doesn't also equate to them not liking guys. To say or believe that would be an assumption that is grossly false. Lesbians can love men friends (platonically) because these guys are beautiful human beings, but just because these women are not sexually attracted to them in no way means they don't like them. See?

There's a misconception in society that lesbians are men-haters. Not so. At least not as an all-inclusive, blanket conceptual fact, because most of them have no objection whatsoever to having friendly relationships with men as business associates or personal friends. So my comment to your question is that lesbians are the way they are because that's inherently who their natural beingness is . . . they're being true to self, just like you are true to your self. This last fact is why the self-righteous religious leaders show such ignorance when they persecute these good folks by claiming they're a "perversion" in society. Nobody is born a perversion. I repeat: *nobody is born a perversion.* God did not create a perverted being . . . ever!

Have you changed your beliefs? You've shifted to a "female" deity instead of the male God of your early writings.

Have I? Have I really? *What is selected to be externalized is not always the composite whole of that which is held within.* Didn't my first writings focus on the Earth *Mother?* The *Grandmother* Earth Spirit?

The messenger aspect of my mission here unfolded precisely as was foreseen and destined. It developed and manifested as a planted seed that grew into a bud before blossoming out into a fully unfurled flower, each stage unfolding naturally within the pages of each successive book. Each book represents a move up into higher and more refined spiritual philosophies that took a gentle journey from interspersing subtle interjections of truth to society's popular belief system in *Spirit Song* to bringing out the full-blown, immutable truths Beyond in *Eclipse.* All these truths and their beliefs have been instilled as an inherent facet of my soul since the writing of my first book and before. Rather than representing an assumed "change" in belief, it exhibits a more complete and full *expression* and *revelation* of it. Ever since the publication of *Spirit Song,* my directional focus was toward bringing awareness of the reality of the Second Coming . . . that of Feminine Spirituality, which the Divine will be here to fully manifest. The Spirit of Grandmother Earth, through the beautiful and innocent, living Consciousness of Nature, has always been my most trusted and true, touchable connection to that singular Divine Mind. Also, the complete totality of the Trinity cannot be even imagined until *each* aspect is recognized as reality first. Once this totality is understood, only then can the Divine Source *above* these aspects be perceived.

How are visions manifested?

I do not disagree with the methodology of visions as described by Jesus to Mary Magdalene when she asked him "how one sees a vision." As revealed in the *Gospel of Mary* (Magdalene) discovered in the Nag Hammadi region in December of 1945, Jesus responds to this question by saying that the soul sees *through the mind,* which is between the soul and the spirit. In other words . . . Consciousness. I've gone into the enigma of Consciousness before. It is the ultimate, virtual passageway to everywhere.

The wrath of God is upon us with all the recent disasters across America and throughout the world. Agree?

No, I don't agree. God takes no wrath out upon the human children. He does not punish or wreak havoc in such an indiscriminate, destructive manner. Well, let me clarify that last statement better: He does not punish, period. Why are you so strongly inclined to blame God for the incredible sorrow and grief happening in the world? This I cannot understand. Why are you looking for someone to blame for the natural workings of nature? Why this need to blame? To pass the responsibility of sorrow and grief onto the shoulders of another? This type of thought negates the very definition of Nature. Nature is natural. It just is. It exists. It is reality. The meteorological aspects of reality are natural. It rains and maybe floods. It snows and maybe creates city-crippling blizzards. The winds blow in currents over the spinning planet and maybe they become intense enough to create hurricanes and tornados. The earth itself breathes released, pent-up pressure and maybe moves the hardened crust above it with earthquakes and volcanos. Nature exists. Don't push its natural forces over onto the shoulders of God. Accept the natural reality of our world. See with clear eyes. Perceive with the clarity of reality's natural logic and reason.

I work hard at advancing my spirituality, yet have never had the experiences that you have. Does this indicate that I'm in spiritual infancy?

Of course not. Since when do spiritual *experiences* equate to meaning a state of spiritual *advancement?* Each individual is unique unto self. Each course in life and the associated spiritual development of that course is also as individual as the grains of sand on the beach. Where is it written that, in order to attain spiritual advancement one must have contact with Starborn, Advisors, and a visionary teacher, or have experiential events of one's Consciousness entering an animal or traveling through other dimensional and frequency realities? There are no formulated criteria for spiritual advancement. An individual who has experienced the above mentioned events does not equate to a spiritually advanced state of being. This state only happens when one has attained the deep wisdom that can be obtained from those experiences. Experiences are meaningless in and of themselves unless the individual has assimilated them in a developmental manner and has come away with an understanding and behavioral appreciation of their attending Wisdom. People who have never had a single mystical experience beyond the recall of their dreams can develop high spiritual status just by living a life of Unconditional Goodness, Acceptance, and tolerance. I don't know where this idea of mystical experiences being equated with spiritual development came from, but the idea is just so much phooey! I've observed folks who are capable of psychic (mentalism) abilities, yet are so spiritually barren in their behavior that the situation is almost pitiful. And then I've seen people who are incredibly wise and full of high spiritual knowledge while never in their life have they ever experienced a single "mystical" event. So what? One does not define the other.

For two decades you have been receiving countless letters of thanks, praise, criticism, and complaints each day from your readers. Has this ever hampered your own personal growth?

I guess I don't understand the question, because I don't understand how the opinions of others can stunt one's personal growth. I'm an individual with a specific spiritual goal that I've kept focus on. Though I'm sensitive and responsive to the emotions of others, I don't lose sight of the solid and firm path of my purpose. Acceptance plays a huge role in being aware of the various opinions others express toward me. Everyone has a right to express opinions and freely make comments. This I understand and accept with neutrality. Those opinions that are unkind are accepted and let go; those that are comforting and encouraging I take to heart and gain greater resolve from. That's it. I don't see how these various attitudes could hamper personal growth.

When we choose to do the will of our Father, how do we know for sure if we are choosing to do God's will or if we are fooling ourselves only to heighten our ego or to obtain self-serving desires?

Well gosh, didn't you just answer your own question here? If your ego gets stroked, then you're actuating a self-serving deed. If you're doing for others, then you're pleasing the Divine. Now this brings up a subtle aspect of this and we'll look at it.

Frequently, when doing for others, we'll have a sensation of fullness within the chest. This is not pride or self-satisfaction; it's *spiritual fulfillment*. It's the "damn good" feeling one receives from helping others. Period. That is definitely, absolutely, not a self-serving, egotistical sense of self. It is our *return* blessing.

I've never understood your need for guns and self-protection measures. Isn't religion all about faith? I'm not saying you need to be foolish and make yourself a target or a martyr like a Christ or Gandhi, but isn't the "gun thing" a sign of anti-faith?

Nope. Nada. Self-protection does not equate to fear or a lack of faith; it's being smart enough to be prepared and self-reliant. I have a specific purpose for being here. I stay aware of my surroundings so that I can remain alive and well in order to finish out that purpose. To not give attendance to that would be irresponsible of me and highly disrespectful to my mission. Why do people attend martial arts programs and classes on self-defense? Why do women avoid walking down dark alleys or through dimly lit parking garages? Awareness of life. Being aware and wise. Why does the pope ride around in a bulletproof bubble? Why do folks lock their house doors at night? Or look into their cars before getting in after dark? They are being aware and performing wise corresponding actions.

Being aware of the violence enacted by society doesn't mean one doesn't have faith or is fearful; it simply means that one recognizes the violent potential of humanity and reacts accordingly with Wisdom. Listen to me. When someone in a woman's household begins to exhibit unpredictable, violent behavior and suddenly, without provocation, charges red-faced in a jealous rage in her face, rants, and then shoves a gun barrel in her chest, she begins to sleep with one eye open all night and a loaded gun of her own tucked beneath her pillow. When someone in this same woman's home suddenly shoves the *handle* of a gun in her stomach and tries to force her hand over the grip and a finger to the trigger to make it look like she shot him, her world suddenly becomes a living twilight zone, where she must maintain an optimum level of acute awareness and swift responses. When someone she thought loved her comes to her cabin and, after letting him in, he just stands there without uttering a word and coldly stares at her with the bulge of a gun showing beneath his leather jacket, her intuitive senses immediately shoot up through the roof and begin screaming at her to prepare to either hit the floor or lunge past him for the telephone to punch in the 911 button. You cannot come to judgment about this unless you've been there. Unless you've been on the receiving end of someone's violence and unpredictability you cannot even begin to understand . . . you cannot even begin. Yet you can understand that those who lock their doors at night and avoid walking through dark alleys are not living in fear, they are simply exhibiting wise behavior generated from an acknowledgment of society's increasingly violent behavior.

The reality of this issue is that faith holds hands with responsibility. We cannot expect the spiritual forces to do it all. We have to help. We are expected to do our own part in this tandem work of protection. We do what we can here in the physical by remaining aware and reacting accordingly with physical means of responsive responsibility and, in turn, the spiritual forces do their part in those circumstances in which we have no control. Remember, the spiritual forces help those who help themselves. Like so many other aspects in life, protection is a joint effort. It's one of the main reasons we were given the gift of intuition and insight in the first place. It's a bit egomaniacal to say, "Okay God, you protect me while I lay back and do nothing to be aware and protect myself." Nope, doesn't work that way.

I dreamed that my girlfriend gave me a ring with a barite gem in it. What the heck did that mean?

Barite symbolizes longevity. I would say that this dreamscape element means that she wishes your relationship will be an eternal one.

Did the Shekinah simultaneously incarnate as five racially different Eves?

The Shekinah was never Eve.

*My sister attends Virgin Mary channeling sessions. I
don't tell her that I think they're bogus, but can there
be some positive value in them for the attendees?*

False hope? Belief generated by an imposter entity? What
spiritual value comes from a foundation made of quicksand?
How can that possibly hold up and become a treasured
touchstone of enduring strength and lasting faith, which our
spirituality is supposed to be? What if your sister were attending one of these sessions, intently listening in awe-struck
wonder to the so-called channeled words of Mary while the
real, incarnated Mary was sitting there beside her in the
physical? Well, first of all, the real Mary wouldn't be sitting
in attendance at such a meeting, but if she were and your sister discovered her there, how meaningful would those messages continue to be after that? Do you get what I'm saying?
In your letter you wondered if this channeled stuff was com-
parable to the empty images of Mary that have been technically manifested throughout time by the Starborn for the
purpose of returning the people's focus back to Spirituality?
An image is not at all the same as someone putting words
into Mary's mouth.

*Fireside seemed more about those dogs of yours than
anything else. And another thing, why Sally?*

I'm not saying, "love me, love my dogs," but *Fireside* was
created for the singular purpose of trying to invite my readers into my cabin's living room with me so they could listen
in on one of the many evening-long conversations that take
place and give some sense of being a personal part of that
evening. Those dogs are a big part of my home life and the
evening wouldn't have been accurately portrayed without
their inclusion. Maybe you'd have a better perspective of the
book if you went back and "read between the dogs."

Why Sally? This question appeared to really bother you
because you asked it more than once, as if you just couldn't

fathom why I'd hook up with a woman instead of a man. That was it, wasn't it? Well, for some women there's only one man in their life and mine came and went. Another intimate relationship is not for me this life. Sally and I go way back . . . back to before recorded history. Before I incarnated this time, while still on the spirit plane, alternate contingencies were provided for—every plan comes with contingencies. If, for whatever reason, I were left alone before the mission was completed, another was waiting in line to carry on as helper and companion. In ancient times, Sally, as a female biblical personage, stepped in to fulfill the identical supportive role when my husband of that time left me because of jealousy and an interest in a more "interesting" life elsewhere. Now, as then, history has repeated itself by paralleling the past and coming full circle. In the spiritual reality, there are, for want of a better phrase, angelic beings who perform a multitude of various support roles to the messengers here in the physical. Has that concept never occurred to you? You need to elevate the level your thinking is on—raise it *way* up.

How does one choose between a pull toward following a spiritual quest and staying in place to attend to responsibilities of the physical, when each is in direct opposition to the other?

Mmmm, this is such a common happening in life and causes all sorts of problems. The magnetic force of one's spiritual direction can be a strong pull away from an individual's current life situation. I admit that this is extremely difficult to deal with and manage, but always—always—one's personal life responsibility to other individuals takes precedence. Children, mate, an elder who must be cared for, such as a father or mother, all come first if they are one's direct responsibility.

I'm going to share something with you. This question came from Sally. She thought it'd be an excellent question for *Eclipse* because she had to deal with this dilemma herself and, throughout her life, had observed others in the same position. I agreed it was a relevant and timely question.

I know that many people are dealing with this situation because I receive correspondence in which people are telling me that they've decided to leave their family to pursue their spiritual quest or that they must leave responsibilities behind to follow their new path. But you see, that choice isn't the *spiritual* one to make. To leave another, especially a dependent or someone you're responsible for, is not spiritual behavior. The two obligations must be synergistically merged and managed in a blended manner. In this way, *both* will be greatly *enhanced* rather than one being abandoned.

Sally was caring for her elderly mother when it became time for her to move into place after certain events in my life made it clear that the contingency plan for the mission had suddenly and urgently manifested. She lived in another state and cared for her mother, so how could she get to the place where she knew she had to be? She moved here and temporarily entrusted her mothers care to her sister. She arrived here at the precise moment when the transitional shift of the identity of one helper/companion to the other reached its critical cusp position. Later, when things were more settled (us moving out of the tiny, stone cabin), she went back to Kansas and took care of all the details of moving her mother (and her schnauzer) out here to the mountains to live with us in the new place. Her mother was not yet with us when I wrote *Fireside*—she arrived a month later. Now, there is Sally, Grandma, me, two birds, two aquariums, and six dogs . . . never a dull moment, I guarantee, but Sally's two magnetic pulls were successfully merged into an enhanced spiritual resolution for both aspects, which were once individual and seemingly separate, problematic situations.

It's important to not abandon any life responsibility, especially when a *person* identifies and equates to that obligation. Spiritual pursuit is good, it's wonderful, but not when one turns his/her back and walks away from another for it.

What makes you so ditzy in autumn?

This one made me laugh. You got this from No-Eyes, didn't you? Like the mountains have an inexplicable draw for folks, or the ocean, or desert, so too do the seasons emanate energy and influence upon the receptive sensitivities of people's Consciousness. Autumn. Autumntime is real—alive, for me. The mask of chlorophyll is gone from the leaves to expose their true faces. And what spectacularly beautiful faces they are! The air is crisp and fresh. Autumn is ALIVE! It says, "I live. Though I will soon sleep for a while . . . I celebrate the soul of my beingness!" Oh, and the scent of wood smoke! So sensuous, bringing the touchable sensation of warm coziness from home fires brightly burning and visions of dancing amber reflections flickering over the pine walls! Autumn is filled with beautiful sights, the sound of leaves shushing when shuffled through, the fragrance of crisp air and heavy wood smoke . . . autumn is so *sensual!* And yes, I am not ashamed to admit that my pure joy in it makes me incontrovertibly, absolutely, undeniably . . . ditzy! Come winter I have plenty of time to mellow back out.

How come people aren't very nice to each other? I've observed a lot of unspiritual behavior in life.

So you've noticed it, too. But know what? It'd be bad enough to observe this lack of spiritual behavior in society, but the way I see it, it's decayed more than that. People have forgotten the basic concept of *common decency* and have lost the sense of it through the growing emphasis placed on self. They've forgotten how wonderful it feels to turn away from gossip. They've forgotten how uplifting it is to accept others instead of criticizing them. They've lost the art of common decency that once was more widely practiced throughout society before it became suffocated by self-centeredness.

Yes, society presents multiple examples of its deepening

unspiritual behavior, but when you realize that this same behavior reflects a loss of the simple, common decency it once had, the true state of affairs becomes even graver, more deplorable, so much sadder for the soul to see. It's been reduced to pettiness, but that pettiness will vanish when people are forced to focus on the basic necessity of . . . just surviving. Things will change. Circumstances will alter and people will go through them and come out the other side transformed.

I've heard you comment that there would never be another man in your life, but I don't see how you can go through the rest of your years without love.

Huh? Oh my, I think you think that, for a woman, a man is her only source of love. Is that what you think? Clearly your question and expressed opinion conveys this idea. However, you're perceiving life through extremely narrow tunnel vision regarding this concept. There is no way I'm going to be without love if I don't have a man. Just no *way.*

Maybe I'm the strange bird here, a rarity in society, but I'm able to feel filled with a sense of deep and warming love just by being out in the incredible sensuousness of nature, where I'm always aware of personally being a strong and vital facet of its very life force. I feel very loved and filled with encouragement from my readers whose deeply emotional letters, hugs, and tear-filled eyes touch my soul and warm my heart. I know I am loved. How can you think this isn't love? How can you think these aren't powerfully moving and tender expressions of emotion directed toward me? This is powerful stuff! I feel loyalty, faithfulness, and love from my little four-leggeds who are so much more expressive with their emotion of love than most people are. When I hold and pet a wild bird, I feel love. When I'm trusted enough to walk a few feet in front of a buck, I feel love. When I stand out in the dark woods, look up, and become lost in the embrace of the vast, sparkling night sky, I feel love. When I meditate, I'm engulfed in enormous waves of love. When I pray, I experience a pure exchange of love. And the support person who was sent to me provides continual companionship, joy, laughter, spontaneity, intellectual conversation, and daily assistance for my work. My heart and soul, my world, is full of abundant, overflowing love. Now . . . exactly, what more love could I be missing when I feel it emanating from every direction I turn to? Or . . . were you perhaps equating love with sex? Confusing the two? Maybe that was it. But that couldn't be, because your expressed concern was termed "love." So, in that respect, be concerned for me no more, for I am blessed with unbounded measures of love. It's what inspires me. It's what motivates my spontaneity and maintains my continued sense of humor. Love is the beat of my heart, the breath of my spirit.

Let me express what "companionship" is to me. It's having someone who understands your moods and lets you be silent or talkative when you feel the need. It's having an intellectual sounding board for when you have the urge to toss complex theories around and figure them out, so they can be relayed to others in simple terms. It's having someone to go out to dinner with and be a buffer for the men who try to hit on me (I don't do well with those situations). It's a personal relief that I don't have to deal with the hectic traffic pace of the city and I can depend on another who, with never a hint of complaint, transports me around town as though she has a dozen cases of fresh eggs in the car. It's having a deep, shared respect for another. It's being able to truly and always know I can depend on someone; not "dependence," but knowing and being confident that she'll actually do what she says she'll do. It's having someone around who thinks as you do, so much so that twin thoughts begin to be voiced at the same moment. And though I could continue this for many more pages, the bottom line is that the companionship I now experience is one that couldn't be more rewarding or more warmly fulfilling.

And regarding this correspondent's equation of a man to

love which, indirectly and politely, implied sex—the rest of my years without sex, well . . . like I already said, maybe I'm a rare bird. I don't believe there's a conceptual term to categorize me regarding this issue. Asexual sounds so cold, and I'm definitely not a frigid human being, but the pure love I so strongly feel from so many aspects of life supercedes all else to the point of feeling so greatly blessed by it that its high and pure nature negates thoughts of all else. I am whole. I am loved. I am whole because I am loved in so many, many beautiful ways and am intensely receptive to every one of them. I'm in love with the love with which life's natural beingness blesses me.

I've become complacent about the "Changes" and have used up all the foodstuffs I'd stored. Do you still have a mind toward storing supplies?

Complacency is all right as long as you're still adequately prepared. Just because catastrophe hasn't hit your locale yet doesn't mean that it's not happening elsewhere in the nation or world. You know it is striking in many places. You can't think it will never strike your town or neighborhood. Look at the current state of the economy. The hurricanes, the flooding, and the suffering going on from them. The personal losses are incredible. The point you're missing here is that what you need the supplies for may not be caused by a local event, but rather by one affecting the entire nation. You have to consider the possibility of all grocery stores running out of stock. What then? You have to keep a mind on having no electricity for an extended period of time. What then? The huge ramifications of that alone is catastrophic because it affects all aspects of life, including business, banking, and the movement of goods. What if water systems were contaminated and you couldn't draw from them? Recent events have shown that we cannot solely depend on organizations such as the Red Cross to supply the needs of those experiencing mass catastrophes. With Hurricane George, they needed donations to supplement their supplies. If an event great enough to affect the entire nation occurred, nobody would be volunteering or donating anything, because they'd all be trying to save what they had for their own families. Complacency is okay *if* you're still prepared.

Yes, I have supplies and add to them as I think of things to include. Recently we came across flashlights and a radio (used in Third World countries) that operate by cranking them; they're pretty amazing, not to mention useful. Solar-powered equipment, on the surface, seems like a good choice until you factor in the possibility of diminished sunlight caused by diffusing or obliterating dust particles and/or clouds. A major volcano can make many dark days, as can fallout from other sources where sunlight will have no effect on powering the solar-energized equipment. Store extra clothing, such as good, durable hiking shoes. Think about the hygiene items you use and have an adequate supply of those. We even have canes, crutches, and a walker. You can eventually run out of water purifying tablets, so bottles of bleach go much farther, as a few drops will purify a gallon of water. If country folks have a well, they should also have a backup hand pump for it. We are gathering hand tools (the old kind) like crank drills. With a stored holding tank of gasoline, we can have enough fuel to run our generator a few minutes at a time as needed for water and toilets, thus making our fuel (and the ability to produce electricity) last many months. I have cases of long-burning candles. It would be wise to have a woodstove installed somewhere in your home. Kerosene heaters are useless without the availability of the fuel. Same with propane heaters. Build up a standing supply of cordwood for it. The first-aid kit is one of the first considerations folks give to their supply cache, but don't forget the Betadine for wound sterilization and a good sewing kit. Though the need for the stored supplies has not yet arisen, and I keep my mind focused on today, the probabilities of tomorrow have not been forgotten.

I dreamed that a homeless person jump-started my car battery. Can't figure this one.

It means that you think homeless people are worthless or have nothing to offer when, in reality, they have much to teach you. This dreamscape homeless person represents someone in your life to whom you don't give a second thought to as far as being capable of offering anything useful to you; however, this individual possesses the potential to bring you some type of assistance or enlightenment. A self-examination is being indicated here. You need to look at your perspectives regarding certain segments of society and attain a more accurate understanding of people's inherent value.

I'm thirty-four and can't seem to rid myself of the racial prejudice I was raised with. How can it be so ingrained?

It's not; you just think it is. Thirty-four is way long enough time to recognize the negativity and wrongness of such destructive thought and come into your own elevated level of "raised" enlightenment. Too often people use this "raised with" reasoning for their behavior, when it's no reason at all; it's an excuse to rationalize why they're still doing it.

I recently heard the same excuse when, after hearing that one of my close friends killed a deer while hunting with his dad, he said: "I tried to scare it away but it wouldn't leave. I had no choice." What, he couldn't shoot *over* it? Then he admitted, "Well, I hope you don't stay upset with me, we were just raised differently." I wasn't raised with any ideology regarding the issue of hunting. I don't believe the subject ever came up while I was young. However, once an individual reaches the age of reason and understands the difference between right and wrong, the difference between a respect for life and a wanton lack of same, that individual has a responsibility to do the spiritually right thing.

I can understand the act of hunting if there's a situational *need* to hunt, but not what men call "sport." Sport? Sport! What is the sport of enticing the deer in range of your aim with sweet feed grain? I found this out when I went into the feed store and the lady regrettably told me that the reason there was only one bag of the deer grain left was because the hunters bought them up. It literally turned my stomach when she said that. A hunter isn't a hunter because he was raised that way. He's a hunter because he likes the feel of power by shooting off his big gun and making a successful kill with it. The excuse of getting meat for the table doesn't fly, not when you live within walking distance of one or more grocery stores.

People are raised with all sorts of negative attitudes, but they voluntarily refuse to hold them as their own. What about the child reared by drug addicts who grows up and *never* even tries it once because that's how he/she believes? What about the child growing up in a neighborhood where gangs try to prove that you're nothing unless you belong, and that child grows into adulthood without ever having joined a gang? What about being raised in a meat-eating family and the child grows up to be a vegetarian? There are all types of examples of individual thinking. The parental minds we were all raised by are not *our* minds. We have our own.

As we live, we learn. As we learn, we grow. As we grow, we raise our vibrations higher into greater spiritual behavior and enlightenment. If right behavior is not given acknowledgment and we make the voluntary decision to ignore it in deference to desires or maintaining the status quo, then we're lost. How one is raised has nothing at all to do with making the decision to do what is recognized as right. I was raised hearing constant ethnic slurs. My father was a hard-core racist who never gave a thought to his daughters hearing his derogatory remarks about Jews, blacks, Asians, women, etc. This is what I grew up with. Yet, as my individuality developed, so did my reasoning. It was wrong to hate. It was wrong to call people names, to denigrate them, to use offensive slang terms for them. No matter what I heard while growing up, I knew in my heart that it was a fact that all people were created as human beings. That we were all Children of the Divine Essences, that we were supposed to love one another—not just because my Catholic schooling said so, but because it just *felt* so. Don't tell me you can't help your racist attitude because that's what you were raised with. Don't tell me that. Worse, stop telling yourself that.

What does a "fringe tree" mean in a dream? I dreamed I was sleeping beneath one.

A fringe tree symbolizes peripheral elements; hidden aspects. If one of your dreamscape fragments showed you sleeping under one of these, then it's attempting to point out that, in your awake state, there are facets of your life that are important but not being recognized and acknowledged. You're perceiving some elements as being insignificant when they're not. These elements could be associates, family members, friends, a job-related situation, or other facets. Now that this has been pointed out to you, you should be able to identify this aspect.

In dreams, can you tell me what a "kingbird" represents. Also the "skylark" and "junco" birds?

Sure. The kingbird symbolizes aggressiveness. This will not be spiritually related, but rather associated with the psychological defensive mechanisms of someone in your life, perhaps self.

The skylark represents joy and happiness.

The junco, friendship.

I've always personally perceived Jesus as being the Alpha. Will he also be the Omega when he comes?

No. You got the Alpha part right, but not the gender of the Omega. This was a really interesting question, because it evidenced higher thought. Presently, there exists a spiritual situation that, in some ways, parallels the ancient, biblical past. In other ways, the situation displays facets that are meant to be in direct contrast to it. Both aspects of the Alpha and the Omega were here two thousand years ago (but *please* . . . do *not* make an assumption as to the identity of the Omega two thousand years ago). At that time, the Alpha persona presented as a male and was recognized as a *male* who took on a *personal public* image. This time the Omega persona of the *female* will come to manifest the same purpose, only through a silent, anonymous manner by way of the *spirit*. Where before there were miracles to convince people and draw attention to the *male* entity of the Alpha; now it's been deemed that people must make recognition of the work (i.e., Word) of the *female* entity of the Omega through their hearts and spirits *without* the dramatic, convincing displays of magic. Before, it was a male; now it's a female. Before, miracles inspired faith; now it must come from within. Before, there were physical followers; now there is to be spiritual recognition. Before, the message was focused on the individual; now it is to be focused on recognition of the Word. This time, the emphasis is not on a person; it's on the words. What remains the same is . . . The Word. It began with the Alpha; it comes full circle with the Omega.

In **The Visitation,** *the archangel suggested that the millennium was more of an inner transformation than physical. Will the earth physically shift on its axis, or is the shift only a shift in Consciousness?*

The entity wasn't specifically speaking about the "millennium" as being an inner transformation, but rather the book of Revelation being symbolic of an event taking place within everyone. The millennium was mentioned in regard to the misunderstandings and the assumptions the general public has perceived it to be.

The "shift" is not symbolic and remains the physical event it was always predicted as being.

If God is all-merciful, then why do we endure suffering here on earth?

If we didn't, then earth would be paradise, wouldn't it? Don't forget, God does not create the suffering. We live on a planet that has meteorological aspects of climatic weather and the physiology of its geologic makeup. These evidence by way of earthquakes, volcanoes, sinkholes, hurricanes, flooding, tornados, etc. God does not control or create these at will. They are "natural" facets of our planet and have nothing to do with the lack of God's mercy.

So too is sickness not God's doing. Our bodies are of the physical. They comprise living cells and systems, both of which are positively and negatively affected by outside physical elements and inner psychological facets. Our bodies are affected by both the external (physical) and the internal (mind). We knew all of this before we entered into this physical, third-dimensional realm. How is it that this has been forgotten and now, when suffering happens, people look to God and ask, "why?" Most of the psychological suffering comes from self. It comes from a lack of acceptance of our world, the people in it, and oneself. Guilt, intolerance, egotism, hatred, prejudice, manipulation, jealousy, etc., cause 99.999 percent of psychological sufferings. People generally create their own soil mix out of which their lives grow. What sort of nourishment that life receives is directly related to how they've prepared the soil content. And that soil is not underfoot; it's within the mind. It can be made to be a fertile, thriving garden or a fallow field full of suffocating weeds. Rich mulch or hard clay. Moist and rich in minerals or cracked and parched. How the soil of one's mind is conditioned is solely up to the individual. But remember, this condition is also in direct relation to the extent of one's psychologically generated suffering and the life problems it produces.

What do you think of X book?

Obviously, I didn't reveal the title of this book because I must reiterate that I don't comment on specific book titles or authors. I used to offer my opinion on these, but found that the opinion was perceived as a firm spiritual directive or fact. Knowing folks received my personal opinions as such; I've since refrained from offering them in a public manner. I express them to close, personal friends, but not to the general public.

I thought it was a little silly to have symbols such as "Mickey Mouse" and "jock itch" in your dream book. What was up with all those types of entries?

Giving folks a comprehensive dream book was what was up with those. *Everything* that exists in reality and whatever one can *imagine* can be a dream symbol. And every dreamscape element is sending a message to the dreamer. You're not fully comprehending the technicalities of dreams if you think *any* symbol is silly to give an interpretation for. Just because you've never dreamed of having jock itch doesn't mean another man didn't and wouldn't love to know what it personally meant for him. In a dream symbol interpretation book, no symbol is silly because people can dream of anything and everything.

How can a dream book help anyone when symbols will have different meanings for everyone?

If this woman's statement were phrased a bit differently, it'd be factual. Dreamscape elements are not different for *everyone,* but they *may* be different for *some.* That is the fact of it. Okay, I absolutely agree with this and that's exactly why I included a statement in the form of a "Note" in the very front of the dream book. I wanted to present that fact up front, at the outset of the book. Did you miss that note?

There are a greater number of people for whom a dream symbol will mean the same than those who will interpret it differently. Also, for those who will interpret a symbol differently, those symbols are selective; therefore, the entire rest of the body of symbology will hold true for them, too. For instance, for a jeweler, gemstones or jeweler's tools will hold a different meaning than for the general public, but the rest of the symbols in the book will be viable interpretations for her/him. Same with ethnic associations. Same with personal life experience, such as someone having a bad experience in an amusement park: any symbology related to such a place will bring a varied message to that particular dreamer. You see? It's obvious that not every dream element will present the exact interpretation for everyone, but on the *whole,* dream elements carry *general* messages and remain immutable in their meaning. Water equates to spiritual aspects in one's life. The air is associated with mental factors such as psychological and emotional elements. The earth relates to the physical, grounded facets of life. The vehicles we drive correspond to our physiologies and the condition of same. So there are general associations that are solid and true for those who don't have a specific individual life aspect that then shifts that generality into a personalized, refined category of interpretation. I think the "Mickey Mouse" interpretation would be the same for everyone unless they went to Disneyland as a child and Mickey accidentally dropped their ice cream cone or something like that and this child grew up with an entirely different perspective about the "Mouse."

Also, as stated in my dream book note, circumstances in one's life can change through experiential events, causing a symbol that heretofore held true to the generalized meaning to now hold an entirely different and personalized one. As life changes, so, too, do the meanings of *select* dreamscape elements. We are all unique individuals having unique dreams. Most of these dream elements can be successfully understood through the use of general interpretations, others are clearly meant to bring a "qualified" message. I think we all know that. It's obvious.

When the spiritual hierarchy makes an appearance to you, are they multicolored? My experience was with someone who appeared iridescently, crystal blue.

Other than perceiving the presence of a few archangel personalities, I've not witnessed appearances of spiritual hierarchy beings. Remember, they are of pure light and, therefore, manifest a physical form as they wish.

Now that you are single, do your beings/spirits make love with you? I mean just a consciousness sharing of spirit—none of the messy, physical crap.

Crap? Messy crap? Is that how you perceive physical love? Let's leave that one alone. Do spirits make love with me? Clearly your intent was to reference the "high" spiritual beings and not the low, earthbound ones who are drawn to physical pleasure. The higher spirits have an all-enveloping love that is expressed through a melding of energies. These energies comprise their very beingness, the totality of their Consciousness. I've felt this nearness, in other words, a peripheral sort of emotional warmth and fulfillment that touches one in an unmistakable manner, bringing a deeply sensual sense with it, but a sensual sense emanating the true essence of what love *really* is.

What does a peridot mean in dream symbology?

A peridot symbolizes a gentle healing, a long-term healing process.

How come you don't write about the universal truths of the UFO races instead of only the spiritual truths?

What? They're one and the same. If you mean writing about the truths of the Starborn *issue* (relating to the reality of their existence and all about them), well, I have no plans to write more about them because I've seen too much of a need for the people of earth to gain a common ground, *average*-level understanding of *themselves* and their relationship to the spiritual universal truths of the Divine Source. All humanoid, intelligent life is bound by the spiritual universal truths of the Source. To attempt to qualify them as being separate "Truths" is to proceed in gross, conceptual error. The Starborn are us. Think about that. To other planetary intelligences, we are the Starborn of earth. We, and all others out there, are all Children of the same Divine Mind and are, therefore, bound by the identical spiritual universal tenets of truth. And one of these tenets is unity. We are all one—one creation—to the Divine Source.

I dreamed that you were in a foreign country—in a Protestant section of it—and they discovered you were Catholic, so they surrounded you and kept you from leaving the circle where a fire was burning. You died of smoke inhalation. Are you planning on going to a foreign country in the near future?

Nope. Your dream was a symbolic one generated from a subconscious fear. This fear is clearly from your perception that my free expression of the universal spiritual truths will cause my eventual demise by religious factions. My opinion of this idea is that it's certainly not an improbable scenario, due to the intense intolerance and rampant crimes of hatred on this planet, but I wouldn't be diligent in performing my mission if this sort of religious fanaticism instilled fear in my life and ruled my words.

The symbology of the dreamscape elements in this dream are: a foreign aspect, specific religious sects, me, fire, smoke, and death. Let's take them one at a time. The "foreign aspect" symbolizes *new and different ideas*. The "specific religious sects" represents *spiritual beliefs*. I, of course, indicate *my own spiritual philosophy*. The "fire" refers to *extreme emotional intensity*. "Smoke" symbolizes a sign that *something is amiss* in one's life. And "death" means a *termination or a finality.* So, clearly, you've got a dream that depicts the attempt to passionately terminate another's spiritual philosophies that are different than one's own or those categorized as being the generally accepted belief system. But we're not so naive as to think this wouldn't happen, are we? Like I already stated, the rampant intolerance and hate evidenced in this world naturally lead to intensely emotional acts of judgment and swift condemnation, where the unspiritual individual perceives self as the righteous judge and executioner who takes upon self the quest of purging individualized thought and behavior from their world. This particular dream included my persona because the spiritual philosophy I represent is not the religious party line and it depicted the desire of some to want to silence it. This intolerance certainly is not a new concept and shouldn't shock any of us. I knew this attitude existed when I first wrote *Spirit Song,* so people's intolerance and hatred have been a *peripheral* aspect shadowing my life for a long time. These shadows don't interfere with my work because I keep my face turned to the sunlight. The Light is fulfilling and is a powerful force that keeps drawing me forward. Though ignorance and hatred are vile aspects of life on this planet, they need not also be allowed to lessen my resolve.

I took my mother in. Her memory is going and she's constantly suspicious of me. I can't live with the things she tells people on the phone about me. She's not the mother I once knew. What should I do?

Her mind may not be operating like the mind of the mother you once knew, but, no matter how you cut it, she is still that same mother. She's still that same mother who took care of you when you were young. The same mother who nurtured you, stayed by your bed when you were sick, read you bedtime stories, and was a sounding board throughout your youth. The same mother who was at your side when you delivered your children and who was the best grandma ever.

Alzheimer's alters the mental process. There is no getting around that fact. This condition has altered your mother's mental process, but it has not altered the fact that she is still your mother. I do have empathy for you, though. In previous responses to former questions in this book, I've mentioned that Sally brought her mother to live with us. She's reached the stage where living alone in her townhouse was no longer a safe option for her. Sally drove back to Kansas, put all her mother's affairs in order, packed the whole townhouse by herself, and made arrangements with a real estate friend to sell it. She loaded up a U-Haul and, with Mary Belle and her dog in the cab, drove through a blizzard to bring them to a new home in the mountains where they'd both be cared for. Mary Belle had reached the stage of required "assisted care." Sally did all of this because, back in Kansas, the hospital doctors in Shawnee Mission were about to transfer her mother straight to a nursing home. Sally would have none of it. Mary Belle has been here for almost two years now and, on an hourly basis, the pleasure of predictability never is in evidence.

There are many aspects to Alzheimer's behavior. Suspicion is but one. Accusation is another. Two or three sides to the personality are normal for this illness. Forgetfulness and an inability to bring thoughts to the fore by way of simple verbalization is common. You can get used to this last one through familiarity and can usually help the individual out by finishing out their sentence or by asking them leading questions that can be answered with a yes or no response. Another facet of Alzheimer's is repetitiveness. This comes from forgetting that one just did something, so the person does it again, and again.

I'd like to share some of our experiences with this situation so perhaps you won't feel so frustrated and at wit's end. We took Mary Belle swimming in Cripple Creek and, when she was done with the Jacuzzi, she went and got dressed. It was a chilly autumn evening when we went, so we all wore car-coat-length jackets. When we got home, Mary Belle took off her jacket and she had her underwear on *over* her slacks. It was absolutely the funniest sight. We all made a huge joke of it. Mary Belle laughed the most. We try to keep up her routine living skills and have her use the kitchen (if she remembers to eat), but sometimes she can make herself a sandwich and other times she'll stand in front of the coffee pot and not remember how to pour herself a cup of coffee. Last winter I awoke at 3 a.m. to find Mary Belle sitting out in the cold car in her nightie. She said she'd been "having the best conversation with a most wonderful man." That one sent a chill or two up my spine. I brought her back in and put her to bed. Another evening when the three of us were sitting in the living room watching television, she pointed to the picture window beside my reading chair and asked, "Who are those little children peeking in?" More chills. Nobody was there of course, not out here in the middle of the woods with no neighbors. But then again, when the mental acuity goes, who is to say that these people don't become more psychically sensitive? Maybe there *was* some guardian entity out in that car talking to her. Maybe she perceived the little Starborn ones peeking in that window at us (they do look like children). This fall I was running the steam cleaner on the carpet and Cheyenne began barking at me. I turned off the machine and my dog went to the window and continued barking. I looked and there was Mary Belle, walking far up the driveway. This is no ordinary driveway. It winds a quarter mile up through woods. Sally went and retrieved her mother. Another day, Sally and I returned home from appointments in town and I took the mail over to my desk. I'd just received a royalty payment and was about to sit down and write checks for the stack of bills I had piled up. The bills were gone. I'd never been late paying a bill in my entire life and now a whole "urgent" stack of them were nowhere to be found. Talk about an anxiety attack! Well, Mary Belle comes down the stairs and is absolutely furious. With daggers in her eyes, she accuses us of using her name on all the bills and says, "I'm so mad I could just spit! And just wait till everyone finds out what you've been doing!" We had absolutely no idea what she was talking about. All I knew was that our bills were gone and I needed to get them paid—today! I was so upset I couldn't even talk. Sally explained to her mother that Sally had the same last name as her mother and that my name was on those bills too. Mary Belle saw her *last* name (which is also Sally's) and somehow connected that to my *first* name (which is the same as hers). She thought all our bills had her name on them. She'd been combining my first name with Sally's last name and came up with hers. She was completely mortified when she finally understood her mistake, so now we had to get the bills out of her hiding place, trouble was—she forgot where that was. Sally and her mother searched and searched Mary Belle's bedroom. Sometimes hidey things get shoved in the bottom of her laundry hamper or in a shoebox. They searched for half a day up there, while I looked in the hidey places downstairs. In the microwave, between the pages of books, under throw rugs, in the freezer, the potato bin. Nada. Zip. Finally Sally found the stack of bills shoved in the cabinet by the back door where we keep the dog leashes, flashlights, and work gloves. What a relief! Most often Mary Belle doesn't remember our names or those of her two other children. More than once she has asked, "Is there a bathroom in this place?" I could give dozens more examples, but you get the idea that we're experiencing the same thing as this correspondent.

This type of condition also evidences a wide range of moods. We've experienced sweet and kind to physically combative. Sensitivity and emotional tears of "thanks for putting up with me" to very harsh and angry words. But that's just the nature of the situation. You see? A mother *is* still a mother. She doesn't mean the meanness. She doesn't mean the accusations and suspicion. Because if you confront her with it, she'll just deny it ever happened. Maybe she really did forget she said those things, or maybe it becomes a spontaneous defense mechanism that's all too handy to use. Whatever it is, it's still your mom. Although Mary Belle is not my mom, she's still an elder who needs to be taken care of on a daily basis. She's still an elder in need. So my advice to you is to just chill out. Oh sure, there are days when I really need to get away, but I don't. Especially now that it's getting to the point where we don't trust leaving her by herself for more than a few hours. But there are ways to be creative in living with this. That creativity comes from love. The reason you're caring for your mother is out of love. Make that be your grounding force that rationalizes the daily unpredictability and serves to balance out the stress. It's so easy to say, "This isn't my mother." It is. And you love your mother. Put yourself in her place forty years from now. Wouldn't you want your own children to care for you out of love instead of sticking you in a nursing home because you became someone who seemed other than the mother they once knew?

What's happened to love? To familial responsibility? What's happened to this nation as a whole in respect to caring for our elders? What I see happening out there sometimes makes me feel ashamed to be a part of this human race. Yes, it is incredibly hard to care for those with this kind of illness. Yes, it's deeply frustrating to tell the individual the same thing over and over again because, a minute later, they forget what you've said. *Yes,* some days you feel like nothing more than a twenty-four-hour babysitter. Yes, time to yourself is rare. Yes, some days you're sure you're going to just explode. Yes, they can be incredibly childish, but there are the bright, lucid days too. And yes, *it's all worth it.* And yes, someday you're going to realize what a wonderful thing you did to help the quality of life for another human being . . . especially if it's for an elder as precious as a parent.

Society is so centered on the "I" that we forget that the singular reason we're here is for the spirit's "I" and not the *physical* I of self. Caring full-time for a parent who you've taken into your home is, indeed, a full-time job in and of it-self because the person is not self-sufficient enough to get a cup of coffee sometimes or stands in front of the phone just watching it ring because they're afraid to answer it or forgot how. So the caregiver slips into thoughts of self. Thinks of the things self could be doing or how this new situation is hampering or stifling self's activities or freedoms. You've raised your kids; you don't need to be doing it all over again with your parent. But listen, if we're all here in bodies to carry out the higher behavior of the spirit that inhabits that physical body, why wouldn't using that body for the spiritual work of caring for an elder be a wonderful act of Unconditional Goodness? What a perfect opportunity! And how convenient can it get being right in our own home! In the old days, there weren't a zillion nursing homes in one city. Family took care of family. What ever happened to that beautiful custom?

What does balsa wood mean in a dream?

This dreamscape element symbolizes talents and/or thoughts that lighten one's burdens. This is associated with perspectives or abilities that ease life by way of positive thinking, optimism, acceptance, or utilizing one's inherent skills of analytical thinking.

I dreamed that my boyfriend was concealing an asp snake in his pocket. I can't figure out what that means. Do different species of snakes carry different meanings?

Yes, they do. Just as different species of flowers, trees, fish, and birds carry specific symbology, so too do the variet-ies of snakes. The asp indicates a "threatening relationship." This association may not currently present any visible type of problem; however, the asp element clearly comes as a cau-tionary warning to be aware and watchful.

I'm generally a very optimistic and outgoing person. At work I always have a smile and am bubbly (I like my job). How is it that some co-workers find fault with that?

Bah! Humbug! Don't you know that misery does love company? Sure you do. Jealousy. Envy of your lightheartedness is the answer. Their outlooks aren't as bright as yours so, therefore, anyone exhibiting happiness or anything mildly close to it gets criticized. Don't allow their negativity to affect you. They have to deal with their own life just as you're dealing with yours. The difference is *how* this is managed. Clearly, you have Acceptance and can deal with life much more effectively than your co-workers. Hey, keep that face to the sun. Keep smiling; your bubbly personality is putting some sunshine into the lives of those you touch. Isn't it a shame that people would rather criticize the happiness they see in others instead of putting in the effort to raise their own perspective up into a higher level of optimism? They must think it's easier to stay negative than to shift into a more positive mode. In today's world, people understand people with problems far more than they understand people who go around with a happy face. Like the song goes, "Be-e—e Happy."

Are you going to do any more children's books?

At one time I had manuscripts for six of them in my desk. At one time I'd sent them out to a trillion publishers (or so it seemed) who declined them. At one time I cleaned out my desk and tossed them all into File 13. I may resurrect a couple of them. Who knows? I've learned to never say never about writing. Right now I have tentative plans for a couple of highly unusual and unique writing projects that I'm keeping under wraps because one is very different from anything I've ever done. The idea for it came to me in a dream. When I awoke and replayed the visual, I actually laughed at the creativeness because it amused me that I'd never thought of doing it on my own. Where the idea *originally* came from, well, "heaven only knows." I've not breathed a word of this idea to anyone as yet and don't plan to until it's completed and ready to go. It's so different I may even self-publish it . . . wouldn't want someone mimicking my idea. I've had a wee problem with that sort of thing.

Do we meet the Starborn ones when we become spirit?

All intelligent life forms in existence everywhere are just borrowing physical bodies. When they die they return to spirit. Spirits are of Light. On the spirit plane, we are all the same and communicate with one another.

When we're in spirit can we incarnate to other planets?

Sure, usually a spirit experiences many planetary lives. Karma can be balanced *anywhere*.

I cry when I read certain passages in your books, or see another person crying, or hear of a sad experience someone had. Is that empathy? My tears can't help anyone, so maybe I should be praying for them instead of shedding tears.

Yes, that's empathy. That's spiritual sensitivity and this type of emotional response to another is the same as prayer. It can effect the same results as prayer. Thoughts are things; they are energy. Prayer is thought. Emotional expressions are thoughts energized. And true tears strengthen the energy of those thoughts. True tears for another become prayer.

Why is there so much hatred in the world?

Ego and a gross lack of acceptance. The tendency to compartmentalize people into ethnic, religious, social status, gender, lifestyle, geographical region, etc., causes the massive extent of separatism we witness in the world. First and foremost we are all, every one of us, an earthly race of human beings. But that isn't perceived. It isn't even seen as the reality. Yet being a human being doesn't soothe the ego nor stroke it enough. People have to designate additional characteristics to distinguish themselves from others so that they can stand out from the rest. This then creates a better than/lesser than graduated level of perception followed by judgment followed by condemnation followed by persecution. It's the ego from which hate is born. Pure ego. I too am guilty of strong hatred. I hate hate. I abhor prejudice, expressions of elitism, snobbery, intolerance, etc. I'm going to stop right here because I feel a soapbox marathon coming on. The answer to the cause of hatred is ego—an overblown, superior sense of self. Plain and simple.

When we survive close brushes with death, does that mean we've not yet fulfilled our purpose in this life?

Mmmm, not necessarily. You see, you could've already fulfilled your specific purpose, but may also be situated in a unique position to be beneficial to others. Small children also survive close brushes with death. Elders do, too. It usually indicates that your time to board the Train to Beyond has not yet arrived. Your ticket for the heavenly realm hasn't been stamped yet. It's just been looked at and returned to you until you're ready to present it another time.

I have read so many knowledgeable people write that prayers should be done in a subservient position because it shows respect for God, yet that feels uncomfortable to me. What do you think?

Strange knowledge. Strange and contradictory because the Divine Trinity doesn't want servants. They want intelligent thinkers with free wills and individuality who reflect their understanding of Spirituality through reason and logic.

People were not created to be slaves nor servants, but rather to be true Children of the Divine who show respect through *living* the Word in their daily lives.

Prayer, as I've previously commented on, is not confined to any kind of strict technicality such as bodily position, format, rote recitation, emotional state, or any other condition. Prayer is free expression of the heart, mind, and soul. Prayer can also be a good deed, a kind word directed to another, a helpful gesture, a smile, holding to Silence when compelled to voice an unkind thought, etc. Life is full of opportunities to express prayer in an endless variety of ways. Have you ever thought that admiring a beautiful sunset is a form of prayer? Sure it is. So are feelings of empathy. When a lump in your throat arises when watching a newscast of starving children in another country, that's a prayer expressing compassion. Giving someone a much-needed hug can be seen by God as an act of prayer. Give-aways of possessions are an active expression of prayer.

Generally, religious folks tend to perceive prayer as a bended-knee type of position while verbally or mentally making a request of God or giving thanks for something. Although this visual is okay, true prayer is not normally accompanied by a supplicant position nor pious attitude. One's entire life can be a never-ending prayer depending on what he/she perceives as prayer. One can choose to make moments of prayer, or one can make life an eternal prayer that never reaches the Amen stage until the last breath is exhaled.

Why are people dumber than dirt?

I liked this question because it was so open and honest. I could give what No-Eyes would say was a "smart-mouth" answer, but generally, people act dumber than dirt because they just don't use their minds. They're lazy. They don't apply any effort to logic or reason, much less any common sense or rationale. What's even more amazing is that they don't seem to care, either. Being dumber than dirt is a psychological defense mechanism that people seem to think makes personal responsibility run off of them like water off a mallard's back.

I know how important Acceptance is, but, for me, it's becoming a dreaded word. How can I get past this?

Uh-huh, I know what you mean. We know that Acceptance is how we should behave and, at times, this quality can be a bugaboo, a drudgery to pull into our lives when it'd be so much easier to just let the natural reactions or emotions to have their way and be done with it. Yeah, it is hard at first because it has to be a conscious choice to choose Acceptance over natural responses. It's real easy to think: "Oh Lord, I've got to accept this. I've got to work at accepting this. I'm tired of putting in the effort to accept so much." But believe me, the effort is well worth the time and frustration put into it, because one day you'll notice that it took no effort at all to automatically accept something you *thought* you'd have to really work at.

I'll give you a helpful hint to assist in perceiving this Acceptance as less drudgery. Acceptance is a quality of the powers of Wisdom. It is *Wisdom* you're using when you accept things in life that you can't change. Now, won't it be much easier to think of gaining acceptance for something by realizing that you're really gaining and practicing Wisdom by doing it instead of the negative practicing thought of working at having that ol' Acceptance word? Every single time you practice Acceptance, you practice Wisdom. You gain greater spiritual strength (power, if you will) by practicing Acceptance. Acceptance is Wisdom.

In your opinion, what is the very worst aspect of society as you see it?

Hatred/intolerance and the persecution it brings.

Why do incidents of societal "mass celebration" so easily turn into mass violence?

An example of this is a city's baseball team winning the pennant. Masses of celebrants throng the streets with excited joy that quickly becomes uncontrollable demonstrations of pent-up energy. The individual energy coalesces into a joined monster of mindless movement that expresses itself on everything in its way. This has been witnessed time and time again. Mob mentality creates mob action and reaction. The momentum gains in strength and plows through the streets without respect to person or property. So how can this happen? It happens because society is in an acute state of incredible stress. Magma roils right beneath the thin skin of societal decorum. I made comments about this before—road rage, remember? Road rage is a like example of the reason why this mass celebration so quickly turns to mass violence. There is deep frustration and anger within people. For whatever reason, they are ready to explode at the slightest provocation or reason. Whether that reason is someone cutting you off on the road or winning the pennant makes no difference, it still creates the spark that sets off the internal ignition switch. But why?

Without realizing it, people are surrounded by noise and other people. The pace of the world has increased at an amazing rate. Traffic, communication, workload, etc., all add together to create a state of internal pressure. People need solitude. People need quiet. People need to release the vent on the pressure cooker and leave it open for a while. I have plenty of quiet up here in the mountains with no neighbors or traffic, yet the constant drone of a television and its endless yakking can drive me right out of the cabin. Though I understand that an elder in the family can easily watch an entire day of the Game Show Network on television, I cannot. So I find a way to work around it and gain some time of respite from it. I'm up here in a semi-remote region of the mountains and the television drone can drive me up a wall. What of most folks who have to work and live in the city, dealing with horrendous traffic and stress-filled jobs all day long? People are inundated by noise and pressure. They're frustrated. They're stressed. Every small opportunity to release that pressure is taken. But we're all still human beings who know and can identify bad behavior. There is still a puzzlement as to why people's stress needs to be released in a violent manner instead of a productive one. Their decency and reason is compromised by the actions of others. In a mass situation it becomes a condition of a hysteric contagion infecting the intellect. And the energy builds while it is carried forward in mindless motion. Solitude. Quiet. Time to reflect and hear our own thoughts. Hear the beating of our own hearts. Peaceful and tranquil atmosphere. Experiencing a state of Beingness . . . just being. These are the rejuvenators. The Balancers.

Do you think the emphasis many people are placing on the Virgin Mary is sacrilegious?

I think the term sacrilegious is too strong to use for this issue. The fascination with a female personage of *semi-deity* is as close to preserving the ideology of a Goddess and worshipping her as present-day society can get. Notice that the Virgin Mary groups are mostly women. These women are seeking out some sort of a Feminine Spirituality to hold within their hearts. What I question is this: Why the Virgin Mary? Why that *particular* historical character? Well, clearly it's because people today aren't familiar with history. They don't know about all the other virgin mothers who birthed saviors and messiahs before Christ came on the historical late scene. They have no idea that the Virgin Mary was the *last* religious legend maker. Before her—*way* before her—was the virgin Maya who birthed Gautama Buddha in 600 B.C. There was the virgin who gave birth to the savior Mithra in a stable on December 25th. Or the virgin Ishtar who was called "Holy Virgin" and birthed the Babylonian god Adonis. Or the virgin who birthed the Greek God, Dionysus, in a stable.

The virgin who gave birth to Indra in Tibet around 700 B.C. And the virgin Devaki who birthed Krishna in 1200 B.C. So you see, to center on the Virgin Mary for one's focus of worship is simply because she is the only semi-deified feminine entity of the Bible's recent history. Virgin mothers go back centuries before then. It's more than interesting why these other famous virgin mothers don't "channel" or make vision appearances to the faithful. It would seem that ignorance of spiritual history is the prime reason, because, well, where are the channeled messages from the virgin who gave birth to Mithra on December 25th? Or the sightings of visions of the virgin Devaki, who birthed Krishna way back in 1200 B.C.? No, I don't think these Virgin Mary situations are sacrilegious, only obvious, obvious that folks are ignorant of spiritual history and, therefore, have only the recent biblical characters to resurrect and animate.

I must be a wicked person because I sure have no rest in life.

Why are you characterizing yourself by way of a silly saying? If you're going to do that, I have a better one for you. "No rest for the *righteous.*" Now there's one you can hang your hat on.

What does it mean to dream that you work at the Better Business Bureau?

It means that you have professional integrity. The dream is emphasizing support for your professionalism and business conscience. It means that you possess a business perspective that's fair and that you put it into practice.

If our Consciousness is the "real" us, are the terms subconscious and superconscious misnomers?

Nope. They define the different depths of consciousness. Yes, the dream state is the subconscious-at-work, as you thought. The superconscious is a far deeper level where Quantum Meditation takes place. The entire Consciousness holds all experiential events that happen on each level, though our awake level is primarily confined to thought and reason. The subconscious and the superconscious are active regardless of the state of one's physical body.

Out of all your family members and friends, who knows you best?

Those who lived with me the longest know me the least because they were continually exposed to two people's (parents) perspectives, opinions, and personalities simultaneously. More often than not, those three qualities were in opposition and never presented a "pure" perspective of either individual, or any specific situation, or spiritual experience. This was not always obvious; therefore, some came through life without the clarity, higher knowledge, and comprehension that I would've wished. With some, spiritual commitment faltered. With others, focus shifted to self. And with some, negativity, resentment, and absolute denial set in. There's a stanza within the ancient Gnostic writings of *The Thunder, Perfect Mind* section that I particularly identify with because it hits home and has proven to be so true of my personal and spiritual life. It is the following:

"Those who are close to me have been ignorant of me, and those who are far away from me are the ones who have known me."

Those who were closest to me have the barest, surface understanding of me, my work, and how it originally manifested on multidimensional levels. They remain clueless. And I've seen evidence of those I don't even know who have reached a natural, inner Knowing of me through clear insight. Yet there is but one living individual who has an absolute comprehension and spiritual alignment with my beingness and purpose.

Have you become a feminist?

Become? I am a woman, am I not? A large part of why I'm here is to release the ideology of the Feminine Principle of the Consciousness from the designation of myth and to cut the bonds of Feminine Spirituality that patriarchal religion has kept captive in its dank, dark catacombs. For two thousand years the myth of an all-male Trinity has prevailed. The millennium marks the beginning of the end of this myth. The millennium will mark, among other events, the return to Spiritual *Reality* by bringing the Feminine Aspect of Divinity to the fore. Feminist? If bringing Truth is being a Feminist, then shouldn't we all be one? This ideology not only applies to the spiritual world, but within the general populace of society as well. It's a fact that women are still being treated like second-class citizens and the chattel of men. The Church of Latter-day Saints held a trial for their church organist, Sonia Johnson, who they discovered supported ERA (Equal Rights Amendment) and she was excommunicated. Former congresswoman Pat Schroeder writes a revealing memoir of her many years in government and called it "an over-age frat house, a boy's club." Let's get real here and address the reality of society.

Sometimes I have strange moods come over me and I do weird things like go out and sit in my wooded yard in the middle of the night. Do you do odd things, too?

Strange moods? Odd things? Never, I say "never" because I don't think these kinds of things are strange or odd. Do I suddenly run outside in *bare feet* when the full moonlight is dancing with the gently falling snow and my joy compels me to twirl around and around in the blue curtain of snow? Yep. Do I suddenly find a tear of love pooling in the corner of my eye while hugging and staring into the tender eyes of one of my little pups? Yeah, I do. Do I jam on the brakes of the truck and pull over to get out and talk to an owl I spied in the treetops? Of course! Do I lie down and roll in the fallen autumn leaves? Yep. I've also been in an electronics store when Sally has had to gently escort me out, so I wouldn't embarrass myself because I couldn't stop tears rolling down my cheeks from feelings of empathy for something I'd seen on a newscast on one of their television sets. Strange moods? Odd behavior? I call it sensitivity . . . an "all my relations" connection to life.

Do you still have a Prayer Circle out in your woods?

I had one out in the forest a little ways from my former stone cabin. It was a time when it was a very important and supportive facet of my life. Sally was the only person to ever witness several of my moonlight, altered-state prayer times, because she sat a distance away as a guardian. I would leave the circle with leaves in my hair or be out there for so long I'd be completely covered in snow. In my new place I have felt no need to create such a place for prayer. The necessity isn't there, for all extraneous elements to prayer have been naturally shed and left behind. Now *everywhere* is a good place to pray.

Regarding a comment you made in your last book about people who profess to have conversations with God, do you not think it is possible that others can do this, too? That it's not just you who has this ability. I admire you greatly for bringing so many truths to the world, but that comment made you sound like you thought you were the only "guru" to bring out truth and knowledge for the new millennium.

Whew! There's some confusion here. What do you mean when you say "me *too?*" I never claimed to talk to God. I never said I had this ability. And how is that an "ability" anyway? Anyone can talk to God. For heaven's sake, don't we do that when we pray? I think it's clear that you mean "bringing messages back *directly* from God's *mouth.*" Now, that I never claimed to do either. It implies that God picked that individual to be His personal spokesperson, like a modern-day Moses. I rather think that God indirectly communicates to everyone on this planet (and others) in a very private and individual manner.

Now, what is this "guru" word all about? Jeez, Louise, don't I continually stress how I'm just like everyone else out there? That I'm no better, higher, or holier than thou? That I am equal? You do me a great disservice to misquote me as if I've ever implied or considered myself to be a guru when I've continually stressed over and over again to never do that . . . regarding anyone.

Also, I think this is a good time to finalize this subject matter. This issue wasn't even an issue until some books came out regarding it. But I must remind you, long before these books became an idea in the author's mind's eye, I'd made definitive comments on this subject way back in *Daybreak*. Let's keep some rationale with this. It would appear that some folks think I'm in some kind of author "sour grapes" mind-set because of several books that were published about talking to God and Him talking back. My published opinion *predates* these books by several *years* and, when my opinion was published back then, not a single soul thought anything of it. But now my opinion is treated like it's something entirely new and I'm, for whatever reason, bad-mouthing these other books. I am personally fed up with that attitude, because it shows how quickly and easily people tend to believe negatively about someone rather than going back and looking at the recorded facts or using a smidgen of logic. Better go back to the book I published in 1991. However, if I ever did have an ongoing communication with a Deity, I would hope it would rather be with the Mother Goddess Herself. Don't hold your breath for it; I'm certainly not. And I hope this finally closes the door on this ridiculous and wildly presumptuous issue.

I'm a bookseller and I'm wondering why I never see you make an appearance at the annual ABA (American Bookseller's Association) conventions? I'd sure like to see you there.

You most likely would if it were ever held in Denver, but it seems that California and Chicago are the preferred sites. You know, people snicker when I suggest Denver, but it's not the cow town folks think of it as being. I don't travel to California or New York because of premonition dreams of warning I've had of those two locales. These come for a reason and I give them a lot of credence. My reason for not attending a California site has nothing at all to do with possible earth movement, but rather because I take my personal premonitions seriously. The same goes for flying. I don't fly because of a strong warning dream I had many years ago. I have no reservations about friends or family flying, because my dream was not about them, just me. Consequently, having to drive everywhere, especially across country, takes a great deal of extra time and expense. I have other considerations in my life now—an elder who needs daily assisted care—and I can't just take off whenever I want or schedule appearances that take me away from home for more than a day. I have responsibilities and considerations other than those associated with my writings; I won't leave them for the purpose of increasing book sales. I thoroughly enjoy doing book signings where I meet my readers and have an opportunity to personally thank them with warm hugs of appreciation, but I also have to work within the framework which situational home responsibility keeps me balanced within. We all experience changing stages of circumstances in life that alter our priorities and the extent of ability for free movement (to be able to just take off at one's whim). That's just part of life and our ongoing experiential variety that keeps life interesting. So when the ABA comes to Denver, I'd be most happy to bring Grandma along and attend with bells on my toes . . . maybe on Grandma's toes, too.

What does a stonefish mean in a dream?

Spiritual fanaticism, which could be coupled with intolerance of anothers religious belief system.

What about the dream symbology of a goby (fish)?

You're dreaming of some odd fish. The dream symbology of a goby represents individuality—individuality of spiritual thought.

In Fireside, you had a lot of conversational interruptions. Between the dogs, and feeding the fire, and other events, it was very distracting.

I conceived of *Fireside* as a way to invite you into my home and spend a typical evening with me. If you didn't like it there, you didn't have to stay . . . all you had to do was close the book.

What do you think of same-sex marriages? And how about racially mixed marriages?

We need to reduce this question down to the main issue—love. Nobody has the right to tell another who they cannot love. Love is the most beautiful emotion humans have; to put restrictions on it is an abomination.

This is a state election year and our ballot has an abortion amendment. What do you think of this issue?

Spiritually speaking, a spirit does not enter a fetus until such time as it becomes a viable "birthed" infant. A woman's body is her own and no one should have say over any decision she makes regarding that body. It is the height of absurdity for males to have one iota of input on this subject. It is a woman's issue. For males to be active in this issue, whether religiously or politically, is the same as women being active in trying to establish laws forcing every man (or boy) who gets every woman (or girl) pregnant to become a father and take responsibility for that child. Reasonably, men and boys should be prepared to accept that kind of parental responsibility, women and young girls shouldn't be forced to bear the sole life burden of something it took two individuals to create. Perhaps if there were a law that didn't let the male participant off the hook so easily for his actions, the number of anti-abortion proponents would dramatically dwindle. That's just something to think about, because, as it stands, the men and boys who get these women and girls pregnant turn their backs on them and walk away from the situation scot-free; though they created the embryo, they have no intention of being a father to it.

How come you think there's so much hate in the world? I don't see that much of it.

Do you wear glasses? Have you misplaced them? And that was not being sarcastic, it was merely an honest question. I'm going to give you a little mental exercise. Sit down and write every word society has established that relates to hate and intolerance. I'll get you started. Apartheid. Sexism. Genocide. Ethnic Cleansing. Religious Persecution. Gay Bashing. Racism. Chauvinism. War. Holy War. Revenge. Supremacy. Ku Klux Klan. Okay, now you finish the list.

Is it true that medicine people must walk in the Light alone?

I'm sure some medicine people hold to this belief, but they all don't. This really depends on what you mean by "medicine" people. If you mean "spiritual" people, then the answer is a definitive No.

Do we only have one soul mate for each lifetime?

This depends on what your interpretation of the term is. Actually, the idea is a misnomer. There can be several options for that "perfect" mate in a lifetime.

If you are around people with very negative attitudes, do they drain your energy? If so, is there any way to counteract this apart from avoiding them? I do pretty well, but when I'm tired they seem to get to me despite my best effort to retain a positive attitude. I know that the answer is to never let yourself get tired, but this is not always possible.

Whoa, never let yourself get tired? There are lots of times that I'm so damned tired I can't see straight. Everyone gets tired. That's why we sleep—to rejuvenate us physically and mentally.

People with very negative attitudes do not drain me. There are also people who I call "sponges" or "users," who either consciously or subconsciously are natural zappers of everyone else's energy. These don't bother me either. I don't do anything special to shield myself from these types of negative people; I just don't get affected by them in any way. What does seem to zap me is being down in a lower elevation where the atmosphere is much denser than what I'm used to. Then I feel suffocated and smothered. My aura feels like it's being compressed. The other life element that bothers me is being among a mass of people such as with holiday mall shopping and rush-hour city traffic. The hectic, panicky pace and mind-set is incredibly spiky and bothersome. At these times I'm right in the middle of experiencing people's incredible rudeness and self-absorption.

Don't berate yourself for getting tired. Don't beat yourself down for instances when others get to you. My goodness, that's just part of life. Being affected by others is part of our sensibilities. Just don't internalize it. Okay?

People certainly can be tiring, some more than others. Likewise, some folks are more sensitive to their behavior than others are. You sound as though you get angry at yourself over this, or maybe slip into a state of melancholia. The anger is an internalization that you definitely do NOT want to let in, but I can understand the melancholia. I, too, get days when I feel like a sad song. And that's okay. It's really okay.

I think it'd help society if everything associated with an addiction was made illegal. Don't you agree?

No way. That'd be like saying we'd have to remove the cookstove from the kitchen so the child will not touch it and get burned. Your premise removes the option of choice and free will from life. Your supposition is also quite impossible. Why? Because you've not thought through all the ramifications of what an addiction can be associated with.

Okay, say we remove everything anyone can be addicted to or, as you suggest, make all these things illegal. What that means is that candy (especially chocolate) would be illegal to eat because millions of people are addicted to chocolate. Alcohol, of course, will mean no glass of red wine with holiday dinners, no more communion wine for Catholics, no champagne at weddings. Would morphine also be illegal to use? Well, let's go on. There'd be no food in the stores, because thousands of people are addicted to eating. And we'd probably have to take away the merchandise in stores, because many, many folks have this compelling, addictive behavior called kleptomania. Games like Nintendo for the kids and the Internet for the adults would have to go, too, because these have been addictive for many. Oh, yeah, another little item that psychiatrists see a lot of is sex addiction. That'd definitely have to be illegal. No? Well then, are you going to selectively pick and choose which addiction will be made illegal? You said *all* of them. Yeah, after thinking it through, it'd be a good idea to just pitch the entire idea in File 13. Society has already selected which ones are to be illegal. Their random selection has been illogical and leaves much to be desired. They've gotten on the bandwagon about tobacco, yet thousands of people are killed every year by drivers drunk with alcohol. It's okay to purchase, consume as much as you want, and drive on the streets, and go home and beat your wife and kids, because alcohol isn't banned from public buildings like tobacco is. Where's the logic in that? If tobacco is banned, why isn't alcohol? It's the alcohol that "alters" the mental faculties and impairs and changes behavioral patterns.

The analogy of the rising Phoenix was very meaning-ful, but I'm not sure what the Phoenix represents. Does it mean Grandmother Earth's spirit?

Partially. It represents an aspect of her spirit, a rejuvenated and completely renewed spirit which is cleansed from mankind's contaminates. But for the most part it, represents the *Spirit of Truth,* which is set free after being confined within the prison of mankind's pollution of falsehoods. The Phoenix represents the freeing of Pure Truth. You see, over time, Truth becomes contaminated and buried beneath the hundreds of man-made religious dogmas that are heaped upon it over the passing centuries; consequently, a major cleansing must occur in order for Truth to break free of its bonds and rise up again in all its beautiful, living reality. Hence the analogy of the Phoenix. And now, because of modern-day technology, the contaminates shoved within the earth are causing her spirit pain. The nuclear waste buried within her breast, chemical dumping in her waters, pollutants spewed into the air from manufacturing smokestacks, etc., all require correction in order for her to maintain a healthy environment for us to survive in. A correction period is imminent.

Some of your books were dark (depressing) and I'm glad to see that you've come out of that phase.

Phase? The phase wasn't due to me, but to something I was required to do—hold up a large mirror so society's behavior could be accurately reflected back on self. It's always an unwelcomed experience to be forced to look reality in the face without the aid of rose-colored glasses. I agree that there were depressing issues that were covered, but it's societal behavior that made them so. Calling a spade a rose is not why I'm here. There are plenty of other books and authors who will tell you what you want to hear; I'm here to tell you what Is. Sometimes that reality isn't as pretty as we'd like it to be. Sweetness and Light is okay, but it will not serve advancement unless reality is first acknowledged and used as a basis for change. I will always call a spade a spade, but so will I always call a heart a heart, a rose a rose. Balance is the key. Yes, the reality of society's behavior contains much darkness of hate, intolerance, and ego, yet there is also much unconditional goodness and spirituality in evidence. My work involved exposing both; when it entailed the negative side, that phase did seem depressing. Now you noticed that the books seem to have more of an up side and that's because they do (and will). The negative phase of exposing the darker side of society's reality is over. I don't intend to be redundant with it.

I don't have that all-consuming total faith that I so desperately want. How does a person get that? Saying "just DO it" doesn't work for me.

Faith in one's belief system comes from having confidence that what you believe is true and right for you. It's a comfortable and settled feeling. I'm not sure how you personally identify "faith" or the supposed, expected feel of it. Perhaps you're in overexpectation regarding how faith is *supposed* to feel. Generally, if you're comfortable with your beliefs and don't find yourself having outstanding doubts, then you already have faith. Faith is a quiet quality. It doesn't have to be a Mardi Gras thing that jumps up and down in front of you (or inside you). Most often, faith is a subtle serenity. Faith; I personally don't ever recall questioning it or even thinking of it. It just is.

I once went to confession and admitted to the priest that I was having a problem with faith. He told me to not come back until I had a handle on it. How could he do that?

You'd have to ask him that. I've observed members in religious orders behave as though they're in their spiritual prime when the congregation is highly devoted, yet when that devotion comes into question, the religious men are thrown into a dither and don't know how to handle it. The people's faith makes and keeps the religious leaders strong, but a lack of faith is something they don't deal well with . The religious leaders are supposed to be there for their faithful, to give advice, counsel, and succor. They do little good to tell a parishioner to go away and not come back until the problem's fixed.

Your photograph on Fireside *and in your 1999 calendar makes you look thirty. How can you stay looking so young after all you've been through?*

That photographing session was the last time I looked that way. It amazes me how I've aged since then. Yes, my life experiences have finally caught up with me. The aging process has made up for lost time. You may not even recognize me if you come to a future book signing.

Hint: don't look for someone with a young face and long, black hair. In the last year, the silver hair has taken great strides in overtaking the dark color and it's done a good deal of natural thinning and shortening (genetic—both my mother and grandma wore wigs by the age of 45). My "feminine elder," the Crone, is having her coming-out party. And I gracefully, and gratefully, welcome her entrance.

My friend believes that before we evolved into human souls, we were all a particular animal and that we still carry that animal energy as our present-day totem. Can you explain what animal totems really are?

"Before we *evolved* into human souls?" We never evolved into human souls; we were originally *created* as such. Except for a brief phase directly following Creation, human spirits were never confined within animal physiologies.

Totems. What are those things anyway? Totems are really all the naturally influencing life energies of various vibrations emanated from differing life forces. Belief in these energies (totems) has crossed culture bounds since ancient times and has been in evidence in people's belief systems from the "Nature/Mother Goddess" ideology of the Celts all the way into our present time by now showing up in the recently discovered theories of modern-day physicists.

I've received so much correspondence asking about this matter that my readers brought my attention to a void in the subject matter in my writings. Consequently, I wrote an informative reference book on the energy influences with which various living aspects of life gift us. I wrote it simultaneously while working on *Eclipse.* The book is called *The Singing Web,* and should be invaluable to those wanting to know more about the energy influence of different species of trees, flowers, birds, animals, fish, gems, rocks, and metals. For each entry, I included the dream symbology along with the specific type of influencing energy the particular living essence emanates. This body of work is closely associated with the conceptual content of *Earthway,* because the natural life and essences of Grandmother Earth and the many beautiful ways She gifts us with Her graces is all part of the interrelatedness of life. The work is a natural addendum book to *Earthway.* We are each a strand of Life's DNA Web that sings with the vibrating Song of Life. *The Singing Web* will be available in the fall of 1999 from Hampton Roads.

Being in a bookstore can sometimes be so overwhelming. Could you make a few title suggestions for me?

Sure, be happy to. For nonfiction, I suggest the following: *The Jesus Conspiracy: The Turin Shroud & the Truth about the Resurrection,* by Kersten & Gruber, published in the U.S. by Element; *Revelation: St. John the Divine's Prophecies for the Apocalypse and Beyond,* by Peter Lorie, published by Simon & Schuster, *Mysticism—The Preeminent Study in the Nature and Development of Spiritual Consciousness,* by Evelyn Underhill, published by Doubleday; *Nostradamus: Prophecies for Women,* by Manuela Dunn Mascetti and Peter Lorie, published by Simon & Schuster; *Amazon Beaming,* by Petru Popescue, published by Viking Penguin.

For enjoyment and leisure, I suggest the following worthwhile fiction: *Foucault's Pendulum,* by Umberto Eco, published by Ballantine Books; *The Prophetess,* by Barbara Wood, published by Little, Brown & Company; *The Fountainhead,* by Ayn Rand, published by Signet; *The Memoirs of Cleopatra,* by Margaret George, published by St. Martin's Press. These listings could be quite long, but these are enough to get you started . . . and thinking.

Have you completely shed all native aspects of your life?

I know you meant "American Indian" aspects. The answer is no, because within the totality of my consciousness I retain a "nativeness" to Egypt, France, England, and North America. Each of these are vitally alive facets of the total "who" of the person I am today. There is current evidence of these nationality characteristics in how I've decorated my home, in things I'm drawn to, and how I dress. My cabin contains items from the Egyptian, English, and American Indian culture. At home, my attire is most often peasant blouses and long, ankle-length calico skirts worn with knee-high moccasins. I don't load down with the turquoise jewelry as I once did, because, quite frankly, I find that I'm uncomfortable wearing more than a couple of favorite antique pieces. I'm just not much of a jewelry person. My home has a mountain/trapper feel to it due to the many furs and beautiful pelts readers have gifted me with. These are accented by intricate and colorful beaded work in the way of medicine pouch necklaces people have made me, walking sticks, and handcrafted pottery along with the dozens of country baskets and hand-picked herbs hanging from the rafters. I'm very attracted to the artistic work of Thomas Kinkade, who paints English cottages. For me, these are extremely reminiscent of the Cottswold cottages I was so accustomed to seeing in my experiential past lived in England. Another aspect of this same lifetime is a high attraction to heavily carved, dark wood furniture.

So to think that any aspect of my consciousness' past has been obliterated is an assumption. All of them are very much within me and a part of my current totality. They are all evident in the items I choose to surround myself with. Now, instead of choosing just one nationality to identify with, all of them have become a pleasing *blend* comprising my current identity. Everyone is a composite of everyone they've ever been, of every nationality they ever were. All of these are the components making up one's present-day spirit consciousness. When you realize this through the recognition of the "carry-over" experiences and traits of past lives and are open to that totality of consciousness, you naturally exhibit that wonderful blend of the real who of you and understand your true identity. When you're only aware of the current ego, you're stuck, so to speak, in the singular ethnic identity you now experience in this life. In our consciousness we are all ethnic composites.

Is it being fatalistic to accept the coming Changes as being inevitable?

Having the wisdom to recognize an inevitability is not the same as having a fatalistic worldview. Is it being fatalistic to believe that your physical body will one day expire? No, that's simply admitting to an inevitable fact of life. Inevitable and fatalistic are not synonyms for each other. Fatalism is a voluntary attitude. Inevitability is a fact that is not affected by choice. If an event is inevitable, it will happen. However, the exact aspects of the happening can alter due to the probability of affecting elements that cause the ultimate manifestation. An example of this would be a foreseen event, such as a hurricane striking the South Carolina coast. What probability factors do to this foreseen event is to have the ability to alter the speed, wind intensity, and direction of said hurricane. It still strikes the coast, that was seen as an inevitable event, but the *severity* can be affected by the probability of affecting factors coming into play. Just because an event is foreseen as being inevitable doesn't also mean that it can't be affected by altering factors. Having acceptance of the inevitable is not the same as having a fatalistic view. Having recognition and acceptance is having the wisdom to know the difference between fatalism and inevitability.

My spiritual teacher told me that all sickness comes from the mind, that all disease is karmically related. I'm having a difficult time putting total faith in those statements.

And well you should. In *Daybreak* I responded to a similar question by reminding the questioner that animals also get sick and have diseases. How then can they manage these when they don't experience karma? It's true that the mind can bring about sickness and disease through negative thought and stress. But these causal factors are simply instigating elements—an impetus—that *activate* a state of physical vulnerability and susceptibility. Mental negativity and stress degenerate the effective strength of the immune system, whereby the whole of the physiological being becomes more open to invading germs, viruses, bacteria, and inherently present conditions that have heretofore been existing within the system in a benign and neutral state, possibly as one of the retroviruses. Herpes simplex is an example of this. This viral aspect is present in the human body, but through negative thought and stress, coupled with the overingestion of the amino acid L-Arginine, through the intake of chocolate, peanut butter, and nuts, stimulates this virus into an active high gear instead of sustaining its former state of benign existence within the system. Yet this example has been given by using a natural "existing" viral aspect that is always present within the body. The premise of your teacher suggests that the mind creates *all* sickness and disease, and this just is not so. Neither is it true that all sickness and disease is karmically generated. When we incarnate, we can choose to enter into an imperfect body if we want. But even that choice does not emphatically indicate a "karma-related" event. All choices of the spirit are not indicative of a *necessity* to balance out karma. They merely represent the spirit's personal choice. The reasons for each choice are so multitudinous that it would be foolhardy to attempt to pinpoint the precise reason for such a decision.

Let's apply deeper reason here. If an entire village in Africa or South America were wiped out by flash floods, does that mean it was all those people's karma? Phooey! If a plague ravaged ten villages, was that their karma? No way. Their minds did not call that plague to them. They did not create that fatal sickness to be visited upon them and their children. I don't know why folks can't seem to understand that life is life. Viruses and germs are a living aspect of our planet. To think that our minds bring these things upon us is ignorance. The sun shines down on us too. Do our minds cause that? Do our negative thoughts cause our child to be born with a disease? No. Every body contains DNA that carries a certain amount of naturally *inherited susceptibility* to certain physiological diseases or unhealthful conditions. Perhaps your own genes carry a marker for bone cancer or Parkinson's. Negative thought and stress can act as a factor that *stimulates* this existing condition into an active state, but the negative thought and stress did not *manifest* the condition from *nothing*. That's why it's so important to keep a positive attitude in life; have acceptance instead of always bucking those aspects you can't change; ride the waves instead of fighting against the current. Yes, attitude and emotions have a great deal to do with health, but they do not have the ability to actually "create" germ and virus cells, only activate that which already exists within the system. In a sense, by maintaining a positive attitude and practicing true acceptance, we let the sleeping dogs within our systems remain asleep. Only the Divine Source is capable of true creation. We are only capable of pacifying or aggravating those creations. It's important to understand the difference. Reality is a preexisting condition. We cannot *create* our own reality, we can only *shuffle* reality around in an attempt to bring about a more personally pleasing arrangement of it. There's a world of difference between contracting a disease because our thoughts and stress have brought about a susceptible physiology through the running down of the immune system and believing the human mind actually created the disease from nothing.

It seems to me that if people could successfully manage Quantum Meditation that they'd no longer have a need for hypnotists performing past-life regressions or organizations teaching the technicalities of psychic experience.

You've come to an accurate conclusion. Within the consciousness lie the recorded and imprinted experiential events of each individual's existence since Creation. To be able to enter the living core of that consciousness is to know the full extent of one's complete identity. Quantum Meditation is the vehicle that carries one's awareness into this full and expansive consciousness. When this occurs, the individual becomes intimately acquainted with every personality she/he ever was. Here the individual clearly examines every facet that formed her/his living crystal of spirit consciousness. The singular facet (personality) that represents our *current* identity is but one incompleted square on the huge patchwork quilt of our composite identity. The current identity is so incredibly minuscule when contrasted to the reality of the whole. People are so beautiful. Their spirit consciousness possesses such brilliant and diverse identities, skills, accomplishments, and goodness. The seen and observed "who" of folks is so fractional and limited in scope. Perception of others is like thinking you know the whole picture when only holding and knowing one tiny fragment of a 1,000-piece puzzle.

I think society's attitude toward aging is so unfair. Aging men are perceived as being "distinguished," while aging women are seen as "getting old."

Well, why have women allowed society to be overrun with male attitudes? In ancient times, in nearly every culture across the world, aged women were perceived as being the "wise Crone" of the family or community. Women's age equated with great wisdom. She was accepted as the matriarch, and a grand one she was, too. But now, because of the predominant attitude of the male and his generally accepted perception of feminine "beauty," women have adopted the false assumption that real female beauty is a shapely form and a lovely face. Today the wrinkles of experience and the thinning, silver hair are viewed as "lost beauty." But you see, the Grandest Crone of all is going to be returning to your world. And the crones within all women will be inspired to recognize their aging process as something wonderful and most beautiful, while men will hang their heads for focusing on the self-centered physical rather than the universality of the spiritual. The true idea of beauty will once again gain its rightful and respected place in the world. So it's really not an issue of unfairness, because it's more due to women not maintaining their inner, spiritual status as matriarchs and wise women. If you want a true example of the world's unfairness, I have a real example. Our pets age faster than we do. Their untimely deaths cause us great heartache. If I were the Creatrix, I would've made their metabolism the same as ours. I think our pets should have a life expectancy at least as long as 70 years, not the stretch to 20 years as it stands right now. To me, *that's* really unfair.

Are you advocating that the Goddess should replace God?

I'm advocating a return to spiritual *reality*. My goodness, your question implies that I might be out to tip the Deity scale off balance in the opposite direction. What would that serve, other than creating the same situation we now have? We must never ignore or ban any aspect of spiritual reality in deference to the desire to gain and maintain sexist control in society. By this I mean solely patriarchal or matriarchal beliefs. The reality of the Trinity contains both Mother/Father aspects and, as a developed, intellectual people, we need to return to the balance of that reality. My intent is to rekindle the knowing of this true Trinity and to encourage equality of reverence and respect for both. Women and the object of their beautiful feminine spirituality have been forcibly subjected to a singular, male Deity for twenty-plus centuries, as their Mother Goddess was suppressed and deemed heretical throughout all that time. I'm here to resurrect Her by removing the burial shroud that had been placed over her in ancient times. Like the Phoenix, she is preparing to rise to glory once again so that all may see her luminous Light and shining Truth. God Himself well knows that a Mother Aspect to the Trinity exists and I'm sure He wouldn't be jealous if His people again elevated Her to Her rightful place.

What do you think of mixed marriages?

"Mixed"? Isn't that qualifying marriage, like saying "same sex" marriage? Marriage. Just "marriage" is a good thing that bonds lovers together for life. It says, "I love you so deeply and wholeheartedly that I want us to share the whole of our time on this earth together." *Marriage directly and singularly relates to love between two people.* Period! Love. *Unqualified* love. So why has opinionated, intolerant, prejudicial, racist, sexist, bigoted society put qualifiers on love? Nobody has the right to say who can love whom. A Jewish mother will have fits if her son wants to marry a Gentile girl. A Catholic is supposed to only marry a Catholic or else make sure the pagan partner agrees to a conversion. A black/white couple receives dirty looks and suffers unkind comments in public. And a woman who has grown to love another woman equates to two women scorned. Wake up, people. Look what you've done to love. Your high-and-mighty egos and little minds have dirtied it. You've turned a beautiful, emotional gift into an ugly, twisted monster. You've successfully morphed love into hate. Righteousness comes in many forms. Self-righteousness is not one of them.

Is there a spiritual dimension called Summerland?

Sure. It's also known as Heaven, Nirvana, Valhalla, and many other terms.

In Soul Sounds, you recounted an event that Sarah experienced by having an accident generated by the Dark Side, yet in Fireside you tended to imply that those negative ones didn't really interfere with your life. Has that changed or what?

I suppose you could say that it's changed, at least for us it has. There was a window of time when their influence was actively directed toward us, but that's been long passed. Clearly, now that I'm nearly finished giving all the messages I've come to relay, why would they even waste their energy any longer? They've found brand-new messengers to focus their energies on, ones who have egos to influence. No, I can't even recall the last time I gave a thought to those dark ones. Out of sight, out of mind. Out of mind, out of sight. Both seem to apply. Guess they've been replaced by my concern over people's intolerance, hatred, and . . . road rage.

I think I'm doing the White Light of Protection wrong because I can't really see it.

No, no, it's not an actual visual seen with the naked eye; it's a strong *mental* visualization done. It's an imagined visual. A mental *image*. If you can mentally visualize an orange, or a house, or an angel, then you can mentally visualize a brilliant white light surrounding yourself or your vehicle. See? It's the same thing. Thoughts have energy. Remember that.

Are you going to publish an update to the Phoenix Files from the back of Daybreak?

None needed.

I've noticed that people aren't giving much concern over the many dams in our country. Won't they be a major threat during geological upheavals?

Yes, few will hold. Same with bridges. Both man-made structures will quickly lose their integrity, causing massive water inundation and creating a huge number of useless and impassable routes. It's not hard to imagine what it could be like if you can envision the Golden Gate Bridge, the Mackinaw Bridge and others collapsing, or the Hoover Dam cracking from earth pressure and movement.

Does praying for someone's enlightenment interfere with their free will?

Not really because even though they finally "see the light," they still have the choice to accept it or not. Rather than praying for specifics in regard to others, it's better to pray for "that which is best" for them. When praying for specifics, such as a physical healing, we're taking it upon ourselves to determine what is best for the individual when, in actuality, that healing may not be a best-case scenario event in view of this individual's destiny or purpose. To us, because we have such a limited, linear view, a healing would seem to be the obviously best thing to pray for. However, it is because of this linear perspective that we can't see the multidimensional totality of the situation, nor can we imagine the reasons for same. Therefore, directing prayer to what is best in each situation for individuals is far better and more effective.

Each Christmas I manage to give family and friends presents, but this year I just don't have the money. Things are really tight. My sister and mother are having a fit because I can't exchange presents this year with my brothers and sisters and their kids. What's happened to the real meaning of Christmas?

It appears to have been buried beneath greed and selfishness. I've had the occasion to observe this very same situation and I'm so incredulous over this kind of attitude that it leaves me absolutely aghast. This behavior is just pitiful. These people are, in actuality, saying, "I don't care if you can afford it or not; I'd rather you went deeper in debt to get your family presents for Christmas." Jeez, Louise, get a clue. Get your spiritual priorities right.

My suggestion to you is to give of yourself instead. When my own daughters come up against this same dilemma, I tell them to bake cookies for people and put a pretty bow on the plate wrapping. One of my girls has a breadmaker and I suggested that she could bake a variety of fresh bread for people as gifts. And I also tell them if anyone complains about her gift, then they don't deserve to get one in the first place. Christmas is about joy, the joy of celebrating Jesus' birth.

The tradition of gift giving for this holiday came from emulating the acts of the three kings who brought the infant gifts. Perhaps this tradition should've kept more to the subject than shifting to giving others gifts. Perhaps tradition should've stayed with giving *Jesus* gifts of self, such as doing good works, volunteering, practicing extra acts of unconditional goodness, gifting to charities, etc. This whole situation of Christmas being the retailers' dream has buried the entire purpose of the holiday beneath wrapping paper, stress, push 'n' shove shoppers, debts, and a race to achieve the award for best neighborhood house decorations.

I once had a conversation with someone about this situation and their comment was that Christmas has been "Christianized." I didn't see it as being quite that way; I saw it as being bastardized. My friend didn't see our perspectives as being that far apart.

Getting back to the specific point of your original statement, why don't you go with whatever you're comfortable with? You don't have the money for gifts and you want to give them. That's your dilemma. I see the solution as a compromise. Forget the idea of bought, retail gifts and bake some goodies. Or here's another idea that just came to me. One year I had absolutely zip money to buy Christmas presents, so I gave my favorite possessions away to people. How about telling people to give what they'd normally spend on your present to the Salvation Army bell-ringer instead? That takes care of their uncomfortable feeling of not giving you anything if you agree not to exchange.

Over the years I've tried to propose a no-gift Christmas and it never worked. People just cannot seem to attain a real sense of Christmas unless presents are exchanged. You ask where Christmas has gone? I can't answer that one. I can't tell you where it's gone; I can only tell you where it's meaning has gone—out of Christmas.

My husband is not a firm believer in God. He believes that there is "something" out there, but that's all. This disheartens me. What should I do?

You also expressed that your husband is a good man. The world is brimming over with religious people who don't live their beliefs. They are highly verbal about their religiousness and they are bloated with self-righteousness, yet their behavior is full of intolerance, greed, ego, infidelity, etc. They do not live a life of Acceptance or Unconditional Goodness. To the Trinity, actions speak louder than words; actions tell the heart of one, not the mouth. A truly good person naturally emanates a bright living light from their beingness, while the self-righteous religious need flashlights. Spiritual beliefs, the extent of or lack thereof, do not define one's spiritual goodness or worth. If your husband is a good man, he is a blessing to count and cherish. Living the "spirit" of the law is far more important than mouthing the letter of it. The foul-mouthed construction worker with the heart of gold whose steel-toed shoes never set foot in a church can be living a far more spiritual life than the minister. True. Beliefs do not define or equate to one's real inner goodness.

The real spiritual people are vegetarians. You are.

Well, two wrongs here don't make a right. Both statements are wrong. Both are assumptions.

Please understand that physiology has no elements affecting the spirit. A paralyzed body can house a beautifully developed, high spirit. Same with ingestion of substances, food included. *The spirit is THE entity regardless of what body it's housed in and the condition of same, or outside influences upon same.* **The spirit is the total Consciousness. The spirit is not the body.** Can this be made any clearer? The idea of fasting affects the body but in no way cleanses or improves the spirit. The idea of vegetarianism is fine for the body, but it in no way affects the spirit or makes it one iota purer, lighter, or more enlightened. Please, I can't make this any simpler. To hold to this is believing in a false premise, a false assumption based on nothing—no conceptual fact or basis of spiritual reality. To believe otherwise is unwise.

Yes I love animals very much. They are the true innocents of this earth. Yet all earthly gifts of Grandmother Earth were given for a reason. In time of starvation, these animals provide humans with sustenance and, therefore, they are hunted. Hunting. I covered that already. I covered it in respect to the "white hunters" and "sport hunters" who lure the kill for the pure pleasure of it, for so-called enjoyment. When I commented on hunting in the former response, I was not including the American Indian people. Here's something to think about. Do you have any Indian artifacts or hand-crafted effects around your house? What are they made of? A deerskin medicine bag? A beaded elk-hide pouch? Suede? Pelts? Leather belts? Claws? All these didn't come from a manufacturing plant. Do you wear any leather shoes? Nikes? Boots? Sandals? You know, the difference between sport hunters and Indian hunters is ideology and cultural tradition. One hunts for the hell of it; the other hunts out of necessity. One hunts with no thought to an animal's energy or Consciousness; the other hunts with centered thought on both. One hunts to take, while the other hunts to receive. One has no respect for the hunted, while the other gives thanksgiving for the offering of life. No similarity between the two. No comparisons. Only contrasts.

I have many American Indian items throughout my cabin. Most of them have been crafted from some part of an animal. I have a beautiful turtle pouch necklace (these turtles are not killed, but harvested after natural death). I have rabbit, coyote, fox, and timber wolf pelts. Sheep and lambskin furniture coverings, huge elk antlers (which Sarah and I found during a woods hike). And I have a 100-year-old Shoshone wedding dress that, I can assure you, is not made of Chantilly lace and brocade. I have knee-high moccasins. I have a wide variety of feathers and wings all over the house. These were gifted from the birds of my own forest and found during my woodswalking times or tree-harvesting labors. Nature and all aspects of it are a strong aspect of my life. I'm surrounded by its facets and elements, both inside my home and without. Both living and the remnant reminders of same.

I am not a vegetarian. I eat almost everything. Remember the admonishment about this—moderation. I'm not a big meat-eater; I like a "loaded" pizza as tasty as an Italian mama can make it. Don't ingest liver or heart, though. I've never tasted venison because I've had no reason to eat it as long as there's a grocery market still open and stocked with a wide variety of other offerings. I won't fish; don't have the stomach for it. But keeping in mind that moderation is the key to healthy eating is important.

Now while we're on this subject, I want to address an aspect of this that some of you may have thought of. What of my mentor's suggestions regarding eating and some of the associated concepts she'd mentioned throughout the books? Am I not living according to my own words? That's what some folks would think, but those were her words and suggestions, not necessarily my own, personal attitudes. This is important to understand. The books relayed her ideas; while 99.999% of them coincided with my own, I still live my life the way I'm most comfortable. Same with you. You read what my mentor and I have had to say on a wide variety of subjects, yet you have a free will to do what's most comfortable to you. Do I treat every illness I have with the total Gateway Healing System as outlined in *Earthway?* Not usually. This is mainly because I rarely get sick, but the chart was given because she wanted all the healing aspects brought together so people could take advantage of the totality of the system if they so chose. It's all useful information and suggestions.

So let's not make wrongful assumptions with any material read, or about anyone in our lives. Use rational thought and logic. We are all such unique and beautiful individuals. And we are all even more beautiful and unique spirits. Just remember, please, the spirit *cannot* be affected by the physical—especially the body's condition or what it ingests. Spirit is of spirit. Spirit is immaterial Consciousness. The body is of the physical. It is of matter and touchable substance.

I see so much negativity in society—the hate crimes, the intolerance of each other's differences getting worse, more and more incidences of children having no respect for life and committing murder so wantonly—is this situation going to get any better?

The differences caused by people's individuality and uniqueness will be recognized with the wisdom of perceiving each as shining jewels, and the respect for life will be brought to the fore as a beautiful perceptual priority. The important aspects of life become clear only after the former priorities have proven to be shallow and destructive. There will come a time when the true spiritual priorities stand out like a diamond gleaming among the coal. Necessities will take priority over inconsequential material possessions (the "stuff" No-Eyes frequently referred to), neighborly helpfulness will be above neighborly competition, unity will replace separatism, and cooperation will come before individualism. Though these will be evidenced through a "forced" situation of cumulative events, the end result will be as a great shift to spiritual behavior. In most of our lives, we've experienced events that bring about an attitude adjustment, by way of highlighting the real priorities and exposing the shallowness of those we once thought were important. In the future, this will happen worldwide.

Since the earthly civilizations are composed of the Five Starborn Tribes, are we being affected by their differences? I mean, do we have some type of inner sense of this separate heredity, whereby we have an innate feel of separatism? I'm still not sure I got my concept across.

You did just fine. You want to know if humans exhibit perceptions of separatism based on an inherent sense of the five separate races of Starborn from which they originated? And the answer is no. The intent of this "creative" Creation idea was to eventually have *one* earthly race evolve, a synergistically blended *tan* one. It didn't work because ego got in the way. Since the races developed, an ethnic sense of superiority and separatism became stronger, and the distance between them grew greater rather than closer as ideally projected.

This concept of blending Starborn races has effectively manifested on other planets, yet those on Earth managed to allow ego to smother Spirituality and unity. That's why the archangel agreed with me when I voiced my perception of Earth being the Ego Planet. When *spiritual* messengers and leaders place the emphasis on self—placing *self* before the public eye instead of placing their *words* upon the altar of life for all to see—then that pretty much emphasizes how far earthly society has taken ego. The truth is, the little human ego is not bigger than Truth. It is not bigger than Spirituality. It is *not* bigger than the Divine. And, one day, those facts will be brought home in a big way—a way nobody will misinterpret.

Is there still hope for this planet and its people?

Oh, yes! Though I would remind you about the concept of being in Expectation. Some imagined and visualized events in one's life don't always manifest in reality as in one's thoughts. Certainly hope is alive and well. A turnaround is evident. Just allow it to come into being as it will, rather than according to the human will.

The Phoenix in **Phoenix Rising** *represents the Second Coming, doesn't it? I just figured it out.*

You did well. Actually, to be more accurate, it represents the return of true *Spirituality* by way of people *living* their beliefs rather than just "mouthing" their beliefs. It symbolizes the return of the true Aspects of the Trinity and that's why Feminine Spirituality will blossom once again. The Second Coming? You could say that. That would be an accurate analogy because the true reality of the Divine will be clear to all. The crisp delineation and separatism of the different religions will dull as it blends into a more unified, conceptual spiritual ideology. The hand of man will be recognized as having no place in the making of the spiritual bread that sustains our souls.

Is there color within the realities of other dimensions?

Color beyond imagining. Color that vibrates with the lively molecules of living energy.

I heard that you've announced that you're the Messiah. I never read that anywhere in your books.

That's because I never wrote such an absurd statement, nor have I even implied such. You will hear a lot of things about me because public opinion is, by its own nature, diverse. That statement is the most outlandish idea I've ever heard. It wouldn't be too strong to even say it's blasphemous and sacrilegious. Can't even imagine where someone would come up something as far out as that. I've always emphasized the role as a messenger, never anything greater or higher. I've always emphasized my equality with everyone else. How someone could misread that is beyond me. A friend of mine made an interesting observation about people's various perceptions of me. He said: "You gift people with a beautiful, symmetrical sculpture. Some people just observe its beauty and come away with a sense of fulfillment for having been exposed to its essence; some people take it as a possession and build an altar around it; and others melt it down into some misshapen form and claim that that was your grotesque gift to humankind." I think my friend was not only extremely perceptive, but also very accurate in his observation of people's view of me. Some see simple truth and are touched, some see an imagined deity and feel the need to elevate, and some twist and deform with hatred. Yet all the while, regardless of people's perception of me, I remain the same . . . just me.

Your popularity is declining. It's about time.

I didn't come here to be popular, so I can't imagine what the purpose of your statement would be. If I'd wanted to be popular, if popularity had been my goal and purpose, then I would've been giving seminars, lecturing, writing workbooks, devising my own board games, constantly traveling about the country and overseas to place myself before the public eye at every opportunity. To my way of thinking, those sorts of things are only devices to wring a readership's wallet. The words of my message are already out there, so, in reality, the fact of the matter is that I don't even need to be here any more.

You made your mentor sound like a bumbling idiot with no sense of grammar.

Since when do we criticize and put people down for their manner of speech? Is the manner of delivery more important than the wisdom conveyed through that speech? Since when are someone's natural characteristics an embarrassment?

Are all of your experiences real?

I already addressed the realness of my experiences in *Fireside,* when I talked about the virtual reality of Quantum Meditation and the concept of places like a parallel universe.

All the experiences, conversations, and events recounted in every one of my books are (were) real. The problem that people have with it is not understanding that all the dimensional levels of reality . . . are . . . real. They are just as real as you sitting there and holding this book. Today, in 1999, neuroscientists are still scratching their heads over what consciousness is, much less being able to understand the most rudimentary extent of the experiential possibilities that exist within the realm of true Consciousness. When we dream; when we have out-of-body experiences, or virtual reality experiences during Quantum Meditation, have visions, or engage in remote viewing, our Consciousness is actively having *real* experiences—real experiences within real dimensions manifested in other dimensions of Reality. Are angels, archangels, angelic beings, and the Divine Trinity not real just because they are not three-dimensional? Are your out-of-body experiences not real because your *consciousness* traveled instead of your three-dimensional *body* when these events happened? Are the worlds and realities of the Indian shamans the world over not real? Consciousness. It all comes down to understanding the vast potential of the consciousness. The out-of-body experiences people have are real. Just as real as those movements and activities and awake-state thoughts made with your three-dimensional body. Do we believe in other dimensions or not? Are people just "saying" they believe in these or are they *really* believing in the concept of other realities? Are people just saying they believe in the real experiences that occur during the end of vision quests or are they *really* comprehending the realness of them? If solid validity is where the verbally expressed belief is, then there'd be no problem in understanding how the consciousness can have multidimensional experiences that are just as "real" as those in the third dimension.

My series of writings has been addressing this issue more and more in an attempt to bring greater clarification to this concept. Multidimensional—the term and concept—means just that . . . *multi*-dimensional (as in *many*). Multidimensional where time is not linear, but where the consciousness also experiences "vertical" time, where vibrational frequencies are of non-space/non-time. My books represent a recounting of *actual* events, persons, and conversations that took place on multi-levels of Reality. In the literary field, there is a technique called "composite" writing, which consolidates a number of events into a *compressed* time frame. In this manner of writing, the author takes advantage of using a method that allows him/her to highlight and place greater emphasis on the more important actual events rather than recounting all the mundane ones that may have happened in between. Some writers use what is called a "composite character," whereby a singular *character* may represent many (one character performing or displaying the acts or attitudes of many). I've never used that particular device, but my books reflect the composite recording of the real and true *multidimensional* events that have taken place throughout my life.

When my deceased grandmother appeared to me at the end of my bed, she was not three-dimensional, but she was as real as that bed. The dream experience I had with the archangel was real. Are dreams not real because they don't take place in the awake state? We're inching back to the main issue of consciousness and the incredible possibilities it holds for experiences on all levels of reality. I've had real visions, experienced virtual reality after journeying into Quantum Meditation, been to a different dimensional parallel earth, been out-of-body, experienced the consciousness of others, witnessed physical and nonphysical manifestations, seen other beings who inhabit this earth and possess the capability of altering form and vibrational density . . . all *real,* as real as this keyboard I'm typing on.

To my natural way of thinking, I inherently recognize all of these multidimensional realities as Real. To me, whether an event took place in the third dimension or on one of the others isn't relevant, because the event still was actual—it still took place and was real no matter what level it occurred on. An experience is an experience. An individual is an individual on all levels. A conversation is a conversation no matter what level it took place on. *The Visitation*—the event and conversation—took place during a dream. It was an actual dream that I recounted. It was a *real* dream. Just because the archangel didn't appear out of thin air in a three-dimensional body and start a conversation with me in a mall parking lot does not mean the event was not actual.

This whole thing with "real" is far too narrow and qualified within society. The reality of Reality has got to somehow make an inroad into the general public's mind-set regarding consciousness, pierce that hard shell of ignorance and reluctance surrounding the subject. Presently, people's perception of what is real and what is not is solely tied to the confinements of the five tactile senses—the "touchable." Anything one's consciousness experiences in another dimension is real. Any person one interacts with on that other dimension is just as actual as their neighbor next door. Trying to explain this makes me feel like how Copernicus must've felt when he tried to explain the fact that the earth was not the center of the universe, but rather the sun was, that the earth revolved around the sun. *Understanding* the technicalities of consciousness and its vast potentialities does not become a *prerequisite* to *experiencing* those realities or even having the basic acknowledgment of them. Sort of like it not being a requirement of having the ability to build a computer in order to experience and utilize its vast potentialities.

Religious history is full of recounted happenings involving other dimension events. This is not something that only happened in ancient times, it happens *all the time* because it is the reality of Reality. It is the reality of the consciousness. Every event I recounted happened. Every event, and every person, and every conversation happened. The books are a composite of *real* events, *real* individuals, and *real* conversations taken from experiences on *various levels of Reality*. Fiction? The answer to that is an individualized one, because it solely depends on if you truly believe in other dimensions and frequency fields to reality, or if you think this heavy, third dimension is all there is. That depends on whether or not you believe the consciousness is truly the spirit and that that spirit has potentialities beyond human comprehension. Me? I happen to firmly believe in both of these two tenets because my experiences leave me absolutely no room to doubt them; my experiences leave me no alternate recourse but to believe in them—incontrovertibly. I've seen and experienced what the consciousness is capable of and . . . it is *all* real.

Just because people haven't had like experiences of the consciousness doesn't mean that such events or possibilities don't exist and are not actual. People can't see the different bands of light rays, but we know they're real. People can't see germs or atoms, but they're real and we all believe in their existence. Just because the capabilities of the consciousness have not yet been likewise solidified in the public's eye, doesn't mean they don't exist yet. People's "belief" in a reality isn't what verifies its existence. *Reality exists in spite of belief.* Reality exists in spite of doubt or disbelief in it. I've always tried to be as open as I could while recounting my experiences. The reality and capabilities of consciousness must begin to be better understood—it *must.*

From what I understand of The [Robert] Monroe Institute, one of its purposes is to educate people about the consciousness, that their consciousness can indeed explore the beautiful realities of other dimensions. People the world over have visited this famous institute and have experienced the vast immensity of reality. Their experiences were real. Those of you who have had like experiences of the consciousness will understand exactly what I mean. Those of you who haven't, may have to wait until the neuroscientists finally figure it out and make it a commonly accepted belief like the germs and multispectrums of light and sound. Society as a whole is just not there yet, but I'm trying to bring a little more clarity to the nature of the human consciousness—the inherent qualities and far-reaching extent of our spirit's magnificent potentiality. I can't stress how important this is to grasp. Our little third dimension is so minuscule, so fragmentary contrasted to the massive whole of Reality. There are literally worlds—*universes*—out there just existing and ready for our consciousness to discover and interact within. The expression that "with prayer, anything is possible" can also be applied to the consciousness—"with the consciousness, anything is possible." Reality awaits the untethered consciousness. Until it is fully explored, for some, Reality—the only reality recognized as real—will remain bound to the confinements of the third dimension. This same idea was set forth by the famed biochemist Kary Mullis, who was awarded the Nobel Prize for chemistry in 1993. In his recent book, *Dancing Naked in the Mind Field,* published in 1998 by Pantheon (ISBN 0-679-44255-3), he made many interesting and thought-provoking comments regarding Reality and society's current perception of it. One of them was "We are only watching a couple of channels. There are a million." I feel that he stretched it a bit and gave society the benefit of the doubt when he said "couple," because I don't see society being aware of any more dimensional channels than the singular, third dimension they seem to be stuck on. Having to explain that my experiences were (and continue to be) based within a conglomerate of separate, multidimensional realities proves that society does not understand the true potential of consciousness. More than once I commented that some things I've experienced have been held back from being exposed in the books because I personally felt that the general conceptual beliefs of society have not yet equated with the true reality of Reality. It's as though there's this problematical glitch with people (in their minds) with time and understanding needing to catch up with Reality, because society's conceptual comprehension isn't quite there yet. Almost, but not quite. So then my readers say to me: "Please don't hold back information. You can tell us; we're big boys and girls; we can handle it." I believe some can with complete understanding, because they've had some of the same types of journeys of consciousness I have or have been successful while experiencing the potential of his/her consciousness while at The Monroe Institute, but for those others, reality will be a problem and will be perceived as nothing more than fiction until they themselves take that initial, validating journey. I have been open and honest with you—always. To do otherwise would defeat my purpose. Whether or not you believe in multidimensional realities and the powerful potentiality of one's consciousness to have actual experiences on them comes down to individual opinion based on the personal experiential events of each person, or a mind open to the vast possibilities of Reality. To quote Stuart Sutherland, a noted psychologist, "Consciousness is a fascinating phenomenon; it is impossible to specify what it is, what it does, or why it evolved." And neuroscientist Susan A. Greenfield has stated, "Another group (of scientists) believes that although consciousness is generated by the brain, it is such a special property that it currently defies scientific understanding." Einstein was quoted as stating the following: "The most beautiful experience we can have is the *mysterious* . . . the fundamental emotion which stands at the cradle of *true* art and *true* science."

The books of my series were written exactly as they were supposed to be. Remember that page from the handwritten notebook I reproduced in *Daybreak?* It was among those written while I sat down one late night to begin recording my experiences? The following morning, when I was ready to type up the first part of the manuscript of *Spirit Song,* the handwriting in the notebook was not my own. I believe it was my mentor's. I believe it was her's because, from her dimension, she wanted to be sure the books contained the proper wording of conversations we'd had and included events in proper sequence. I believe that, perhaps, she didn't quite want to leave it all up to me. That notebook ended up with both *Spirit Song* and *Phoenix Rising* written in it. The amazement of that notebook was too special—too validating—for me to ever destroy. Although I've burned all of my own handwritten notes, scribblings, and working manuscripts from the other books, I cherish that singular initial notebook as my own "grounding object," which serves to personally underscore my work with reassuring validity.

There's another incredibly interesting situation that happened to me, which was an amazing confoundment at the time it happened and again served to verify the validity of my experiences in multidimensional realities. My mentor had a special rattle. She had some unique markings in the wooden handle that were etched by her fingernail. Six years ago, before I even met Sally, she'd seen something in a shop that she couldn't get out of her mind. The item nagged and nagged at her until she finally went back and purchased it and sent it to me as a gift. It was a rattle, *the* rattle . . . with No-Eyes' same markings on it. That incident was a clear and certain verification from the Old One that Sally was meant to be involved in my purpose. Though we don't always understand the workings of Reality, it exists just the same. It exists in spite of our mind's incomprehensibility. To underscore this fact, all one has to do is take a cursory look into history and societal beliefs, which have been in a continual state of flux due to ongoing, revealing discoveries. Experiencing something firsthand or the event of tactile, sensory occurrence is not a prerequisite to make Reality real. The famous physicist, Enrico Fermi, came up with a question he posed to his colleagues in 1950, which became known as Fermi's Paradox. The question related to the possibility of extraterrestrial life. The question was "Where is everyone?" meaning that we'd surely have been contacted by now if these Intelligences existed elsewhere, because of the simple fact that the universe is so vast and old. For a while, this posit shamed astrophysicists into silence about queries into extraterrestrial life until . . . they realized that *experiential proof* of something *does not* take away the *possibility* nor the *probability* of it being *real*. In other words, just because something *hasn't* happened, that in no way proves that it *can't* happen.

I would like to close this response with a quotation from a letter that the famous Greek philosopher Epicurus wrote to Herodotus twenty-three hundred years ago. "There are infinite worlds both like and unlike this world of ours. For the atoms being infinite in number are borne far out into space. For those atoms have not been used up either on one world or a limited number of worlds, not on all of the worlds which are alike, or on those which are different from these. So that there nowhere exists an obstacle to the infinite number of worlds. We must believe that in all worlds there are living creatures and plants and other things we see in this world."

If the Virgin Mary was reincarnated in the world today, what would that mean?

Not a thing. It'd mean absolutely nothing more than there's someone walking around on earth who was once the Virgin Mary in a former life and is someone completely different now. Society, for two thousand years, has elevated this biblical mother to the status of a near-deity and that's wrong, really wrong. She was a mother who birthed and cared for a great spiritual being when he was young. End of story. Worshippers need not apply.

Jesus was the main event back then. *He* was the focus. *He* was the divinely designated one destined to bring a realignment to spirituality. *His* life example, works, and words were the prime purpose. This current fascination with his mother has, over hundreds of years, slowly but steadily escalated into a situation where she is perceived as a demigoddess of some type. The fact of the matter is that she was a mother, a mother just like all the other mothers in the world. She scrubbed clothing, cleaned eating utensils, drew water from the well, shopped in the market and argued over prices, cooked, cussed when she spilt lamp oil, chatted with friends, babysat neighbor's children, etc., just like all mothers today do. Her days were mostly mundane, with routine chores and thoughts of what her son was up to. Because of how modern-day society has raised her status, it's difficult to picture Mary as a commoner, a housekeeper, a normal mother. Back then that's exactly what she was. Back then she never perceived herself as anything but. It's today's societal perception that seems to think her reincarnated return should represent or symbolize something special. Why would *society* think that when *she* wouldn't? Especially when she'd be someone absolutely different now, someone with a completely separate, new personality and purpose? If she were walking among you now, she'd be very puzzled over why anyone would think she was anyone special just because of a past-life identity. She would have her own past life in proper perspective. She would see it as a life lived as a commoner, a housekeeper, a mother who often wondered about the whereabouts and health of her son. Today, she would not perceive her biblical personality as society currently does, because she was the one who lived it and knows how common and mundane her life was back then while, on the other hand, society only has illuminated legend and mysticism to define her existence. The former is fact, the latter is not. Perspective. The alignment of perspective with reality should be everyone's priority if they have any interest in recognizing truth. Never underestimate an individual's worth and never overestimate it. Allow reality to exist within its own beauty. Reality doesn't need human elaboration, dressing, or golden gilt to make it meaningful.

When the worst of the earth changes are happening, will you be off with the Starborn somewhere?

I'm certainly not planning on abandoning my homeland—Grandmother Earth. I've been routinely adding to my stock of supplies as time and funds allow—so why would I be doing that—going to all that trouble and expense—if I were planning on not being here with the rest of you? I don't think any of us would be evacuated off this planet against our wills; it'd be a voluntary choice for each individual. My choice is here.

I've heard that you've changed your lifestyle. You lesbian, I'm not buying any more of your books.

Let's see now. I've been called a Clown, a Visionary, a Messiah, a Phoney, a Hermit, an Intellectual, Satan's advocate, a Nobody, a Goddess, a Light, a Crazy Person, a Wise One, a Megalomaniac, an Idiot, an Introvert, a Blessing, a Curse, and a Lesbian. Jeez, if people like to call me names so much, I sure am thankful that they've at least not called me a Republican.

Okay, what is this lesbian thing, anyway? I don't think the general public has a clear definition of the term, because, from what I've seen and heard in the last three years, it appears that any woman who chooses the single life is looked at with suspicion. When I was a little girl, there was a pair of elderly ladies sharing a house down the street. They were friends—companions—and believe me, if they'd been lesbians I sure would've heard the aspersions flying out of my father's mouth about them. A friend of mine has two spinster aunts (sisters) living together. Are they considered lesbians just because they never married and chose to live out their days enjoying each others companionship? I know two women who have lived together for many years and I also know (for a fact) that their relationship is purely platonic. Just because they each independently chose not to marry a man, does that define condemning criteria for making them bona fide lesbians? Of course not. Are sisters living together in a sorority house considered lesbians because they openly run around the halls in their underwear? What of nuns who chose the convent life? So is sexual *intimacy* what defines this? Is just the fact that choosing not to marry a man (singlehood) criteria? See where society is sitting with this? It doesn't know what it thinks; therefore, every time two women who are seen together on a regular basis—or if they choose to live together because they're more comfortable with being with their own gender for whatever reason—these ladies are erroneously labeled something they're not. Please, let's be loving. Let's not make assumptions about others. Labels are so hurtful and cruel. They exacerbate "separatism" among humanity and serve to fragment unity instead of empowering the concept of "all my relations" and oneness. Labels are not terms of endearment, they are signs of hatred, intolerance, and prejudice. Until all the labels are weeded out from this world, love will not have a chance to grow and thrive. Can't you see? My God, can't you understand that every single time you call someone a name or label them with some derogatory term you're not only being a vilely cruel and spiteful person, you're also killing kindness and love? You do this and you still have the temerity to hold your head up before God inside your church? What incredibly huge egos you must have.

My thoughts on this "labeling" issue are certainly not solely focused on this most recent one I've been called. My thoughts on this extend to *every* label people attach to *anyone* in this world. It's just plain meanspirited and cruel. I don't care if it's directed toward an overweight person crossing your line of vision in a shopping mall, or related to someone's style of clothing, or the color of their skin, or spiritual belief, hairstyle, occupation, etc.; when you feel the urge to label someone or call them a derogatory name, better you keep your mouth closed and show the wisdom of Silence rather than opening it and letting the stench of your stupidity and cruel nature to spray out and contaminate the air. I purposely chose the word "stupidity" instead of "ignorance" because the act of calling people names is far beyond ignorance. It's plain stupid. Not only is name calling a spiritually bankrupt act, it also shows a complete lack of common sense and simple politeness. It shows an absolute lack of respect for others. This knee-jerk cruelty and hatred has got to stop if we're to survive and ever . . . *ever* hope to evolve. People have to shift their focus from the incredible puny, pettiness that consumes their lives to the grander behavior of centering on Unconditional Goodness.

Associated with this labeling and name calling issue is the concept of gossip and hearsay. These are often the result of observations people make but don't have the intellectual logic to realize that these observations, more often than not, represent circumstantial evidence of rumor. Okay, suppose I'm in the grocery store checkout and the checker (who knows who I am) scans chewing tobacco, beer, and a couple of hunting magazines. The checker then tells others that I chew tobacco, drink beer, and am really interested in hunting. Was that what my purchases proved? Was that what it proved when I was picking up items for a neighbor who was housebound after an operation? Another example of circumstantial evidence is when I went into a popular Colorado Springs music store, Independent Records, that sells music, posters, incense, pop jewelry, bumper stickers, and drug paraphernalia (oh my!). Someone seeing me come out of that shop could easily say I was seen coming out of a drug paraphernalia shop with a full bag of stuff. That individual could easily tell others that I bought stuff for drug use based on their observation of me exiting the shop with a full bag when the truth of the matter was that I went in there to purchase three Taco Bell dog T-shirts (that I thought were hilarious) for my three daughters to use as nightshirts. A friend had told me about these shirts and I wanted to get them for my girls as a joke. You see how easily observations can be misinterpreted as to the *actual* "reality" of them? Jeez, Louise, let's get on with the business of attending to our *own* lives; that's a full-time job all by itself.

How come you're against churches?

How come you think that? You've made a false transference of a statement I've made about one concept to another. I believe that churches make wonderfully serene places to contemplate in, to pray in, to experience the Silence and go within. What I have a big problem with are the "religious leaders," such as ministers, priests, reverends, etc., who devise ceremony and tell those people in the pews what to say, sing, and believe.

Churches, as buildings, provide incredible solitude and a place of deep tranquillity, which allows an individual a much-deserved respite from the hectic pace of their world. A church can provide much-needed breathing room, a place to release a big sigh and . . . just exist for a few moments or as long as a person can stay before worldly responsibility calls them back into the crazy pace. Churches should be open to all and always be a quiet place where people can find spiritual solitude and peace for the soul. This is the vision I've been given for the Magdalene Abbey I've been encouraged to establish once *Pinecones and Woodsmoke* has been published. It is the next phase of my work after the writing is done and I anticipate the abbey taking quite a few years to complete. When it's ready, it will have no ceremonies, no meetings, no tithing, no prescribed prayers, no sermons, no ministers, and no priestesses. Its sole purpose will be a women's spiritual sanctuary where they can connect with the Divine Within in a quiet and personal manner without any intervention by the patriarchal dogma or ceremony within which today's established religions currently confine them. Its main purpose is to provide a place where women can gain some spiritual solace away from the tightly regulated established religion churches. Churches? Originally, society's idea of a spiritual "building" was right; what messed it all up was the people who tried to head it up and tell others what they had to believe, how they had to pray, and participate in ceremonies in order to belong. Nope, none of that stuff for this abbey; just come and rest for a little spiritual sanctuary for a couple of minutes or a couple of hours of peaceful quietude. If you'll be looking for more than that, there are lots of other places to go to that will satisfactorily fulfill all your ceremonial needs. Churches? I prefer the phrase, "Spiritual Sanctuary."

Now, since folks get really off-the-wall ideas in their heads about me, I want to clarify at the outset that, regarding this Magdalene Abbey, I will *not* be in residence there. It's *not* intended to be a place of active worship. It won't be dedicated to *any* deity. I'm *not* establishing it as "my" church or sanctuary. Please get this clear right now, because I know how people twist things, especially beautiful spiritual concepts. The abbey sanctuary will be empty for the most part . . . empty except for any woman who is there enjoying a few hours of solitude and spiritual respite. Please, people, don't misconstrue or twist the reason for this abbey. It has been a part of my mission from the beginning, and now that the message phase of my purpose is nearly done (the books), I'm beginning to be involved in moving on to the second phase.

I'm impressed by the wide range of subjects you address in your writings. Your head isn't stuck up in the clouds with just metaphysical or God-related concepts.

Spiritual concepts are nothing without the spiritual human behavior to put it into action. In order to accomplish this bond between the two, one has to address the related societal issues, such as the current superiority of the established religions (especially the Religious Right) and their unbridled persecution of others through their intolerance. One has to address the lack of equality and extreme prejudicial behavior among humans, the suppression of women and the cruel inferiority with which men treat them. One has to address the current technological and scientific discoveries and breakthroughs in order to clarify their relatedness to spiritual aspects. A spiritual messenger cannot have her/his head stuck up in the clouds and only speak of spiritual or meta-physical ideologies; the messenger must tie it all in with the working world reality and the behavior of those living upon it for the words to be meaningful and effectively related to people's everyday life. Spirituality is not something up in the clouds; it's something we live . . . every hour of every day. It's what we breathe.

How many planets exist with intelligent life on them?

I couldn't begin to guess, but astrophysicists and astronomers greatly disagree on this answer. I read that, before his death, Carl Sagan was planning on writing a book about the possibility of intelligent life existing in the many galaxies of the universe. In the book, *Probability 1,* written by the mathematician, Amir Aczel, Ph.D., he relays that Carl Sagan believed that the number of civilizations in our galaxy that can communicate with us is about 1 *million.* Our galaxy alone contains 300 *billion* stars and our solar system is situated within one of its arm extensions. I don't know about you, but before I experienced multidimensional, quantum realities, understanding that the volume of the sun could hold one million earths was one hell of a mental exercise in visualization.

The moon, a luminous orb of reflected light symbolizing not only knowledge, wisdom, and enlightenment but, more importantly, human-kind's "reflected" behavior of same. Eclipse. The moon in eclipse, when that brilliantly illu-mined enlightenment is momentarily darkened by shadow, is when knowledge, wisdom, and enlightenment is temporarily forgotten and minds slip back into a Dark Age of Ignorance full of hate, intolerance, and persecution. Rather the eclipse be a reminder of that precari-ous intellectual possibility. Eclipse, a sign that we must never let our ascending enlightenment be pulled back into its dark depths—a sign that despite a moment of darkness . . . the Light of Wisdom prevails.

Hampton Roads Publishing Company

. . . for the evolving human spirit

Hampton Roads Publishing Company
publishes books on a variety of subjects including
metaphysics, health, complementary medicine,
visionary fiction, and other related topics.

For a copy of our latest catalog,
call toll-free, 800-766-8009,
or send your name and address to:

Hampton Roads Publishing Company, Inc.
134 Burgess Lane
Charlottesville, VA 22902
e-mail: hrpc@hrpub.com
www.hrpub.com